A SURVIVAL GUIDE *for the* ELEMENTARY/ MIDDLE SCHOOL COUNSELOR

SECOND EDITION

A SURVIVAL GUIDE *for the* ELEMENTARY/ MIDDLE SCHOOL COUNSELOR

John J. Schmidt

JOSSEY-BASS
A Wiley Imprint
www.josseybass.com

Published by Jossey-Bass
A Wiley Imprint
989 Market Street, San Francisco, CA 94103-1741   www.josseybass.com

The materials that appear in this book (except those for which reprint permission must be obtained from the primary sources) may be reproduced for educational/training activities. We do, however, require that the following statement appear on all reproductions:

A Survival Guide for the Elementary/Middle School Counselor by John J. Schmidt.
Copyright © 2004 by John Wiley & Sons, Inc.

This free permission is limited to the reproduction of material for educational/training events. Systematic or large-scale reproduction or distribution (more than one hundred copies per year)—or inclusion of items in publications for sale—may be done only with prior written permission. Also, reproduction on comput-er disk or by any other electronic means requires prior written permission. Requests to the Publisher for permission should be addressed to the Permissions Department, John Wiley & Sons, Inc., 111 River Street, Hoboken, NJ 07030, (201) 748-6011, fax (201) 748-6008, e-mail: permcoordinator@wiley.com.

Jossey-Bass books and products are available through most bookstores. To contact Jossey-Bass directly call our Customer Care Department within the U.S. at 800-956-7739, outside the U.S at 317-572-3986 or fax 317-572-4002.

Jossey-Bass also publishes its books in a variety of electronic formats. Some content that appears in print may not be available in electronic books.

Library of Congress Cataloging-in-Publication Data

Schmidt, John J., 1946-
 A survival guide for the elementary/middle school counselor / John J. Schmidt.— 2nd ed.
     p. cm.
Includes bibliographical references (p.   ) and index.
 ISBN 0-7879-6886-2 (alk. paper)
 1. Counseling in elementary education—United States. 2. Counseling in middle school education—United States. 3. Student counselors—United States. I. Title.
 LB1027.5.S259 2004
 372.14—dc22

                                                2003021670

Printed in the United States of America
FIRST EDITION
PB Printing   10   9   8   7   6   5   4   3   2

Contents

9

BELONGING AND BEING WITH THE SCHOOL

In memory of

Dr. Nicholas A. Vacc,

whose immeasurable contributions to the preparation of counselors have given the counseling profession an identity and credibility among mental health practitioners.

About the Author

John J. (Jack) Schmidt, Ed.D., is professor of counselor education at East Carolina University in Greenville, North Carolina. During his career, Dr. Schmidt has been a social studies teacher, elementary, middle, and high school counselor, school district supervisor of counseling and testing services, state coordinator of school counseling programs, and a university department chair. An active writer and presenter, he has published over fifty articles, book reviews, and manuals and more than a dozen books, including *Counseling in Schools: Essential Services and Comprehensive Programs* (Fourth Edition), *Intentional Helping: A Philosophy for Proficient Caring Relationships, Making and Keeping Friends, Living Intentionally & Making Life Happen,* and *Invitational Counseling: A Self-Concept Approach to Professional Practice* with Dr. William W. Purkey.

Dr. Schmidt is past president of the North Carolina Counseling Association and the North Carolina Association for Counselor Education and Supervision. He has received recognition from several professional associations and universities for his leadership, research, and publications in the field of counseling, particularly school counseling. Awarded the Elementary Counselor of the Year Award by the North Carolina School Counselor Association in 1978, he also received the Ella Stephens Barrett Leadership Award from the North Carolina Counseling Association in 1997 and the Ruth C. McSwain Distinguished Professional Service Award from the North Carolina School Counselor Association in 2002. In 1999, the College of Education at East Carolina University named Dr. Schmidt Distinguished Professor for his teaching, scholarship, and service to the university.

Dr. Schmidt is a National Certified Counselor, a Licensed Professional Counselor, and member of Chi Sigma Iota, the international counseling honor society. From 1997 through 2004, he served on the North Carolina Board of Licensed Professional Counselors.

Acknowledgments

It has been both a personal and professional pleasure to write *A Survival Guide for the Elementary/Middle School Counselor*, and I am indebted to Jossey-Bass for the opportunity to update the book for this second edition. I am particularly grateful to Steve Thompson, editor, and Elisa Rassen, his assistant, for their guidance during this revision.

As I travel around the country talking with school counselors, it is a joy to hear that this guide has been helpful to so many. My hope is that this new edition will be equally useful to counselors in the years to come.

Many thanks to Katy Donahue and Tremaine Young, graduate assistants in the counselor education program at East Carolina University, who helped with research for the second edition. Their work in gathering information and Web sites updated the volume tremendously. Also, I sincerely appreciate the support and friendship of Linda Warren, who was the office manager during the years I chaired the Counselor and Adult Education Department at ECU. Without her support, wisdom, and sense of humor, I could not have survived the university. Finally, I thank my wife, partner, and best friend, Pat, whose lifelong support of my work has enabled me to enjoy my career in counseling so fully.

February 2004

John J. Schmidt
Greenville, North Carolina

About This Survival Guide

A few years ago while working as state coordinator of school counseling for the North Carolina Department of Public Instruction, I met with a group of counselors and posed the question, "Why are counselors needed in schools?" Specifically, I asked, "What is a counselor's primary purpose in providing comprehensive counseling, consulting, and coordinating services to students, parents, and teachers in a school setting?" The discussion that followed speculated that professional counselors are in schools to help people become "more able" in their respective roles. School counselors help students become more able learners, they assist parents in their supportive roles, and they enable teachers to provide beneficial instruction for all children. In sum, everything a school counselor does, every service rendered, aims at helping students, parents, and teachers in the process of human development and learning.

Counselors who agree with this conclusion—that they are in schools to help people become more able—will discover that to accomplish this goal, they, too, need to become more able in their professional functioning. To become more able as counselors, they must move beyond survival toward a proactive stance that permits them to become *identifiable, capable, available,* and *accountable*—four characteristics essential to being a successful school counselor. Being *identifiable* means knowing who you are and what you do and letting others know this identity. Being *capable* means practicing at a high level of skill while recognizing the limits of your competency and professional role. When you are *available,* you are accessible to the students, parents, and teachers that you serve. *Accountability* brings together the first three abilities by assessing how you spend your time and measuring the effectiveness of services that you provide.

A Survival Guide for the Elementary/Middle School Counselor is a resource intended to help counselors become identifiable, capable, available, and accountable in surviving and eventually flourishing as a school counselor. This second edition continues the focus of the original *Survival Guide* to help elementary and middle school counselors design comprehensive programs of services to fit their professional settings and address the needs of students, parents, and teachers in the school.

As an elementary or middle school counselor, you might find the following exchange familiar. Two counselors were talking at a state counseling conference. One new elementary counselor confessed to his colleague, "I have so much to do and so little time to do it. I go from one crisis to the next one or from one administrative task to another." A middle school counselor responded, "Me too! So many things take time away from students—coordinating the testing program and responsibility for exceptional children's referrals take up much of my time. I need practical ideas and strategies to handle students' concerns and everything else that goes on in my school." This exchange reveals that the two counselors are struggling with their identity, questioning their capability to meet all the demands, going in many directions but unable to be available to students they want to help, and looking for ways to be effective and accountable in their schools. In addition, these two counselors are searching for surefire ways to solve problems, "fix" kids, and cure American education. For them and many other school counselors, the transition from learning about the art and science of counseling to being an artful and scientific practitioner is challenging.

Simply learning about art does not make us masterful artists. We might be able to learn about the tools of oil painting and the skills required to create a lifelike masterpiece, but this knowledge, in and of itself, does not make us accomplished artists. Only with sufficient practice and personalization of the techniques that we learn will we approach an artistic level of functioning. At the same time, simply knowing what the research says about a particular issue does not make us scientific practitioners. Consistent application of such knowledge, dependable evaluation of outcomes, and reflection of what we do and why we do it are also required.

Similar to an artist and a scientific professional, you are seeking ways to apply your knowledge in a practical direction and with a beneficial purpose. In elementary and middle schools, where the counseling profession searches for a clear, understandable role but where case loads often reach astronomical ratios, successful counselors establish a professional identity by emphasizing their capabilities, serving a wide audience, and accounting for the services they provide. To be successful, these counselors structure a school counseling program that permits optimal use of the time they have available.

Expanded to twelve chapters, this second edition of the *Survival Guide* continues the assumption that although the developmental needs of students in elementary and middle schools differ, the practice of counseling at these two levels consists of similar goals, objectives, and activities. When appropriate, specific activities and strategies that are suitable at one level more than the other are noted, but for the most part, this guide will be useful across elementary and middle school counseling programs.

The first four chapters define and describe a comprehensive school counseling program. A comprehensive program includes a clear definition and description of your counseling role, input from those who use your services, and strategies to allow the most effective and efficient use of your time. Chapters One through Four address the concepts of *identity, availability,* and *accountability.* An effective and efficient use of time requires planning, coordination, and evaluation, as well as a careful and deliberate selection of services.

Chapters Five through Eight present ideas and strategies to integrate the counseling program with the overall educational mission of your school. These ideas and strategies include aligning your counseling program with the school curriculum, focusing on educational development for all students, reaching out to diverse populations, and preparing for school and community crises that affect student learning and development. Many of the ideas and suggestions in this chapter will enhance your *capability* as an elementary or middle school counselor.

The remaining chapters focus on relationships with professional colleagues and the parent community, and on yourself as a counselor. A school counseling program is as strong as the staff that supports and guides its development. Likewise, you elevate assistance to students to the degree that their parents and guardians are involved in the process. In addition, your ability to function effectively is influenced by your own well-being—your personal and professional fitness. Professional fitness includes a practical knowledge of ethical codes, state and federal laws, and local school policies. These chapters continue the emphasis on your *capability* and *accountability* as a counselor.

A Survival Guide for the Elementary/Middle School Counselor, second edition, bridges the gap between theory and practice. Counseling theories help us understand human behavior and development and enable us to choose reliable approaches to professional helping. Practical strategies and materials, such as those in this guide, give us an opportunity to structure our theoretical stance around useful and effective helping behaviors. These practical suggestions encourage us to include many participants—teachers, parents, and students—in the process of designing and implementing comprehensive school counseling programs.

This resource sets the stage for you to identify who you want to be as an elementary or middle school counselor. It shows you how to develop ways to become available to a wide audience, expand your knowledge, improve your skills, and measure your worth and effectiveness. In each chapter, you will find ideas to move beyond survival as a practicing school counselor toward flourishing as a professional helper in an elementary or middle school. Whereas *surviving* conjures up an image of desperate endurance, *flourishing* conveys a notion of thriving and elicits a positive vision of what you can become as a school counselor. This book encourages you to look beyond basic survival skills and develop into a proactive counselor who provides a comprehensive program of services for your school and community.

Throughout this book, you will find lists of specific strategies, helpful guidelines, Internet Web sites, and reproducible forms to use in a comprehensive school counseling program. Not all of these might be appropriate or feasible to apply in your school and program. Choose the ones that are, and adapt the others if they can be helpful. Some of the suggested techniques and materials may not be useful as presented, but with adjustments, you might spin off new and better strategies from these initial ideas.

In an effort to make the *Survival Guide* a practical, readable resource for professional school counselors, I have used references and citations sparingly. You will find an extensive resource list of references and Web sites at the end of the book.

Thank you for allowing me to share my experience and suggestions with you. I wish you well in your career development, and hope the strategies and tools in this guide are helpful as you move toward higher levels of artful counseling within a scientific framework.

chapter 1

DEFINING *and* DESCRIBING *a* SCHOOL COUNSELING PROGRAM

As an elementary or middle school counselor, you are a member of a relatively young and honorable profession. You belong not only to the profession of school counseling but also to the counseling profession, which spans countless areas of professional helping and service in our society. Having historical roots in the industrial revolution at the turn of the twentieth century, the counseling profession of the twenty-first century has become an important member of mental health services (Schmidt, 2003).

Today's counselors work in settings that include mental health centers, family agencies, prisons, hospitals, funeral homes, crisis centers, employment agencies, colleges, and schools, to name a few. As an elementary or middle school counselor, you have joined one of the largest memberships within the counseling profession.

Throughout its history, the school counseling profession has searched for an identity and role among the helping professions. Today the questions—of why are counselors in schools and what are they supposed to do—are as prominent as they were years ago. As a member of this profession, you now face the same questions: Why are you here? What are you supposed to do?

In preparing to become a school counselor, you studied many areas of knowledge, including human development, psychology, career information and development, tests and measurement, and social and cultural foundations.

In addition, you have acquired skills in specific helping processes such as individual and group counseling, consultation, and facilitative teaching. This knowledge and skill provide a framework within which you are able to formulate and clarify your professional role to identify specific services for students, parents, and teachers.

Unlike counselors who practice in prisons, hospitals, mental health centers, and other settings, your services span a broad program of activities to assist several populations. This program includes preventive services, developmental activities, and remedial interventions for students, parents, and teachers. The challenge of offering such a wide range of services to different populations renders you unique in your practice of elementary or middle school counseling. Although you are similar in skills and knowledge to other professional counselors, you do not limit your role to a single service. Instead, you offer many services within the context of a comprehensive program. This notion of a *program* of services is a key element in school counseling, and your ability to define and describe your school's *counseling program* is a key to your survival and ultimate success.

DESCRIBING THE PROGRAM

The most important steps you take will be in describing and defining the school's counseling program. Although the range and diversity of the expectations placed on you illustrate the vital need for school counselors, they can also threaten your effectiveness by pulling you in too many directions and spreading services across too broad an area.

One element that will influence how well you describe the program is the language you choose. Because school counseling is a young profession, it continues to struggle to find accurate language with which to describe and define what it is and what it does. You want to explain your program with a language that is consistent with your profession and understood by students, parents, teachers, and others in the school community.

Choosing a Language

Terms such as pupil personnel services, guidance programs, and student services are a few of the labels that categorize and classify school counseling services. Since we frequently adopt the language and terminology of our location, you probably identify yourself according to labels and language you learned either in your graduate studies or in your school system.

My preference is to call myself a *school counselor* and the services I provide are part of a *school counseling program*. As such, I belong to a *student services team*, which consists of other helping professionals such as the school nurse, school social worker, and school psychologist. For me, these terms accurately label the program of services I provide in schools. They are contemporary and more definitive than terms such as personnel services and guidance programs that are vague descriptors and often encompass conflicting roles and services for school counselors. For example, personnel services frequently imply and include record keeping, class scheduling, attendance monitoring, testing coordination, and other functions that detract from direct services to students, parents, and teachers. The terms *school counselor* and *counseling program* are also consistent with the language of our profession, as seen by the American School Counselor Association (ASCA) and its journal, *Professional School Counseling.*

Guidance is a term with which I have struggled my entire career. This word has confused me because I have never understood what it means professionally in terms of skills and training unique to school counselors. Yet the word *guidance* has historical significance and remains prevalent in the school counseling profession.

My confusion is founded in the belief that guidance is not the professional domain of any single group. Everything we do in schools and, consequently, everyone who works in schools can relate in some way to the notion of "guiding students." Teachers guide students in daily instruction, as well as in their personal relationships with others. Yet we do not call them "guidance teachers." Administrators guide students regarding policy, curriculum, discipline, and school programs, but we do not refer to them as "guidance principals." Why then should we use the term "guidance counselor" as opposed to "school counselor?"

The entire educational program of the school, including the counseling program, is guidance-oriented (or should be). For this reason, it is inaccurate to confine guidance goals and objectives to a single program such as school counseling. Because guidance permeates every facet of the school, no one person or program has ownership.

The term *school counseling program* encompasses a broad area of services, which includes preventive services, developmental activities, and remedial assistance. The common ground for these three areas is that in each, counselors provide direct services to students, parents, and teachers.

Some counselors believe that the term *school counseling program* is too restrictive because it confines services to remedial relationships. This is an unfortunate and narrow definition of professional counseling. Counseling relationships are for everyone, not only for people who have problems. For this reason, I see counseling as a way of helping healthy, functioning people capitalize on their strengths and reach higher levels of development. Although counseling also supports people who have concerns about the direction and purpose in their lives, school counseling does not need to be restricted to remedial relationships. Individual and group counseling process-es, for example, can benefit a wide audience. In this guide, you will find suggestions of how to use counseling processes in preventive services, for developmental learning, and to remedy existing concerns.

In developing a successful program, you want to select a language and vocabulary that describe accurately your role and function in the school. In choosing such a language, these guidelines may be helpful:

1. *Understand the language.* The terms you choose—counseling, guidance, personnel, or whatever—should have meaning to you. You should be clear about the words you use to describe yourself professionally and be able to defend the language you choose.

2. *Educate the populace.* Once you choose the language of your program, teach it to the people you serve. Let students, parents, and teachers know what you mean by *counseling, group guidance, consulting,* and other terms. A language is useful only if the people with whom you communicate understand it, accept it, and use it themselves.

3. *Use consistent language.* It is confusing to students and others when you use the language you adopt inconsistently. Consistency may be difficult at first, particularly if you have decided to change to new terms. Stick with it, and correct yourself when you confuse the language. Your students, parents, and teachers will be as consistent as you are.

Exhibit 1-1 presents a sample description for a school counseling program and the role of a counselor. You might use this description as part of a school brochure, a student handbook, a faculty manual, or other medium.

If you replaced another counselor who once served the school, the deci-sion about language requires careful consideration. For example, if the pre-vious counselor used terminology different from yours, you may need to adjust your thinking for a while. This is particularly true if your predecessor was at the school for many years and is well thought of by students and fac-ulty. You may feel strongly about the terms you want to use to describe who you are and what you do, and these beliefs may be a healthy sign of your professionalism. Nevertheless, move slowly and as you introduce new terms, explain your rationale. By being considerate and winning teachers' trust and confidence, you will be more likely to have your ideas and suggestions accepted.

Regardless of the language that you choose or how long it takes your school to adopt it, an important aspect of describing a program of services is the leadership role you take in the process. Remember, you are not the program, but your leadership ability is paramount to helping the school build a successful program.

EXHIBIT 1-1

The School Counseling Program and the School Counselor

The counseling program in our school is available to help students, parents, and teachers develop positive learning experiences. The program consists of a variety of services and activities, including individual and group counseling, parent and teacher consultation, group guidance, information services, referral assistance to other programs and services in the community, and student assessment.

The school counselor is responsible for developing, scheduling, and evaluating services of the program and is assisted by the Counseling Advisory Committee and the school principal. Primary services of the school counselor provide direct assistance to students in the school. For this reason, a major portion of the counselor's day consists of services for students. Parent and teacher consultations are usually scheduled in the early morning before classes or during after-school hours.

The counselor is a licensed professional with preparation in human development, learning theory, counseling and consulting, tests and measurement, career development, research, and other areas appropriate to the practice of counseling in a school. The counselor's office is located in the school, and appointments can be scheduled by calling [counselor's phone], e-mailing [counselor's e-mail address], or writing to [school address].

Leading the Charge

To survive and flourish as a successful elementary or middle school counselor, it is essential to identify and embrace the leadership role you have in the program and the larger school community. School counseling in the twenty-first century is not simply providing individual and group services to students. Rather, it is the orchestration of many services, some provided by you, the counselor, and additional ones provided by other professionals. This orchestration, much like leading a major symphony, requires leadership characteristics and skills to develop working relationships, identify goals and objectives, and create appropriate action to demonstrate that everyone is playing the same tune and in the correct key.

A first step in developing your leadership role is to assess your strengths in taking on this responsibility. What skills and knowledge do you already possess that will enable you to persuade people to create a comprehensive program of services and commit their involvement in carrying out its objectives? Next is to determine what additional knowledge you need to be a successful leader in your school. How can you obtain this knowledge—through workshops, professional associations, or more graduate training? A third step to consider is how to begin developing support for your ideas as a school leader. What will you need to do to win the confidence of your administration? Which teachers, support staff, and other school personnel are likely to support a comprehensive program, and how will you secure their support?

Throughout this chapter and book, you will learn about aspects of comprehensive school counseling programs and how you, as a leader, can create a viable and valuable one for your school. Here are some starter tips as you put your plan into action:

- Know what you want to do and understand the literature and research to support your ideas.
- Identify school members—administration, teachers, parents, staff, and others—who will support you initially. Recruit optimistic colleagues and administrators and tell them your plans.
- Respect school traditions and culture. Even though you might want to work toward changing old ways of doing things, understand the emotional ties that some people may have to historical aspects of the school.
- Be inclusive. Although you might identify people who give early support to your ideas, be careful not to exclude other people in the process. People who might disagree with initial plans could have constructive ideas that when incorporated into the plan will help make it better.
- Listen, listen, listen! As a counselor, one of your greatest strengths is your ability to listen fully to others without being judgmental. Use that skill in building support for the counseling program and for your leadership.
- Maintain a consistent stance. In an earlier book, William Purkey and I presented a professional counseling stance that consists of optimism, trust, respect, and intentionality (Purkey & Schmidt, 1996). Consider these characteristics and others that you believe will help maintain a dependable leadership posture in your school.

By learning about yourself as a leader, gaining additional knowledge about the school counseling profession, and creating collaborative relationships in the school community, you are in a stronger position to maintain a wide vision of what the program should be. This means focusing on the development of a comprehensive school counseling program.

Focusing on a Comprehensive Program

All school counselors face the danger of being overwhelmed by the challenges brought by students, parents, teachers, and administrators. Sometimes, when we become overwhelmed, we lock ourselves into a single mode of operation.

In most cases, we choose what is comfortable. As a result, we sometimes spend a major portion of our time in a single activity such as classroom guidance, individual counseling, or program administration. Although these services are important, they do not, in and of themselves, establish a comprehensive school counseling program.

A school counseling program consists of a number of activities and services. These activities and services aim at specific goals and objectives chosen as a result of careful examination and analysis of the needs of the school populations. The services you use and the goals you select do not happen by chance; they are part of a planned program of services. Hence, you want to move beyond routine reactions to situations and crises that emerge and become guided by a well-designed plan of counseling, consulting, and coordinating services.

In this guide, all the suggestions and ideas relate to some aspect of a comprehensive counseling program. To summarize, we can categorize these ideas under one or more of the four components of a comprehensive program:

- Planning
- Organizing
- Implementing
- Evaluating

Planning is the process of assessing school and student needs, formulating a philosophy of school counseling that is consistent with the mission of the school, evaluating the current program (if there is one), and establishing and prioritizing future program goals.

Organizing entails the selection of specific objectives and program strategies. This selection process includes the decision of who will provide which services. In this sense, the selected goals and objectives assign specific responsibilities to counselors, teachers, and administrators, defining their roles in the school counseling program.

Implementing is the action phase of a comprehensive program. It involves the delivery of services such as counseling, consulting, coordinating, referring, testing, and others. Implementation of a comprehensive school counseling program also involves all the personnel who have responsibility for educating students in the school: teachers, counselors, media specialists, administrators, and others.

Evaluating is the phase of a program that determines success, examines weaknesses, and allows you to recommend changes for the future. In this edition of the *Survival Guide,* you will see that program evaluation is essential to a comprehensive school counseling program. Effective programs are not guided merely by the intuitions, preferences, and desires of counselors and teachers. Rather, they are based on the assessed needs of students and measured outcomes of the services provided.

Some counselors believe they are valuable to their schools because they are always "busy." To survive as a school counselor, you want to move beyond the notion of "being busy" toward the realization that the services provided *make a difference* in the lives of students, parents, and teachers. Making a difference means measuring the effect of your services to the school.

These four phases of a comprehensive school counseling program illustrate that to be successful you must move beyond traditional approaches to guidance and counseling programs. The following comparison shows a few of the differences between traditional and comprehensive approaches (see Exhibit 1-2). As you will see, the traditional guidance approach is counselor-centered and informational in nature, whereas the comprehensive model focuses on broad populations being served and a wide spectrum of services.

You can use the Program Assessment Scale presented in Worksheet 1-1 to evaluate how comprehensive or traditional your program is. The scale emphasizes teacher input, group services, program planning, parent involvement, and other aspects of a comprehensive counseling program.

An example of the differences between these two approaches is in the area of career information and development. In a traditional guidance program, the counselor assumes responsibility for disseminating career information to students. At the elementary level, this could happen in the form of classroom guidance, whereby the counselor would present information about "The World of Work," for example. In a middle school, it might happen with individuals or groups of students receiving occupational information from the counselor.

EXHIBIT 1-2

Comparison of Traditional and Comprehensive Programs

Traditional Program

- Predominantly one-on-one activities
- Informational and administrative in nature
- Reactive to situations
- Clerical orientation
- Counselor dominated
- Minimum use of group work

Comprehensive Program

- Balanced program of services
- Preventive, developmental, remedial in nature
- Proactive in planning and goal-setting
- Direct service orientation
- High level of teacher involvement
- Extensive use of group services

WORKSHEET 1-1

Program Assessment Scale

DIRECTIONS: Underline your response to each question, and fill in the respective point values in the blank spaces. Total your points for the twelve questions to determine how traditional or comprehensive your school counseling program is.

1. Do you spend most of your time doing individual counseling and consulting with students? Yes (1 point); No (3 points) _____

2. Does your program emphasize a wide range of services, such as group counseling, teacher consultation, parent education, individual counseling, student assessment, and classroom guidance? Yes (3 points); Somewhat (1 point); No (0 points) _____

3. How many group counseling sessions do you lead in a typical week? 4 or more (3 points); Between 2 and 4 (2 points); Between 1 and 2 (1 point); None (0 points) _____

4. Are you involved with teachers in planning and presenting classroom guidance? Very much (3 points); Somewhat (2 points); Not at all (0 points) _____

5. Do you present all of the classroom guidance in your school? Yes (1 point); No, teachers also do guidance activities with their classes (3 points); No, there is no classroom guidance in the school (0 points) _____

6. Do you spend most of your time in crisis intervention and remedial services? Not most (3 points); No, but I want to do less (2 points); Yes, most of the time (1 point); No, I do no crisis intervention (0 points) _____

7. Do you have a written plan of goals and objectives that you revise annually? Yes, it guides program decisions (3 points); Yes, but only on paper (1 point); No (0 points) _____

8. Do you have an advisory committee to help guide your school counseling program? Yes, an active committee (3 points); Yes, but not active (1 point); No (0 points) _____

9. Are you overburdened with paperwork? Not really (3 points); Somewhat (1 point); Yes, most of the time (0 points) _____

10. Do you use assessment procedures with your students, parents, and teachers to establish program goals and objectives? Yes (3 points); Occasionally (1 point); Never (0 points) _____

11. Are your teaching colleagues an important part of the school counseling program? Yes, their input is sought and they participate (3 points); Somewhat, a few teachers are involved (1 point); No, it is my program to develop and implement (0 points) _____

12. Does your principal understand and support the services of the program? Yes, always (3 points); Usually (2 points); Rarely (1 point); Never (0 points) _____

SCORING: The closer to 36 points you score, the more comprehensive your program. The closer to 0 points you score, the less comprehensive your program of services.

In comprehensive programs, career information and development go hand in hand and are the shared responsibility of the entire school staff. In elementary and middle schools, teachers accept responsibility for integrating career information into their daily instruction. This infusion of career awareness helps students see how the subject matter can be applied in the outside world. It also enables students to learn which subjects relate to their interests and to particular careers in the world of work. You can assist with this integration by planning career guidance lessons and activities with teachers, locating appropriate resources, and presenting special topics in the classroom. Throughout the school year, you design and lead individual and group activities to focus on specific career development needs of all students. In addition, you work with teachers to plan schoolwide activities that focus on career information and development.

Using the ASCA National Model

Over the years, the American School Counselor Association (ASCA) has worked diligently to develop a model for comprehensive school counseling programs. As I was completing this revision of the *Survival Guide,* ASCA was in the final stage of developing a national model. You can find out about the ASCA national model from the association's Web site at www.schoolcounselor.org.

The ASCA national model for comprehensive school counseling programs is intended to help practicing counselors create programs that are data-driven and results-based. The hope is that a national model will help school counselors design, implement, coordinate, manage, and evaluate services that help students achieve success in school. The national model should provide a structure or framework around which counselors design and develop their programs. Because we have a national model, however, it does not mean that all programs should look and function the same. Each elementary and middle school is different, and the comprehensive counseling program designed and implemented in each school should reflect those differences. In this way, you ensure services for all students.

Advocating for All Students

Today, elementary and middle schools reflect the populations they serve. Typical elementary and middle schools consist of students who bring a range of hopes, challenges, and needs to school each day. Counselors who design comprehensive programs of services understand their role in advocating for *all* students, not only those who show promise but also those who struggle to fit in the school.

One way that school counselors advocate for all students is by observing and listening to the culture of the school. At times, schools pass policies or develop programs that, though well intended, might discriminate against certain groups or individual students. When you see this happening in your school, it is imperative that you take action. Point out to the principal and teachers what you have observed or what you have heard, and help them understand the implications for all students in the school. For example, one elementary school started a program for students to bring their fathers for a turkey lunch before Thanksgiving Holiday. The counselor pointed out that not all of the students in the school had fathers at home. Some students did not have fathers and others had fathers away in military service. After listening to the counselor, the principal and faculty decided to change the program to "Bring a Family Member to Lunch."

By advocating for all students, you demonstrate the democratic principles on which our educational and political systems are based. This professional stance is another way that you win support from your principal, teachers, and parents. Their support, in turn, allows you to describe and define the scope and limits of your role as a school counselor within a comprehensive program.

Elementary and middle school counselors who design and implement a comprehensive program of services rely on input and participation from the entire school staff. For this reason, the first step in establishing your program is to seek input and win cooperation from your teaching colleagues.

SEEKING INPUT

A comprehensive school counseling program does not belong to one person and is not the sole responsibility of the elementary or middle school counselor. Therefore, include as many people as possible in your program decisions. By seeking input from a wide audience, you are more likely to win support for the direction you take. When you make program decisions in isolation, out of reach of your teaching colleagues, services get out of touch with the needs of the school. As a result, you may find that the program lacks support from the faculty.

As a counselor in an elementary or middle school, you want the support of your colleagues. You may not win the total support of the faculty, but you do want the majority of teachers to believe that the services you provide and the part of the program for which they are responsible are important to the education of all students. This is what is meant by winning their support.

Winning Support

The first person to include in this decision-making process is the school principal. If you have replaced a counselor, you want to assess how the principal viewed the program in the past. When you are starting a new counseling program, determine what expectations the principal has for this new addition to the school. Or if you are a veteran counselor, you want to maintain a strong working relationship with the principal. In all cases, you should schedule a time at the beginning of the year to meet with your principal and gather insights and expectations about your role in the school.

Before you schedule this meeting, do some preparation. Whether you are replacing a counselor, beginning a new program, or reviewing the existing program, make a list of questions to organize your interview with the principal. You may want to memorize these questions, so your interview is relaxed and spontaneous rather than stiff and structured. The following questions and explanations will help you prepare for an interview in a school where you are replacing a counselor. If you are a new counselor or a veteran counselor, you will need to adjust these questions to fit your situation. For a veteran counselor, an adaptation of these questions will help you and your principal examine where the program is and where it could be heading.

Questions for the Principal

1. *What was the most beneficial service offered in the school counseling program last year?* The principal's answer to this question will help you assess his or her priorities for the program. This information enables you to compare your philosophy with the principal's expectations and determine how close or far apart you are. By comparing your views with the principal's, you will know how much work you have to do to convince the principal of why a comprehensive school counseling program can benefit an elementary or middle school.

2. *Was there an annual plan for the school counseling program?* If there was a plan, you may have seen it during your interview for the position. If you did not see one, ask about it. An annual plan will give you a clear idea of what the past program looked like. If the principal indicates that there was no written plan, this is an excellent opportunity to mention that you would like to create one to give the program specific direction during the year and adequate evaluation at the end of the year.

3. *Are the teachers involved in providing guidance in the classroom?* The principal's answer to this question will indicate how the school views "guidance" and who has responsibility for it. You might ask whether there is a guidance curriculum—learning goals and objectives that are part of the overall school curriculum. Some states and school systems have developed guidance curriculums for every grade level. If this is true in your school, who has responsibility for it? On the one hand, if you find that teachers are integrating guidance activities into their daily instruction, you will know that you have a strong foundation for a comprehensive school counseling program. If, on the other hand, the counselor has had sole responsibility for classroom guidance, much work will need to be done to expand counseling services.

4. *Are teachers involved in an advisement program?* This question aims particularly at middle schools but also can pertain to elementary programs. If teachers are active in an advisement program, what is the school counselor's

role? A comprehensive school counseling program will include some type of advisement program that involves teachers for which the counselor might have coordinating responsibility. The counselor also provides in-service training for teachers. A strong advisement program is the heart of a school counselor's referral system.

5. *Is there an advisory committee for the school counseling program?* A comprehensive program of services will reflect the needs of the school and community. To achieve this, seek input from others. If the counseling program had an advisory committee in the past, encourage the principal to continue with one. If there is currently no committee, ask the principal to suggest names of teachers and parents who might serve. In middle schools, you also could recommend that students have representation. If your school has numerous committees, you may want to recommend that an existing committee serve as the advisory group for the counseling program. The school does not need to add yet another committee, so you will win favor with the teachers by combining this initiative with other committee objectives.

Once established, the advisory committee will help you assess student needs, design a comprehensive program, inform the staff about program goals and its role in reaching these objectives, and evaluate services for the year. An advisory committee enables a counselor to win support from the faculty for program decisions and changes. It also encourages the staff to accept responsibility for various aspects of the program, thereby sharing ownership of the school counseling program.

6. *What parental involvement have you had in the school?* A comprehensive counseling program benefits from volunteers and parents who are involved in their children's education. A school that prides itself in strong parental involvement and volunteer programs is in good shape to establish a comprehensive counseling program.

How your principal answers this question may give you an indication of how welcomed parents are in the school. School climate is essential to school effectiveness and is, in turn, affected by parent attitudes. As the counselor, you can assist the principal in strengthening parent and school relationships, thereby improving student performance.

7. *Is the counseling center located in an ideal place, and is it adequately furnished?* If you have begun working as a school counselor, you have already assessed the facilities and made preliminary judgments. If your assessment is positive, you will not need to ask this question. If, however, there are some aspects of the counseling center that disturb you, you may want the principal's perceptions.

The principal will be able to educate you about funding limits, space restrictions, and other realities that have an impact on the placement and furnishings of the counseling center. If the principal is open to suggestions for changing the center, you may want to have a few ideas in mind. For example, suppose you are in an elementary building with three stories, and the counseling center is in the basement at the far end of a dark hall. You may want to emphasize that student access to the counselor is paramount to a successful program and that kindergarten and first grade children would probably not be comfortable visiting the counselor under these conditions. Would any other alternatives be possible?

When focusing on facilities of the counseling center, it is wise to emphasize their impact on the program and on students, parents, and teachers. Avoid mentioning your own welfare, preferences, and tastes. The most important factor is how appropriate facilities contribute to a positive difference for clients the program intends to serve.

Is the furniture adequate? Are there adult-size chairs as well as student chairs? Is there a telephone for making referrals and following up cases? Is the center sufficiently private for confidential sessions? If some of the facilities are less than adequate, ask your principal how you can help improve the situation. Worksheet 1-2 provides an easy checklist to evaluate your facilities.

Because elementary and middle school counselors are frequently placed in buildings that were designed and constructed before counseling programs existed, adequate facilities are sometimes unavailable. Take heart. Remember, just because the broom closet or boiler room is the only available space does not mean it has to look and function like a broom closet or basement. Use your imagination, ask teachers for ideas, and renovate!

8. *What has been the most successful service offered in the counseling program?* If the principal has an answer, you may want to follow up by asking how the service was evaluated. The principal's response will give you insight into the kinds of accountability processes that have existed in the program. You will want to stress the importance of evaluating services so that the program can be altered each year to meet the needs of students, parents, and teachers.

9. *Was there any service or activity in the past that the principal prefers to discontinue?* Sometimes principals and counselors do not communicate. If your principal has allowed some services to continue despite his or her feelings about them, you should know this up front. If the principal dislikes a service that you believe is important, you can examine what aspects of the service have been discomforting and negotiate changes to make it more palatable.

As a follow-up to this question, you might also ask about activities that the principal wants you to handle but that have no relationship to counseling services. As a member of the school staff, you will want to participate and accept your fair share of responsibilities to help the school run smoothly. Although you want to be involved, extra duties or administrative functions can detract from your primary role of serving students and might even defeat your purpose in the school.

WORKSHEET 1-2

Facility Checklist for a School Counseling Center

Directions: Check *Yes* or *No* for each of the items on the list.

Yes   No

☐   ☐   Adequate space for small group sessions.

☐   ☐   Counselor's office has audio and visual privacy.

☐   ☐   A reception area for waiting and reviewing materials.

☐   ☐   A display area for educational and career materials.

☐   ☐   A telephone and desktop computer for the counselor.

☐   ☐   Storage area for equipment, toys, games, and materials.

☐   ☐   Appropriate sized furniture for students and adults.

☐   ☐   Tables for group activities.

☐   ☐   Access to a conference room.

☐   ☐   A sink for washing hands and cleaning up paint, clay, and so forth.

☐   ☐   A computer for student self-instruction and guidance programs.

☐   ☐   A TV monitor for video, Internet, and closed circuit use.

☐   ☐   A secure room elsewhere in the school where records are stored and teachers can have access without disrupting counseling services.

These sample questions are intended as a starter list that you will want to tailor to suit your situation and needs. Having an open, honest discussion with your principal sets the stage for you to win support for a comprehensive school counseling program. The questions may also help you survey your teaching colleagues to assess what teachers think will make a good program. Without knowing what they think, you are less able to win their support, which along with that of the principal is essential for success of a school counseling program. Teachers' support is also important in helping you convince them of their role in assisting with student development.

Sharing Ownership

Winning support from your principal is the first step toward including your colleagues in planning and implementing a school counseling program. An advisory committee is an excellent vehicle through which to gain their cooperation. After discussing the idea of a committee with your principal, you will want to select members. This selection might come from recommendations of the principal or from volunteers. The persons selected for this committee should advocate a strong counseling program, believe that the program is the responsibility of all staff members, and be willing to attend committee meetings during the year.

If you and your principal decide to seek volunteers, an announcement about the committee could be made to the staff at a faculty meeting or by a memo to the teachers. You might consider sending out an announcement and following it up with discussion at a faculty meeting. Exhibit 1-3 presents an example of an announcement.

During the year, your advisory committee will help you and the teachers plan events and activities to focus on schoolwide guidance, parent involvement, student development, and school climate. As these activities are implemented, the involvement of your students, parents, and teachers will be essential. This is another illustration of how the school counseling program belongs to everyone.

Letting everyone share ownership in the counseling program gives you support that is vital to function as a school counselor in a comprehensive program of services. Such support enables you to define clearly the expanded services of the program.

DEFINING WHAT YOU DO: A GLOSSARY OF SERVICES

Many functions of school counselors are defined and described in counseling literature and research. As mentioned earlier in this chapter, school counseling is a broad professional practice that includes preventive services, developmental activities, and remedial interventions. As such, counseling in schools encompasses a wide variety of activities and services. An important characteristic of a comprehensive school counseling program is the awareness people have about your role as a counselor. To be successful, you need to educate students, parents, and teachers about program services.

One way to help others learn about your role as a school counselor is to list your functions, with a brief description of each, in a faculty manual, student handbook, PTA or PTO newsletter, or other resource. But the first step is to identify for yourself what it is you do.

Identifying Services

The following list will help identify and describe the services of a comprehensive school counseling program. Depending on your audience—students, parents, or teachers—you may need to adjust the language and edit the list accordingly.

Individual Counseling

School counselors provide individual sessions for students to assist with a variety of educational and personal concerns. The primary purpose of these

EXHIBIT 1-3

Advisory Committee Volunteers

Dear Teachers:

The principal, Mrs. Jones, has asked that we form an Advisory Committee for the School Counseling Program. This Committee will consist of teachers, students, and parents, and will guide the counseling program during the year. The committee will

· Design a needs assessment procedure and make program decisions based on the results of this assessment
· Determine how classroom teachers will use the guidance curriculum during the year
· Assist the counselor with the design of a schedule of services
· Help the counselor determine topics for group counseling and group guidance
· Focus on school climate and recommend activities to improve the learning atmosphere
· Help the counselor design procedures to evaluate the program during the school year

The committee is to meet before the end of September, and then will meet three times during the year. The school counselor will chair the committee.

Mrs. Jones will select committee members next week. If you are interested or can recommend students and parents for the committee, please complete the form below and return it to the counselor's mailbox. Mrs. Jones will announce the committee members at our next faculty meeting.

Thank you for your assistance!

Advisory Committee Form

Name _____

_____ I would like to serve on the School Counseling Advisory Committee

_____ I nominate the following student for the committee: _____

_____

_____ I nominate the following parent for the committee: _____

_____

Home Phone: _____

Please return this form to the counselor's mailbox.

sessions is to help students explore their concerns, make appropriate plans of action, and be successful in following through with their plans.

Group Counseling

In some instances, students help each other by working in groups with leadership from a counselor. Group counseling allows students to share ideas about specific issues such as problem solving, career choices, educational planning, and peer relationships, as well as helping them use these ideas to resolve their concerns. Group sessions usually involve small groups of students, who are led by a counselor and meet once or twice a week for a specific number of sessions.

Group Guidance

School counselors often meet with groups to help students learn specific information about themselves and their development. These instructional groups are commonly referred to as group guidance. Ideally, teachers also lead these types of activities in their classrooms. Guidance groups can be small or large, and usually the guidance topic is related to one or more goals and objectives in a guidance curriculum.

Group guidance also can be used in a student/teacher advisement program. Whether a counselor or a teacher leads them, guidance groups are instructional in nature and focus on topics such as self-concept development, study skills, friendship, health habits, career information, and good citizenship.

Guidance Curriculum

Some schools design learning goals and instructional strategies to assist students with personal, social, career, and educational development and write these goals and strategies into the school curriculum. The intent is to have these goals and objectives incorporated into daily instruction by classroom teachers. School counselors assist with this curriculum by planning its integration with teachers, providing resources and materials, and presenting some activities with teachers in the classroom. You will learn more about this service in Chapter Five.

Student Appraisal

Counselors help students, parents, and teachers by gathering information about student abilities, behaviors, and achievement so they can help make appropriate decisions about educational placement and instruction. In helping with these decisions, counselors use tests, inventories, observations, interviews, and other procedures to gather information.

Referral

School counselors serve as referral agents to help students and their families receive assistance from other programs and services in the school system and from agencies outside the school. Counselors work closely with teachers and administrators in these referral processes.

Consultation

Helping children develop to their fullest potential is best accomplished when people work together. For this reason, counselors consult with teachers and parents to plan appropriate services for every child. These consultations typically focus on the needs of the individual child, but sometimes counselors lead group consultations for teachers and parents to focus on specific issues and topics. For example, a counselor might present an in-service workshop for teachers to learn about indicators of child depression, or they may lead an education group for parents to discuss childrearing techniques.

Coordination

The school counseling program includes a wide range of services and activities that require coordination for smooth administration and for which the counselor assumes primary responsibility. In some instances, student helpers, parent volunteers, and teachers can be of assistance.

The preceding list is a sample of typical counselor services. Use it as a guide to develop a list that suits you and your school's counseling program. As you can see, responsibility for many activities is shared. Your next step in program development is to determine areas of shared responsibility: Who does what?

Communicating Your Role

As noted earlier in this section, having a lexicon or description of your services is just the first step in defining what you do in the elementary or middle school. More important are the processes you use and actions you take to communicate your role with students, parents, teachers, administrators, and the community.

This *Survival Guide* devotes considerable attention to ideas and strategies that counselors use to help people understand their role in schools, so I will not devote much space to the topic here. However, there are a couple of essential points that might help you create and communicate a role that is professionally satisfying and rewarding. Here are three starter ideas:

1. *Use existing avenues of communication.* For example, if you have regular faculty meetings, PTA (or PTO) meetings, assemblies, or other gatherings in the school, place yourself on the agenda each time and tell something about what the counseling program is accomplishing. If your school puts out a newsletter periodically, write a "Counselor's Column" that shares useful information for students, parents, and teachers.
2. *Commandeer a bulletin board.* Sometimes counselors shy away from being responsible for bulletin boards in the school, and this reluctance

is understandable. Sometimes managing bulletin boards becomes a full-time job and takes counselors away from their primary responsibility. Nevertheless, having control of at least one bulletin board can be an excellent way to communicate what you and the counseling program are doing in school. Be sure to include samples of student's drawings and other productions if appropriate because they will attract attention to your announcements.

3. *Launch your program into cyberspace.* In this rapidly changing world of advanced technology, it is essential that the counseling program be visible on all school communications, including the Internet. Make sure you ask for space on the school's Web site to have a link to the school counseling program.

These three ideas only scratch the surface of ways to communicate your role in a comprehensive school counseling program. What is most important, and stressed throughout this book, is the effort you make to communicate the role as you understand it so that you take professional command of who you are and what you do in the school.

In this chapter, you have learned about ways to describe and define a comprehensive school counseling program. This guide takes the position that planning, organizing, implementing, and evaluating a program of services are key to your survival as a school counselor. To be successful in this endeavor, seek input from others and share ownership of the program. The next step is to determine the responsibilities that various players—administrators, teachers, and counselors—have in making a comprehensive program of services a reality. Chapter Two offers suggestions for determining these responsibilities, identifying your role in the program, and learning to balance your time across the many services of a comprehensive school counseling program.

chapter 2

DEVELOPING YOUR ROLE *and* CREATING *an* IDENTITY

Before considering various aspects of developing your role in a comprehensive school counseling program, let us reemphasize that a National Model is available from the American School Counselor Association (see Chapter One). At the same time, as an elementary or middle school counselor, you want to be aware of any local or state initiatives that encourage counselors to design comprehensive programs according to particular guidelines. It is inefficient to create a program according to steps you have designed if your school system or state has already recommended guidelines about the role and function of school counselors. If you find that your school system or state has a plan for developing and implementing a comprehensive program of services, this *Survival Guide* will be a useful resource to complement that plan. If you do not find a local or state plan, this guide could be a primary source for developing a comprehensive counseling program for your school, as well as establishing your role and creating your identity as the counselor in your elementary or middle school.

The educational reform movement that began in the 1980s continues to have an impact on state programs and local perspectives about what school counselors should be doing with students, parents, and teachers. Unfortunately, some school administrators, or committees of people other than counselors, often control the school counselor's job description. For this reason, it is imperative and ethical that you learn about comprehensive programs through this *Survival Guide* or other useful resources and apply these ideas within the context of the local school system and the state where you practice as a school counselor.

Once you have checked to see whether any local or state initiatives exist to guide the development of school counseling programs and the counselor's role, you are in a more knowledgeable position to use this guide. The first step after you have described the program is to determine who is responsible for particular services.

DETERMINING WHO DOES WHAT

Some key elements play an important part in helping counselors develop a clear role for themselves in a comprehensive program of services while also identifying assignments for teachers and other personnel. I discussed some of these elements in the first chapter, but it is helpful to repeat them here. First, it is vital that you work with your advisory committee to initiate some type of needs assessment. Through this process, you and the committee are then able to select program goals and objectives. Once you have identified goals and objectives, you can design services and activities to address broad goals and meet specific objectives. As you and the school identify appropriate services, you and the advisory committee are able to recommend assignments for administrators, teachers, yourself, and others to make sure that these services are delivered.

I will explore performing needs assessments and setting program goals and objectives based on the outcomes of these assessments in Chapter Three. By way of introduction, Exhibit 2-1 illustrates ten key elements of implementing a program. Throughout this and the remaining chapters of the *Survival Guide,* you will learn about these key elements and their importance to a comprehensive program.

Describing and defining your broad role as a counselor in the school provides a framework and the parameters for specific services you will offer. This framework is the structure within which to create an identity of who you are and what you do as the school counselor. Creating this identity is the next step in developing a successful program.

As noted in Chapter One, an advisory committee helps you give direction to the counseling program. In addition, a committee can enlist the support of teachers and parents to help with some of the services in the program. For example, suppose the students' needs assessment produces an outcome that says many students want more friends but are unsure how to form friendships. To address this need, your school might decide to have a special schoolwide program that focuses on friendship and call it a "Friendship

---

EXHIBIT 2-1

Ten Keys to Implementing a Comprehensive Program

1. Design needs assessment instruments and processes for students, parents, and teachers.
2. Interview the principal and other administrators to assess their perception of school needs.
3. Review the outcome of the needs assessment with the advisory committee.
4. Prioritize needs indicated by review of the outcomes.
5. Select, design, and create activities, strategies, and services to address prioritized needs.
6. Assign responsibilities for particular services and activities.
7. Schedule activities and services.
8. Monitor activities and services to be certain all students are included in the program.
9. Evaluate ongoing services throughout the year to measure outcomes.
10. Seek feedback from students, parents, teachers, and administrators to assess overall program satisfaction.

Week" program, with various activities planned and assignments made. The plans could call for students to make posters about different kinds of friendships. Teachers would integrate friendship activities into language arts instruction. Parent and other volunteers could speak to classes about important friendships they have formed. You might lead group guidance sessions on how to make new friends. Each of these activities would contribute to Friendship Week, and each would allow different people to assume responsibility for making the program a success. Assignments from the advisory committee would enable each person to accept responsibility for some aspect of this special event.

In managing special activities, it is helpful to have assignment sheets to specify everyone's responsibilities. Exhibit 2-2 gives an example based on Friendship Week in a middle school. Use it as a prototype for schoolwide activities you might plan.

A successful counseling program requires an understanding of who is responsible for what. If people do not clearly understand their assignments and responsibilities, the program becomes uncoordinated, services are duplicated, and resentment might occur because "some people are not doing their job." The following example illustrates what can happen when we do not clearly define functions and have undetermined responsibilities.

EXHIBIT 2-2

Friendship Week Assignments

Monday: All teachers will plan a language arts lesson for the morning to focus on the importance of friendships in life. Stories, videos, and writing projects will be available for review in the media center to assist with lesson plans.

    The counselor will visit all fifth grade classes during the day to make a twenty to thirty minute presentation on "Inviting New Friends." (For a friendship curriculum, see Schmidt, 1997.) Please schedule time for the counselor to visit your class.

Tuesday: Teachers will plan art activities for students to make posters about friendship. All posters will be hung and placed around the school for the PTA meeting Tuesday night. Volunteers will visit classes Tuesday afternoon to speak on the topic, "Friendships That Made a Difference." A schedule of volunteer visits will be sent to teachers the week before.

    The counselor will visit all sixth grade classes to make a twenty to thirty minute presentation on "Ingredients of Positive Friendships." Please schedule a time for the counselor to visit your class.

Wednesday: Mrs. English's sixth grade class will present its original play, "My Best Friend," to all grades in the morning. The play will be repeated for parents at the PTA/PTO meeting. Teachers should plan follow-up guidance activities with their classes after the play.

    The counselor will visit all seventh grade classes and present on the topic "Friendships That Last." Please schedule a time for the counselor to visit your class.

Thursday: Mr. Pritchett from the community theater will present his one-man show, "Huck Finn and Friends." The media center has scheduled times on Thursday and Friday for each class to do follow-up activities. A schedule will be presented to teachers at the next faculty meeting. Peer helpers will be available Thursday and Friday afternoons to see students who want to talk about their friendships. The counselor will have more information about this activity at the next faculty meeting.

Friday: Teachers will meet with their advisees during the regularly scheduled TAP (Teacher Adviser Program) meetings to ask students about the weeklong activities. Evaluation forms will be available at this time for students to complete. Each teacher will tally the evaluations from their advisees and send a summary to the counselor.

A teacher in a middle school was advising a student about how to cope with the separation of his mother and father. At the same time, this student was in group counseling with other students who also were experiencing family changes. The counselor did not know of the teacher's relationship with the student and, as a result, there was no coordination of services. The student became confused because of contradictions between what the teacher advised and the direction of the group counseling sessions. This confusion could have been avoided if the teacher knew that students who need continued counseling should be referred to a school counselor. The counselor in this case had neglected to inform teachers adequately of their advisement and referral roles. Teacher advisement of students is an important part of a counseling program and can help to identify students who need assistance from a professional counselor. When counselors do not clearly communicate with teachers about their functions and relationships, confusion and misunderstanding can occur.

In another school, an elementary counselor realized the importance of determining and communicating roles when a new teacher asked, "When are you going to take my class for guidance?" The counselor inquired, "What do you have in mind?" The teacher replied, "The art teacher and music teacher have scheduled my class so I can get my lesson plans done. Will you be doing the same?"

Fortunately, this counselor had a strong advisory committee who supported the belief that classroom guidance is best accomplished when integrated by teachers into daily instruction. The counselor in this school assisted teachers in this process by helping them plan guidance activities, finding resources and materials for teachers to use, and presenting special guidance lessons with teachers in the classroom. At a faculty meeting, the advisory committee presented this role of the counselor and teachers working together, and this procedure enabled the counselor to work out a suitable plan with this particular teacher. They planned guidance activities together and presented them in a team-teaching approach.

CREATING A COUNSELOR IDENTITY

Establishing a school counseling program and creating an identity as a school counselor are continuous processes. Once you have defined the program, you will want to develop ways to advertise it and promote yourself so people consistently understand and accept your role as counselor in the school. This is a continuous process because people and programs in schools are ever changing. In addition to the new students, parents, and teachers who come into your school each year, other changes commonly occur. Advisory committee members could change, or your school might replace the principal. Each change potentially influences the direction and definition of a school counseling program. Having methods of educating people about the program and about your role as a counselor is essential if you desire to maintain continuity of services and leadership of the program.

Advertising the Program

Plan ways to advertise your program. For example, design a school counseling brochure. Make it attractive with the school logo on the front and your name, phone number, and e-mail address on the back. The contents of a brochure should describe the counseling program and your role as a school counselor. Be brief. Details are not necessary in this type of communication. Generally, it is best to highlight short descriptions and illustrate the overall program. Use Exhibit 2-3 as a guide in developing the content of your program brochure.

In elementary and middle schools, it is wise to avoid the term *therapy*. Also, use the term *counseling* sparingly in brochures and handouts that describe to parents services of the school counseling program. Not everyone understands that counseling is a helping and learning process. Some people, including a few professionals, associate similar meanings to *counseling* and *therapy*. These terms, though useful to professionals, raise unnecessary alarm among parents and move their focus away from the primary mission of the program. That mission is to help children learn. You will therefore want to convey to parents that your services have the educational purpose of assisting children with learning. Your goal as counselor is to help children achieve in school and in life. To do this, you and the teachers cooperate to offer a broad range of services.

As noted earlier, other media for advertising your program are the school Web site and newsletters. Local newspapers and radio programs are other vehicles to use. Ask your principal whether you can have a column in each issue of the school newspaper. You might use this column to announce upcoming schoolwide activities planned by the advisory committee and the teachers or to send home useful information to parents.

Local town and city newspapers are also a good source for advertising school events. When you plan a special event, ask your principal whether it is permissible to call the local newspaper. An article in the local press will establish both an identity for yourself as the counselor in the school and an awareness in the community about your services. Local radio shows can serve the same purpose. Frequently, radio stations are looking for material for public service announcements and information. See whether there is a market in your area.

EXHIBIT 2-3

School Counseling Brochure

Hello, I am *[your name]*, the school counselor at *[school name]*. I am available to help you and your child have a successful school year. As a school counselor, I work with parents and students in different ways through a program of many services. Each service is aimed at helping children learn and develop to their highest potential. Some of the services in the school counseling program are

· Groups to help children learn how to study
· Individual sessions to help children adjust to school
· Classroom lessons to help children learn how to get along with others
· Groups for parents to share and learn ways to communicate with their children
· Conferences for parents to learn about their children's progress in school

These are a few of the services I offer you and your child. If you have questions or wish to see me about your child, please call me at school. The number is *[counselor's telephone]*. The best time to reach me is between 7:30 and 8:00 A.M. or after 3:00 P.M. Check out the School Counselor page on the school's Web site: http://www.schoolname/schoolcounseling.usa.

Parent coffee hours held during the daytime or evening are another vehicle to highlight services in your program. They are most successful when they include fun activities and icebreakers as well as topics of interest for the parents who attend. For example, Tom Carr, an elementary counselor and a past president of the North Carolina School Counselor Association, has used an activity that allows parents to express their opinions about child behavior before they hear a presentation about discipline. The activity asks parents to use a scale of +3 to −3 to rate various statements about children and parenting. Sample statements might include

• Children should have a voice in purchasing large family items, such as automobiles.
• Allowances should be directly related to children's chores.
• Physical punishment is sometimes necessary.
• Television watching and Internet surfing should be restricted for children.
• Parents should ask permission or knock before entering a child's room.

The ratings (+3, +2, +1, 0, −1, −2, −3) are posted on the walls around the room. After the parents rate all the statements, the counselor reads each item and parents are asked to stand near the spot where their rating is posted. As the counselor reads each item, parents move from one rating to another depending on how they scored the items and thereby learn how they responded in comparison to the rest of the group. They hold no discussion or debate about which rating is "most correct," but parents see that there are different points of view in the group. It is a fun icebreaker and a good way to set the stage for a presentation on discipline at home or other, similar topics.

Parent education programs, such as coffee hours, are excellent public relations activities for school counselors. Chapter Eight discusses these types of activities in more detail. In addition to helping you advertise the school counseling program, they also promote you as a school counselor. Self-promotion is another way of creating an identity.

Promoting Yourself

Your success in creating a positive image for yourself as an elementary or middle school counselor is influenced by the methods you choose to advertise your program. Whereas newspaper articles, radio broadcasts, program brochures, and other methods are aimed at advertising the program and informing the public, they also contribute to your professional identity. Newspaper stories, a counselor's column in the school or town newspaper, PTA presentations, workshops for community groups, and a number of other avenues give you an opportunity to highlight services and accomplishments you achieve as the school counselor. This process of *promoting yourself* is not an egotistical posture, but rather a means of focusing on the important contribution that counselors make in our schools. Of course, you will want to be judicious about how you promote yourself, but the point is to let people know about the program and the many services you offer. By highlighting your accomplishments, you elevate the entire school counseling profession.

Volunteer services are another way to introduce yourself to groups outside the school. By assisting in a crisis center, serving on a community board, and participating in local youth organizations, you help community leaders and volunteers learn who you are and what you do in the school. Often, our professional identity is most clearly defined not by what we say about who we are, but by what we do in the community where we live and work. By being active and behaving in an exemplary manner, we paint a positive picture of the counseling profession and ourselves.

One method of promoting yourself each new school year is by introducing yourself to students in all the classes. In elementary and middle schools, new students arrive each year. At the same time, students who were at the school last year may need a "refresher" to help them remember who you are and what you do. To help them, you should develop an introduction activity that tells students something about yourself and what you do as a school counselor.

As you think about this introduction session, remember the developmental levels of the students to whom you are introducing yourself. The level of those students will influence the nature of your introductory activity, especially the media you choose to use. If you are a beginning counselor, you may want to confer with experienced elementary or middle school counselors to benefit from their advice.

Examine your own talents and skills as possible vehicles with which to introduce yourself. If you play a musical instrument, use it in a sing-along activity with young children. Or if you have a skill such as juggling or performing magic, use it. Your skill could entertain the students while relating an educational message. Juggling, for example, could be associated with the idea that some things seem very difficult, yet with a little training and practice, we can accomplish these seemingly impossible tasks. In a similar way, magic tricks can show how we see things differently. Sometimes, what we see is not always the way things are. Counselors help people see and understand things better.

Puppets are a favorite medium of elementary children. Young students enjoy the animation and can easily relate to the counselor. Middle school students enjoy puppets, but only when the activities are appropriate to their age and developmental levels. If you choose to use puppets with middle school students, try them out in small groups with lifelike puppets and a moderate level of puppetry skill. If you have no experience with puppets, or are uncertain about your skills, find out whether there are training programs or workshops available in the community. The local arts council and public library are two places to ask about these types of workshops. Also, several Web sites on the Internet provide information about puppetry.

Some counselors are creative in designing their introductory activities. One elementary counselor uses a simple, empty paper bag in an activity called "The Counselor's Bag" (see Bowman, 1986). This is how it works. Hold the bag at the top with the thumb and middle finger. As you explain what you do in the school, pretend to throw these "services" into the bag. While tossing in a service, snap the fingers that are holding the bag and make it sound as though something has dropped into the bag. Young children enjoy this activity while learning about who the counselor is and what the counselor does.

All of these activities—introducing yourself, being involved in your school, and participating in the community—will make demands on your time. As an elementary or middle school counselor, you will find that time is a critical and elusive commodity. As you become successful and known in your school and community, people will request more services of you. To keep control of your personal and professional time while meeting these demands, you must decide how the time available will be balanced across all the services and activities offered in your school counseling program.

BALANCING TIME

Using time wisely and efficiently is like walking a tightrope. You need good balance. Without balance, you cannot get across to the other side, and similarly, without monitoring your time your counseling program will not be efficient and effective.

Balance does not occur by accident. We learn to balance ourselves by developing skills, accepting the support of others, and using appropriate and available resources. In learning to walk a tightrope, performers first learn basic skills and fundamental rules. They then accept the instruction and support of expert tightrope artists who offer encouragement and valuable experience. Finally, they use apparatuses and equipment, such as a balancing pole, that increase the likelihood of their success.

Balancing time in your counseling program is analogous to learning to be a successful tightrope walker. You begin by designing a system to determine where time is most needed. Next, you establish a schedule of activities, recruit volunteers, and search for resources to assist in delivering these services. You begin by setting priorities for the counseling program.

Setting Priorities

As noted earlier, your advisory committee, other teachers, and administrators can assist in determining program priorities. By accepting their input and assistance, you will be able to decide which services are important to the school and determine what will benefit students the most.

You learned earlier that needs assessments help gather data to use in setting program priorities. Chapter Three describes needs assessment procedures. At this point, you want to develop a process for allotting time to your program priorities. There is no precise way to do this, but if you design some type of process, you can justify to yourself and the school why you schedule activities in a particular way.

One way of allotting time is to list all your services by the priorities determined by your advisory committee. The committee will need your guidance in this process. After the list of priorities is complete, create a worksheet to determine the total amount of time you have to devote to the school counseling program. Typically, a normal work week is about forty hours. Begin allotting time to each of the services listed. As you proceed, your worksheet may look eventually like the sample in Exhibit 2-4.

This balance sheet is a sample and not intended as an ideal program balance. Sometimes, as you can see from this list, the importance of an activity does not necessarily determine the amount of time allotted. For example, referral processes may be a very important service, but if few children or families in your school need referral assistance, you will allot less time to this

EXHIBIT 2-4

Sample Time-Balance Sheet

Individual counseling	10 hours
Group guidance	6 hours
Group counseling	6 hours
Program coordination	4 hours
Student appraisal	4 hours
Teacher consultation	2 hours
Parent consultation	2 hours
Peer helper program	2 hours
Referrals	2 hours
Parent education programs	1 hour
Student orientation	1 hour

activity. Usually, the most important services you deliver as a school counselor will be those that provide direct services to students: counseling and guidance.

Another fact about allotting time to your activities is that as the year progresses, some activities will change in their level of priority. For example, on the list in Exhibit 2.4, *student orientation* has the least amount of time devoted to it. This may be appropriate during the middle or end of the school year, but in the beginning of the year, most counselors would allocate a greater amount of time to it. Of course, program priorities will change during the year, and as a result, you will alter that balance of time accordingly. This also will affect the schedule you establish for the services and activities for which you are responsible. An established schedule helps keep your time well balanced.

Worksheet 2-1 helps set priorities and allot adequate time to each service. Begin by reviewing the services listed and delete or add as appropriate for the services you deliver as a counselor.

Establishing a Schedule

Counselors are different from teachers because they do not have assigned students or a definite schedule of classes. Successful counselors, however, find that a schedule helps them to control their time and informs teachers and administrators about the services of the counseling program.

After you have allotted time for specific services of the school counseling program for which you have responsibility, you will want to design a schedule.

WORKSHEET 2-1

Time-Balance Worksheet

Service	Priority	Time Available
Individual counseling	_____	_____
Group counseling	_____	_____
Group guidance	_____	_____
Program coordination	_____	_____
Student appraisal	_____	_____
Teacher consultation	_____	_____
Parent consultation	_____	_____
Peer helper training and supervision	_____	_____
Referrals to other services	_____	_____
Teacher in-service	_____	_____
Parent education programs	_____	_____
Student orientation services	_____	_____

This will not be a permanent schedule because, as noted above, your program priorities and responsibilities will change as the year progresses. You might find that a weekly schedule is best, or perhaps a monthly schedule will suffice. Whichever you decide, it is important to convey to administrators and teachers that a counselor's schedule is a guide that must remain flexible. Flexibility enables you to address and handle crises as they occur in the school. Crises not withstanding, you should stay on schedule once you announce it to the faculty. A posted schedule that is seldom followed is worse than no schedule at all. Most teachers are tolerant when crises interrupt their plans, but they appreciate dependability and respect a counselor who provides anticipated services reliably.

You may want to post your schedule so that teachers and administrators know your whereabouts should they need you. Some counselors post weekly schedules in the principal's office and the faculty lounge. This not only helps colleagues locate you in emergencies but also advertises the many services of the counseling program.

A sample schedule in Exhibit 2-5 uses the time allotments from the Time-Balance Sheet in Worksheet 2-1. You will want to design your own schedule based on the priorities and time allotments of your school counseling program. Worksheet 2-2 is a blank schedule that you can use in establishing a weekly schedule.

In addition to setting a counselor's schedule, it might also be helpful to have a master schedule for the school counseling program. In the same way

EXHIBIT 2-5

Sample Schedule

Monday	Tuesday	Wednesday	Thursday	Friday	Time
Parent conferences	Individual sessions	Orientation	Individual sessions	Individual sessions	8:00
Group guidance	Individual sessions	Individual sessions	Individual sessions	Group counseling	9:00
Group guidance	Group counseling	Group counseling	Group counseling	Group guidance	10:00
Individual sessions	Testing	Observations	Observations	Parent group	11:00
Peer helper	Teacher consultation	Peer helper	Group guidance	Group counseling	12:30
Group guidance	Testing	Individual sessions	Individual sessions	Teacher consultation	1:30
Program coordination	Group guidance	Group counseling	Individual sessions	Program coordination	2:30

that you decide whether to use a weekly, monthly, or semester schedule for yourself as counselor, a master schedule could cover the same period. In the master schedule, you address major goals and activities planned across the school that are part of the school counseling program. Exhibit 2-6 provides an example of a middle school counseling program at the beginning of the school year. Remember, this is a sample. Use it as a guide to construct a master schedule that is unique to your school program.

In addition to assigning and scheduling services for you and the school staff, you might want to recruit volunteers to assist with the school counseling program. Resourceful people can assist you in meeting the demands of a comprehensive school counseling program. The first step is to identify these people and the resources available and determine how to use them efficiently.

Using Resources

There are many ways to use volunteers in a comprehensive school counseling program. As you saw in Exhibit 2.5, the counselor's sample schedule, a peer helper program schedules two hours a week for the counselor to train and supervise students.

WORKSHEET 2-2

Schedule Worksheet

MONDAY	TUESDAY	WEDNESDAY	THURSDAY	FRIDAY	TIME
____	____	____	____	____	7:30 am
____	____	____	____	____	8:00
____	____	____	____	____	8:30
____	____	____	____	____	9:00
____	____	____	____	____	9:30
____	____	____	____	____	10:00
____	____	____	____	____	10:30
____	____	____	____	____	11:00
____	____	____	____	____	11:30
____	____	____	____	____	Noon
____	____	____	____	____	12:30
____	____	____	____	____	1:00
____	____	____	____	____	1:30
____	____	____	____	____	2:00
____	____	____	____	____	2:30
____	____	____	____	____	3:00
____	____	____	____	____	3:30
____	____	____	____	____	4:00
____	____	____	____	____	4:30
____	____	____	____	____	5:00

EXHIBIT 2-6

Sample Master Schedule for a Middle School Counseling Program

Schedule for September

Beginning Date	Activity	Assignments	Date Completed
September 1	Sixth grade student orientation	Counselors, sixth grade teachers, and peer helpers	September 20
September 1	Other new student orientation	Counselors and peer helpers	September 15
September 15	Last year review: successes and challenges	All teacher-advisor groups	September 30
September 15	"To Your Health" (sixth grade)	School nurse	October 30
September 10	Schedule for individual counseling	Counselors	September 20
September 10	Screen students for October and November small groups	Counselors	September 20
September 20	First "Parents and Students in Transition" night (eighth grade)	Administrators, eighth grade teachers, and counselors	September 20
September 15	Career exploration classes (seventh grade)	Counselors and teachers	October 30

Student helpers can be tutors for their peers and younger students. They can be "buddies" and "welcome counselors" for new students who enter the school. Older students can assist teachers with classroom guidance activities. Some students can learn basic listening and helping skills to assist their peers and make referrals to the school counselor.

Potential volunteers also include parents, grandparents, and retired citizens who can tutor or assist with special students in the classroom. To facilitate volunteer services, you can help the school administrators recruit and train these volunteers. Some volunteers can be buddies or older friends for students who need additional attention or who have few adult role models in their families.

Volunteers allow teachers and counselors to devote more time to their primary functions in the instructional and counseling programs. Coordination, training, and monitoring all these volunteer services is important, and your advisory committee can help you establish procedures and identify volunteer coordinators who can assist with this effort. One caveat is that you do not want to create a program that, although intended to help you balance your time, becomes a drain on the limited time you have available. Program coordination is essential.

All the elements presented in this chapter and Chapter One set the stage for establishing a comprehensive school counseling program. These elements show you how to describe and define a program, obtain input from teachers and administrators in your school, create a clear identity for yourself as a school counselor, and use time efficiently. Now that the stage is set for a comprehensive program, it is time to examine the script—the functions and services you will perform and deliver. Chapters Three and Four focus on the major functions used by school counselors in a comprehensive counseling program.

chapter 3

SETTING SAIL *and* STAYING AFLOAT

By describing and identifying a program of services you take the initial step toward getting ready to set sail. The next step is to plan and organize appropriate services to bring the program to life. In survival terms, you set full sail with your program and learn to stay afloat.

This chapter reviews aspects of program planning, including assessment procedures, organizational structures, and evaluation processes. It also examines strategies for coordinating a comprehensive school counseling program. Coordination is essential to the overall organization and success of your counseling program. You demonstrate effective coordination by how efficiently you use a variety of skills, including scheduling, decision making, team building, program planning, and evaluating. Your use of these and other skills begins with planning, which is a critical function of effective elementary and middle school counselors.

PLANNING

Several years ago, David Campbell wrote a popular book titled, *If You Don't Know Where You're Going, You'll Probably End Up Someplace Else.* His book focuses on decisions about career direction and development, but the title and premise also hold true for school counseling programs. If you are unsure of the direction and focus of your program, you will find it difficult to create effective, comprehensive services for students, parents, and teachers. In addition, two corollaries to Campbell's hypothesis apply:

1. If you do not know where you have been, you probably do not know where you are.
2. If you do not know where you are, you probably do not know where you are going.

In planning a comprehensive counseling program, first evaluate where the program has been in the past and what its present direction includes. This is a process of assessing what was and what is in the counseling program.

Assessing the Program

Chapter One presents some questions for interviewing your principal about a comprehensive program. Through such a process, you will gather information about past activities and services, current needs of the school populations, and expectations for the future of the program. Information about these three areas reveal important aspects of your school and the counseling program and help you formulate assessment questions such as the following:

- What services are valued by the school community?
- What are the needs of students, parents, and teachers?
- What results are expected from the services of a school counseling program?

You may gather assessment data to answer these questions formally or informally. In the same way that you interview the principal, you could also design questions for teachers, parents, and students. If you are replacing a counselor who has served the school in past years, you might want to ask questions of each of these groups. Here are some samples:

For Teachers
- What is the most valuable service offered by the school counselor?
- Why is this service valuable?
- What service would you want to increase this coming year?
- Are there additional services you would like to have this coming year?

For Parents
- What do you know about the school counseling services?
- Has your child benefited from any counseling service or activity at school?

- Have you participated in any activity of the counseling program?
- What are the most valuable services of the school counseling program?

For Students

- Did you like anything the counselor did in your school last year?
- What did the counselor do that you liked?
- Is there anything the counselor did that you did not like?
- If a friend had a problem, would you encourage her or him to talk with the counselor?

You will also want to design methods of assessing current needs of students, parents, and teachers. Usually, to collect this information counselors use questionnaires and surveys. Your advisory committee can assist you in designing some questionnaires. For students and parents, you may want to sample populations by choosing a certain percentage, say 10 to 20 percent at each grade level. Such sample groups will give you data to evaluate needs across the entire school. With teachers, I recommend a survey of the entire staff if possible. Here are a few hints for designing assessment questionnaires:

- Limit the number of questions and assess a few specific areas and services.
- Try out the survey with a "test group" of people to check for clarity and understanding of the items.
- Read the students' survey out loud to young children (primary grades) or students with reading difficulties.
- Word the items in *positive* rather than *negative* language. Avoid "not," "don't," "doesn't," "won't," and other pessimistic terms.
- Design objective items that people can answer by checking a response rather than by writing lengthy answers.

Worksheets 3-1, 3-2, and 3-3 are sample questionnaires for students, parents, and teachers. The student form is for primary children and can be adapted for older students by rewording items and using the responses "yes," "no," and "sometimes" in place of the smiley faces.

In addition to assessing the needs of students, parents, and teachers, you will also want to evaluate the overall school climate. Research has shown that a school's learning atmosphere correlates with student achievement. Student success and progress are enhanced to the degree that schools establish positive climates and invite children to learn. One the one hand, schools that are positive, optimistic, and caring tend to generate optimal learning for students. On the other hand, punitive and negative schools become bastions of disruption, vandalism, low self-esteem, and poor performance.

WORKSHEET 3-1

Primary Student Needs Assessment

Name _____ Date _____

INSTRUCTIONS: Listen to the teacher or counselor as she or he reads each question to you. Circle the face that shows how you would answer the question. Make a circle around the face you choose.

1. I like coming to this school.

2. I am happy with my work.

3. I like my teacher.

4. I have many friends.

5. I like riding the bus to school.

6. I am happy in my family.

7. I like to look at books.

8. I like showing my parents my schoolwork.

9. My friends like me.

10. I am happy when I go home from school.

WORKSHEET 3-2

Middle School Parent Needs Assessment

INSTRUCTIONS: Please complete this questionnaire and return it to the counselor's office at the school. Thank you.

Circle your responses:

1. My child needs to focus more on schoolwork.	Yes	No	Sometimes
2. My child chooses responsible friends.	Yes	No	Sometimes
3. My child enjoys school.	Yes	No	Sometimes
4. I help my child with homework.	Yes	No	Sometimes
5. My child does well in schoolwork.	Yes	No	Sometimes
6. My child spends too much time alone.	Yes	No	Sometimes
7. My child fights with other children too much.	Yes	No	Sometimes
8. My child gets along with most teachers.	Yes	No	Sometimes
9. I would like to be involved in parent programs at school to help me learn about my child.	Yes	No	Sometimes
10. I am interested in volunteering in school.	Yes	No	Sometimes

Name _____ Date _____

Child's Name _____

Ask your advisory committee to design a process for assessing school climate. Do students, parents, and teachers feel welcome in their school? Are they comfortable in the school surroundings? Do they feel safe? Staff morale, student learning, and parental involvement are all influenced by "atmospheric conditions" in the school. When the places in which we learn and work demonstrate caring, respect, and value for our well-being, we are more likely to achieve our educational goals.

To help your school focus on positive ways to improve the learning climate, design assessment processes to seek input from students, parents, and teachers. Worksheet 3-4 offers one example of a student survey, the results from which could help a school plan strategies to improve relationships, enhance its physical appearance, and create an optimal learning environment.

WORKSHEET 3-3

Teacher Needs Assessment

INSTRUCTIONS: Please circle the responses that describe what you would like to see for students and yourself this year. Thank you.

1. Students need more opportunities for group counseling.	Yes	No	Unsure
2. More individual counseling is needed for students.	Yes	No	Unsure
3. Parent education programs are helpful.	Yes	No	Unsure
4. I would like to use peer helpers in my classroom.	Yes	No	Unsure
5. I want more conferences with the counselor.	Yes	No	Unsure
6. I need more information about students who receive services from the counselor.	Yes	No	Unsure
7. I want to do classroom guidance with the counselor.	Yes	No	Unsure

I suggest the following classroom guidance topics for this year: _____

_____

I would like in-service on the following topics this year: _____

_____

Name _____ Date _____

WORKSHEET 3-4

School Climate Survey

INSTRUCTIONS: Please read each of the following questions and circle the response you would make to each question (*Yes* or *No*). Thank you.

1. Are you treated kindly in your school?	Yes	No
2. Is your school a friendly place?	Yes	No
3. Are you able to learn in your classroom?	Yes	No
4. Do the teachers listen to students?	Yes	No
5. Is your school neat and clean?	Yes	No
6. Are parents invited to your school?	Yes	No
7. Do parents and other people volunteer in your school?	Yes	No
8. Does the air smell fresh in your school?	Yes	No
9. Is the cafeteria a good place to eat lunch?	Yes	No
10. Is the playground safe and fun?	Yes	No
11. Do you have a school newspaper or newsletter?	Yes	No
12. Do people say nice things about your school?	Yes	No
13. Do teachers have enough materials for all students?	Yes	No
14. Is the counselor's room a good place to go?	Yes	No
15. Do students treat each other well?	Yes	No
16. Are girls and boys treated the same in your school?	Yes	No
17. Are you told about the rules in your school?	Yes	No
18. Are the rules in your school fair to everyone?	Yes	No
19. Is your media center a good place to find books?	Yes	No
20. Do you feel safe in your school?	Yes	No

William Purkey and John Novak, authors of *Inviting School Success,* 3rd ed. (1996), offer many suggestions for creating a healthy school climate. Purkey and Stanley (1997) offer 101 ways to invite student success in their guide, *The Inviting School Treasury.* If you want additional ideas about "inviting schools" and how to assess your school's environment, contact the International Alliance for Invitational Education at the Radford University Center for Invitational Education, PO Box 7009, College of Education and Human Development, Radford University, Radford, Virginia 24142; telephone, (540) 831–6509; fax, (540) 831–5059; e-mail, inviteru@radford.edu. Or go to the Web site, www.invitationaleducation.net, for information. The Alliance is an international group of educators, counselors, and other professionals who have developed the basic concepts of invitational learning and applied these concepts to schools, hospitals, clinics, and other settings.

When you and your advisory committee have completed the assessment process with students, parents, teachers, and the school environment, summarize these findings and report them to the principal and faculty. These results will help you begin the next phase of planning—organizing a counseling program.

Organizing the Program

Data from an accurate needs assessment enable you to

- Set priorities
- Identify program goals and objectives
- Select strategies and assign activities
- Design the counseling center
- Schedule your time

In consultation with your advisory committee and principal, identify the most important services needed in the counseling program. As noted in Chapter One, the most important services are not determined simply by assessing the desires of the staff. Instead, choose them to reflect the needs of students and parents and to fit the realities of the resources and personnel available to deliver them effectively in the school. All these factors are important to consider as you set program priorities.

Set Priorities, Identify Goals, and Select Strategies

Priorities set the stage for you to establish program goals and objectives. These goals are not restricted specifically to what you will do in your counseling role during the year. Rather, they are global goals for the entire school. They are goals for teachers and students alike. In this way, the activities and services you deliver as a counselor are supported and complemented by the activities of classroom teachers. They, too, are part of the program. In addition, other student services professionals, such as the school social worker, nurse, and psychologist, are included. Worksheet 3-5 illustrates a format to use in designing

WORKSHEET 3-5

Annual Planning Sheet

PRIORITY	GOALS AND OBJECTIVES	TEACHER ACTIVITIES	COUNSELOR ACTIVITIES
____	Goal:		
	Objectives: _____	_____	_____
	_____	_____	_____
____	Goal:		
	Objectives: _____	_____	_____
	_____	_____	_____
____	Goal:		
	Objectives: _____	_____	_____
	_____	_____	_____

your annual plan of goals and objectives. You can expand this form to include more goals and objectives, as well as a timetable for specific goals.

It is possible that your state or local school system has identified goals and objectives for student development, guidance, and counseling services. As noted in Chapters One and Two, the American School Counselors Association (ASCA) has developed a national model for school counseling programs. To help choose program goals and objectives, you can obtain information about ASCA's model from the Web site www.schoolcounselor.org. These aims should be used in conjunction with your school's needs assessment to identify annual goals for the counseling program. Generally, your advisory committee will develop goals across the following student development areas:

- Student educational planning
- Student learning
- Student career development
- Student personal and social development

After priorities are set and goals are established, decide about specific activities and strategies to reach these objectives. Once you have chosen the strategies, assign responsibilities to assure that these activities are implemented. As mentioned, a comprehensive school counseling program consists of a variety of services and activities offered by counselors, teachers, parent volunteers, and student helpers. A well-organized program clearly delineates services and assigns responsibilities to appropriate parties. Your advisory committee can be influential in helping you convince the school principal and faculty of the importance of these assignments. You and your committee members should advocate for wide participation and involvement of teachers in the counseling program.

Design a Counseling Center

The services assigned to you help establish your daily schedule. They also influence the counseling center that you design for your school. Chapter Two stresses balancing your time by carefully scheduling counseling and other services. This schedule should reflect the priorities of your program. In similar fashion, you should design a counseling center to serve different populations of your school community efficiently. In some elementary and middle schools, the challenge of designing a functional counseling center seems an insurmountable task. Perhaps the space or room you are currently assigned looks nothing like an ideal counseling office. Yet the degree to which you are able to make your space organized, appealing, and functional is a measure of your ability to personalize your program and, in effect, survive as a counselor.

Many older elementary and middle schools were designed and constructed without counseling programs in mind. As a result, adequate facilities are sometimes unavailable. We find counseling centers established in broom closets, boiler rooms, off the stage, in a corner of the cafeteria, and other inadequate locations. Yet administrators place counselors in these spaces and expect them to administer comprehensive programs and deliver effective services. Whatever your situation, encourage yourself to "see the possibilities." Privacy, comfort, and function may have to be compromised to some degree, but if you are a survivor, you will be able to look at broom closets, boiler rooms, classrooms, and other spaces and envision functional counseling centers. Ask your teaching colleagues for their ideas. You will find that teachers are a most resourceful group because they, too, often make do with inadequate space and facilities.

Choosing furniture for a counseling center can be challenging because of the different populations served. For example, in a primary school, you will want small tables and chairs that "fit" young children. Yet you will also be consulting with adults, parents, and teachers, for whom it is appropriate to have a few full-size chairs. Some elementary schools house a wide range of grade levels, beginning with kindergarten and going as high as eighth grade. The furniture in a counseling center should reflect the age range of those served as much as possible.

The layout and arrangement of an elementary or middle school counseling center depend on the available facilities and the developmental needs of students. Figures 3-1 and 3-2 illustrate two sample floor plans for elementary and middle school counseling centers. Use them as ideas for planning and furnishing your space.

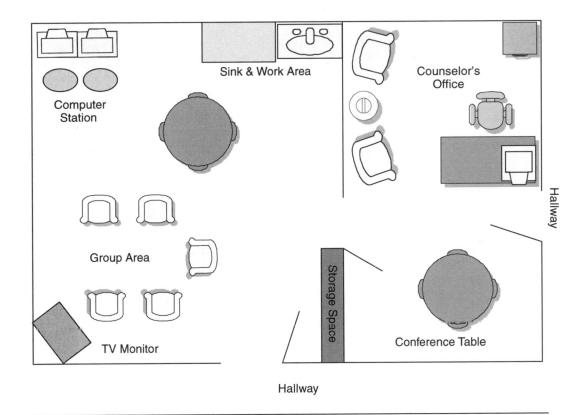

FIGURE 3-1

Elementary School Counseling Center

This diagram of an elementary counseling center includes space for individual sessions, small group guidance and counseling, computer assisted learning, video and PowerPoint presentations, and hands-on activities. The center has a private office, storage space for games, kits, and other materials, and a cleanup area with counter and sink.

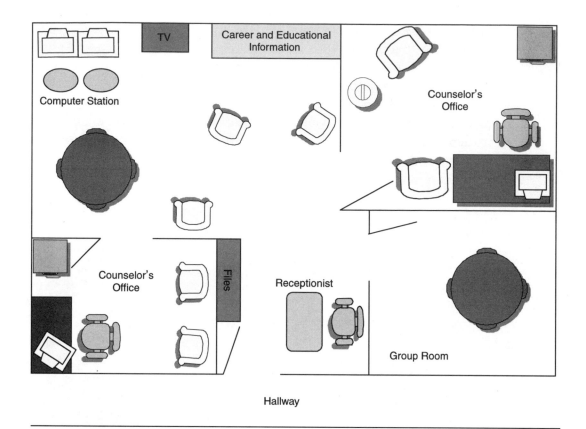

FIGURE 3-2

Middle School Counseling Center

This diagram of a middle school counseling center includes a reception area, offices for two counselors, and space for group guidance and counseling. In addition, the center has computers, a TV monitor, and displays for educational and career information.

A final and perhaps the most important point about designing and furnishing the space assigned as the counseling center is that it must be user friendly. A counseling center encourages and invites customers—students, parents, teachers, and others—to enter and use the services available. Your comfort is important, too, but not at the expense of being available and accessible to the clients whom the program intends to serve. This point became clear to me when I revisited a school counseling center where I had been a few years before. The school had a new counselor, and my immediate impression on walking into the counseling center was how open and friendly it was from what I remembered from a couple of years ago. The previous counselor had structured the center in a way that made it less inviting and accessible to students and others. She had valued privacy over function.

For counselors and clients, privacy is important at times, but if it dominates your vision for a counseling center, the need for privacy may become a barrier for clients and others. As an illustration, Figures 3-3 and 3-4 show the same space designed differently. Figure 3-3 shows a center that is limited in its openness and accessibility because the counselor's office dominates the space available. When the counselor is in a private session, the "In Conference" sign hangs on the outer door, discouraging people from entering. At the same time, if teachers or staff need to get school files, they have to wait until the office is open to them. In contrast, the center shown in Figure 3-4 allows the counselor to use minimal space for private sessions, while leaving the main room open for students and others to enter and wait to see the counselor, browse through materials, play with games and toys, or retrieve school records.

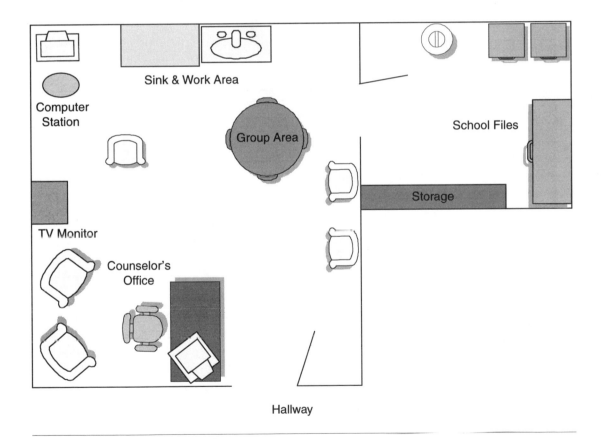

FIGURE 3-3

Inaccessible Counseling Center

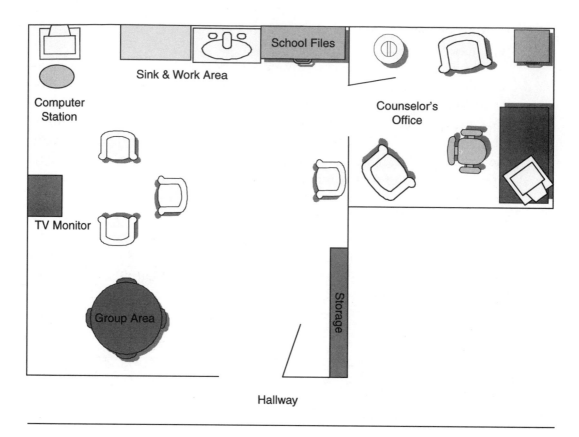

FIGURE 3-4

Accessible Counseling Center

Schedule Your Time

In Chapter Two, you learned about scheduling your time and found ideas about how to do it efficiently. The challenge of getting control of your time will be mentioned again in the next chapter because of its importance in coordinating counseling services. A well-organized program and counseling center facilitate your ability to schedule events, set appointments for students, parents, teachers, and others, and generally manage how you deliver services each day. A graduate student of mine once said, "You don't manage time, you schedule it. Time exists in the same amount and in exactly the same way for everyone." It is an interesting perspective. Although we cannot really manage time, we *can* use it efficiently by scheduling things we want to do.

By organizing your program and counseling center efficiently, you will be able to deliver effective services to students, parents, and teachers. Furthermore, teachers will identify with the counseling program and understand their role in helping meet program goals and objectives. To ensure that the services you and the teachers provide hit the mark, you will want to move on to the next stage of planning by evaluating program effectiveness.

Evaluating Services

Program evaluation is essential to the survival of a successful school counselor. The credibility and acceptance of a counseling program depends on how others perceive its value and worth. Program evaluation helps you complete the assessment cycle by examining data to reassess and reorganize services to meet the future needs of students.

To avoid falling into the same old pattern in your counseling program, implement ongoing evaluation methods to assess the effectiveness and timeliness of your services. Adequate program evaluation focuses on two aspects to measure the value and impact of your counseling services. These two aspects are the quantity and quality of your services.

Evaluating quantity means accounting for the time you spend in program activities and services. By accounting for your time, you assess how the counseling schedule aligns with program priorities selected by you, your advisory committee, and the staff. If you find yourself spending time in activities that are unrelated to these predetermined priorities, you should reexamine program goals and decide what adjustments to make in your schedule in order to meet the intended goals of the counseling program.

One way of accounting for your time is to keep weekly or monthly activity logs. Worksheet 3-6 is one example of a monthly report for a middle school counselor. You can adapt this form to design your own report.

Evaluating the quality of your services is more elusive than accounting for your time. Elementary and middle school counselors who are concerned about the effectiveness of their services usually design methods to assess activities on an ongoing basis, as well as at the end of the school year. Methods of ongoing evaluation include

- Holding regular conferences with the principal and teachers
- Following up teacher and parent consultations
- Receiving incidental feedback from administrators, students, parents, and teachers
- Receiving written evaluations from students, parents, and teachers

Develop ongoing evaluation processes and revise them throughout the year. By collecting formal evaluations from students, parents, and teachers about specific services, you are able to share the results with the administration and faculty. Sharing results accomplishes two important goals: (1) it tells your principal and teachers that you value their opinions about your role and performance in the school, (2) it lets them see the effects of your services and the counseling program. Your willingness to share this information contains some risk, but you will be rewarded in the long run. Counseling is a risk-taking business, so who better than a counselor to risk a public review of his or her performance?

Middle School Counselor Monthly Report

INSTRUCTIONS: Record information on the appropriate blanks for each item. If an activity was not performed during the month, record N/A.

1. Number of individual counseling sessions. _____

2. Number of group counseling sessions. _____

3. Number of small group guidance sessions. _____

4. Number of teacher consultations. _____

5. Number of parent conferences. _____

6. Number of classroom guidance sessions. _____

7. Number of peer helper conferences and training sessions. _____

8. Number of parent education group sessions. _____

9. Number of observations (classrooms or elsewhere). _____

10. Number of individual appraisals (testing, etc.). _____

11. Number of group assessment sessions (e.g., group testing). _____

12. Number of extracurricular meetings (clubs, athletics). _____

13. Number of referrals made to school system services. _____

14. Number of referrals made to community agencies. _____

15. Number of counseling or other meetings attended. _____

16. Number of teacher in-service presentations made. _____

Topics:

17. Special events coordinated during the month: _____

Ongoing evaluations can also ask students to rate services they have received from a counselor. Worksheet 3-7 presents a sample questionnaire for middle school students who have participated in group counseling. You can create forms to survey students about individual counseling, classroom guidance, and special events such as Career Days, Friendship Month, or Drug Education Week.

One way for teachers to give feedback about the effects of services is to ask them about behavior changes they have observed in their students. For example, you can use Worksheet 3-8 to receive teacher input about students who have received individual counseling. Send these forms to teachers at different times during the year and summarize the results to let teachers and administrators know about the progress of particular students and about students in general who receive individual counseling. The summary indicates how many students improved, how many stayed the same, how many regressed, and the average progress for the total group.

As you can see from the preceding examples, some of the forms you create might be primitive assessment tools. They are not intended for scientific research (although with some additional effort, they could be). Nevertheless, they will demonstrate to you and your school that students, parents, and teachers value the services of a comprehensive counseling program. Things that people value tend to last, and counselors who are valued tend to survive.

Another process of program evaluation is to ask students, parents, and teachers to complete an annual survey about your counseling services. The results of these surveys can often serve to assess goals and objectives for the coming year. By summarizing feedback from students, parents, and teachers, you measure how each group sees the overall counseling program. As with needs assessments, you do not have to survey every student and parent to evaluate your program. Sample groups of students and parents are sufficient. I do suggest that you survey every teacher for your end-of-the-year evaluation.

You should tailor your surveys to the sample groups selected. For example, if you want to survey parents who have actually used the services of the program, write the questions for that specific population. Worksheets 3-9, 3-10, and 3-11 are examples of student, parent, and teacher evaluation questionnaires to use as starters for designing your own instruments. The three components of program planning presented here—assessing, organizing, and evaluating—will help you get a counseling program off the ground. Because you offer a variety of services, you also want to keep the program afloat. To do so, you establish efficient program coordination. This is a major challenge to counselor survival.

WORKSHEET 3-7

Group Counseling Evaluation

1. Did you ask to be in this group?	Yes	No	Maybe
2. Did you like being in the group?	Yes	No	Maybe
3. Did the group help you?	Yes	No	Maybe
4. Did you learn any new ways to behave?	Yes	No	Maybe
5. Were you able to help any members of the group?	Yes	No	Maybe
6. Would you want to be in future groups?	Yes	No	Maybe
7. Would you recommend any groups to your friends?	Yes	No	Maybe

WORKSHEET 3-8

Teacher Form for Individual Counseling Evaluation

In *(month)* of this year, you referred *(student)* for individual counseling because *(identified concern)*. Please check on the line below to indicate your observations about the progress being made with this student. When completed, return the form to the counselor's mailbox in a sealed envelope. Thank you for your assistance.

```
    -3    -2    -1     0     1     2     3
  __/____/____/____/____/____/____/___
Problem Worse      No Change    Much Improvement
```

WORKSHEET 3-9

Student Evaluation of a Middle School Counseling Program

INSTRUCTIONS: Please circle the responses that best answer each question. Your answers will help us plan counseling services in the future. Write at the bottom of this questionnaire any comments or suggestions you may have for improving the counseling program.

1. Do you know who your counselor is?	Yes	No	Unsure
2. When you began in this school, did you feel welcomed?	Yes	No	Unsure
3. Are you able to see the counselor when you want to?	Yes	No	Unsure
4. Has the counselor met alone with you this year?	Yes	No	Unsure
5. Has the counselor met with you in a group?	Yes	No	Unsure
6. Have you visited the counseling center to talk with the counselor this year?	Yes	No	Unsure
7. Does the counselor come to your classroom and present information with your teacher?	Yes	No	Unsure
8. Does the school have a peer-helper program?	Yes	No	Unsure
9. Does a teacher advise you about school and educational plans?	Yes	No	Unsure
10. Has the counselor shared information about test results?	Yes	No	Unsure
11. Has the counselor shared information about jobs and careers with you?	Yes	No	Unsure
12. Has the counselor ever talked with your parents?	Yes	No	Unsure
13. Has the counselor helped you with any problems?	Yes	No	Unsure
14. Would you recommend the counselor to friends?	Yes	No	Unsure

Additional comments or suggestions:_____

_____

_____

WORKSHEET 3-10

Parent Evaluation Form

INSTRUCTIONS: Please complete this opinion form to help us plan future services for the school counseling program. Circle your responses for each question. Return the completed form to the school counseling office. Thank you for your help.

1. Do you know the counselor at school?	Yes	No	Unsure
2. Have you talked with your child's counselor?	Yes	No	Unsure
3. Has the counselor helped you or your child?	Yes	No	Unsure
4. Is the counselor available to all students?	Yes	No	Unsure
5. Would you like more information about the counseling program?	Yes	No	Unsure
6. Has your child been in a group with the counselor?	Yes	No	Unsure
7. Does the counselor follow through on your requests?	Yes	No	Unsure
8. Have you participated in programs for parents presented by the counselor?	Yes	No	Unsure
9. Are programs presented by the counselor helpful?	Yes	No	Unsure
10. Do you believe school counseling services are important?	Yes	No	Unsure
11. Has the counselor shared test information about your child?	Yes	No	Unsure
12. Has the counselor met with you about your child's educational progress?	Yes	No	Unsure

Name _____ Date _____

Child's Name _____

WORKSHEET 3-11

Teacher Evaluation Form

INSTRUCTIONS: Please complete this form to help us assess the counseling program this year. Circle your responses to each question. You may write comments and suggestions for future program plans below or on the back of the form. Thank you for your assistance.

1. Does individual counseling help students?	Yes	No	Sometimes
2. Does group counseling help students?	Yes	No	Sometimes
3. Is the counselor available to all students?	Yes	No	Sometimes
4. Does the counselor provide meaningful feedback to you about student progress in counseling?	Yes	No	Sometimes
5. Does the counselor ask teachers for input into the counseling program?	Yes	No	Sometimes
6. Has the counselor been available to consult with you when necessary?	Yes	No	Sometimes
7. Does the counselor communicate effectively with students?	Yes	No	Sometimes
8. Does the counselor communicate effectively with parents?	Yes	No	Sometimes
9. Does the counselor follow through on referrals?	Yes	No	Sometimes
10. Has the counselor presented guidance activities in class with you this year?	Yes	No	Sometimes
11. Has the counselor provided material and resources for you to use in classroom guidance?	Yes	No	Sometimes
12. Has the counselor helped you plan ways to integrate guidance in your daily lessons?	Yes	No	Sometimes

COORDINATING

All the functions and activities of your school counseling program need to be coordinated. Coordination consists of a wide range of behaviors and processes that you use to assure that a service, event, or project is planned, implemented, and evaluated satisfactorily. One study of elementary and middle school counselors identified about twenty activities representing a wide range of coordinating responsibilities. In practice, the actual list is probably longer because every service and activity included in a school counseling program requires some coordination.

Every service and activity needs to be planned, scheduled, delivered, and evaluated within the context of a total school counseling program. You will want to organize information and services for students, parents, and teachers in a way that facilitates appropriate educational planning and adequate assistance yet avoids duplication of services. These goals illustrate the importance of the coordination function.

This section looks at several activities related to program coordination. The examples are presented to assist you in "staying afloat" as you set sail with your elementary or middle school counseling program. Once your program is under way, you will discover and create other management strategies to meet your program needs adequately. The examples presented here will help you design coordinating procedures for a wide range of services. The key to coordinating these services is your ability to be organized. If you are uncertain about basic steps for organizing your program and your time, you may want to obtain a self-help guide, such as Stephanie Winston's *Getting Organized* (1991), and teach yourself, or you could locate training programs and workshops on this topic. Here are a few tips on how to begin:

- Keep a daily calendar, and the first thing each morning review your schedule for the day. Scan the next two or three days to prepare for upcoming events.
- Write a daily to-do list. Put down the most important five to ten activities to accomplish this day and rank them in the order you will do them. Stick to your list!
- Open a helper file. Record names of students, parents, and teachers who are willing and able to assist with program activities.
- Keep a reminder notebook or handheld electronic organizer. As you remember tasks to do, jot them down. At the end the day, add leftover items from the reminder notebook to your to-do list for tomorrow.
- Break down major assignments into manageable tasks. For example, if you are planning a parent education program for next month, you could list the following tasks: set a date, schedule the auditorium, ask the media specialist for a VCR or PowerPoint equipment.

Scheduling, organizing, and coordinating skills help you keep track of the goals and activities for your counseling program. These skills also help you manage and coordinate ongoing activities such as receiving referrals, scheduling services, keeping records, following up cases, organizing a peer helper program, using volunteers, orienting students, parents, and teachers, and coordinating teacher advisement programs. Let us now consider each of these activities.

Receiving Referrals

As an elementary or middle school counselor, you have major responsibility for providing direct services to students who are experiencing educational, personal, or social difficulties. Sometimes these students come to you because they realize there is a problem and hope that a counselor can help them. Other times, teachers and parents will ask you to see a child. In either case, you want to have a procedure in place to receive referrals in a timely manner.

Some suggestions for receiving referrals are

- Place a secure mail box outside your counseling center so when students, parents, and teachers stop by and you are temporarily unavailable, they can leave a note or referral slip. Check your box during the day so that immediate concerns do not go unnoticed.
- Design a brochure for parents to receive at PTA or PTO meetings or at home from their children. The brochure can include information about how parents can reach you at school and the best times to contact you. List your counseling center Web site and phone number.
- Ask your advisory committee to help you design a referral form for teachers to use. Teachers can put these forms in your mailbox in the school office, or you can make a daily tour around the building so that teachers can give them to you personally. Worksheet 3-12 is one example of a referral form. Make it simple. Avoid asking the teachers to fill out lengthy questionnaires or write long explanations. Teachers' time is a valuable commodity.

Scheduling Services

Because you are directly responsible for a wide range of services and activities, a schedule is essential to managing your time efficiently. It also helps you maintain a direction for the counseling program. With a schedule, you have reasonable control of what will happen and when it will happen.

When setting your schedule, be sure to request input from teachers about the best time of day or best day of the week for particular services and events to occur. Teachers at different grade levels can let you know their instructional schedule so you can plan appropriate times to see students individually,

WORKSHEET 3-12

Teacher Referral Form

To: Counselor
From: *(Teacher's Name)*
Date:
Re: *(Student's Name)*

I am referring the above-named student for the reason(s) checked below:

____ self-concept	____ test grades	____ friends
____ fighting	____ inattentiveness	____ absences
____ hyperactive	____ class work	____ homework
____ family concerns	____ withdrawn	____ unhappy
____ bullying	____ anxious in class	____ depressed
____ always tired	____ worried	____ shyness

Other concerns: _____

_____

Comments:_____

_____

The best time for me to meet about this student is:_____

schedule groups, hold parent meetings, et cetera. Because so much goes on in elementary and middle schools, it is impossible to avoid all scheduling conflicts. By asking for teacher input, however, you minimize the likelihood of your services interfering with the instructional program.

Keeping Records

It is helpful to have a counselor's file of students with whom you are working. This file is not part of the cumulative records but is a confidential index of what you have done and what needs to be done to assist children when they are referred for counseling.

One way of coordinating this information is to keep a file of index cards. As you follow each case, write brief notes about what you have done and what you plan to do next to help the student. Use caution when recording details of a case or confidential information revealed to you. You only need a file to recall what direction the relationship is going. A file is for coordination purposes only, so detailed accounts are unnecessary. Write essential notes that help you maintain a direction with each case. Note the sample Case Card in Exhibit 3-1.

Following Up

Most of the counseling and consulting services you provide are attempts to bring about some beneficial behavior change on the part of students, parents, or teachers. To assure that these services are on target, you want to follow up with all the people involved. When you serve large caseloads, as do many elementary and middle school counselors, this process of following up may seem like an insurmountable task. One suggestion is to take time once a week to consult your counselor's file and identify a few cases that you will follow up.

Set goals to follow up on a specific number of cases each week. Depending on their nature and who made the referrals, decide which follow-up activities to use. For example, if you are seeing Johnny in group counseling because his mother called and is concerned about his lack of friends, you might call Johnny's mom and ask how things are going at home. You could also ask Johnny's teachers if they have noticed any changes in his peer relationships at school.

EXHIBIT 3-1

Sample Case Card

Student: *Billy Jones*   Concern: *Peer relationships*

Date	Notes
9/10	First individual session. No one wants to be his friend.
10/12	Second session. Explored how to make friends; role played.
10/30	Third session. Asked if he would like to form a group to work on friendships together. Made a list of potential group members.
11/3	Interviewed potential members of Billy's group.
11/10	First group session. Set ground rules and agreed on group goals. Billy did well.

After you do a follow-up activity, record what you did on the case card in your file. This helps you keep track of what you have done and documents your follow-up activities. One rule of thumb to assist you in determining follow-up activities is *go back to the source within two weeks, and keep in touch at least once a month.* Follow up with teachers, parents, and others within two weeks of receiving their referrals. As you continue working on these cases, you might follow up at least once a month. Usually you can accomplish these contact activities with brief phone calls, e-mail messages, or personal contacts that let each party know what has been done and what progress has been observed.

Organizing a Peer Helper Program

In elementary and middle schools, many students are available and capable of assisting counselors with coordination of services. By developing a peer helper program, you can recruit students to help new children become acquainted with school, assist teachers with classroom guidance activities, work with the administration on improving school climate, tutor students, and provide other assistance in the school.

You will find that it is essential to design and plan ways to select and train potential peer helpers. Teachers can help with this selection process, and there are several good resources for training students in peer helping, such as Myrick and Bowman's (1991) book, *Children Helping Children: Teaching Students to Become Friendly Helpers.* There is also the National Peer Helpers Association (NPHA), which publishes the excellent *Peer Facilitator Quarterly.* You can find more information at the NPHA Web site: www. peerhelping.org.

Using Volunteers

Counselors who keep track of all that is expected of them usually seek assistance from other people. In most communities, there are ample opportunities to tap volunteer groups willing to assist in schools. These volunteers include parents, retired citizens, and business people.

Parents and other adult volunteers can help counselors and teachers in a variety of ways. They can supervise in the cafeteria or on the playground to allow teachers time to meet with the counselor and discuss program planning, student placement, or other issues. Volunteers can help the school secretary with clerical tasks and assist teachers by typing worksheets, making instructional materials, and collecting school fees. They can be trained to help with classroom guidance, supervise group testing, and greet children as receptionists in counseling centers.

Using volunteers in your school requires planning, coordination, and training. As the counselor, you can help with this effort. Let your advisory committee suggest ways that volunteers can help and ask committee members to assist in the planning and training of volunteers. More information about volunteer programs is provided in Chapter Ten.

Orienting Students, Parents, and Teachers

Most schools admit new students, parents, and teachers each year. In our mobile society, some schools admit new students every day. Another role for you is to orient these new persons to the school and to the counseling program. Design ways to facilitate this orientation and use student helpers and other volunteers to assist you. One idea is to design a packet of materials for new elementary or middle school students. Packets could contain data about the school, including a building map, and information about the town, as well as coupons and gifts such as pencils, rulers, stickers, and other promotional goods supplied by local merchants. Orientation ideas such as this one will help students feel welcomed, both at school and in the community.

Procedures to help students in the transition from one school to another are also important orientation services that you coordinate. These services are particularly helpful for elementary students who attend two or more schools before entering their middle school years. Begin early and plan transition activities with your teachers and administrators throughout the year. Contact the counselors at the feeder and receiving schools and make plans for a smooth transition.

Coordinating a Teacher Advisement Program

In most elementary and middle schools, counselors have responsibility for many students. To help with advisement and follow-up of students, ask your principal about starting a teacher advisement program. If your school already has one, be sure to get involved.

Teacher advisement programs assign each teacher in the school to a group of students whom they assist with educational planning and academic progress. In some programs, teachers advise the same students throughout the years they attend the school. For example, in a middle school a teacher would be assigned a group of fifth graders one year and then be their advisor when they move to sixth and seventh grades the following years. This allows teachers and students to develop trustful relationships and helps teachers get to know the students well.

Teachers also provide developmental guidance for their advisees. In some middle schools, a specific time of the week is set aside for students to go, as a group, to their advisor's classroom for guidance activities. You can assist teachers by providing guidance topics, helping plan activities, locating resources, and co-presenting these lessons with them.

Through individual advising and group guidance, teachers are able to assess student needs and refer students to counselors for additional or more intense services. This process of networking between you and the teachers facilitates services and contributes to the overall coordination of the school counseling program. As with other coordination activities, a teacher advisement program requires adequate preparation and planned training. Some teachers may need basic helping and facilitating skills to be effective as advisors. You can help plan and deliver this training.

Using New Technology

The technology available today and in the future will find many uses in schools and in comprehensive school counseling programs (Bloom & Walz, 2000; Schmidt, 2003). It will help with information management, communication, student assessment, guidance information and instruction, and perhaps counseling and consulting with students, parents, and teachers. As you adopt and adapt new technology to your school's comprehensive counseling program, here are some guidelines that might be helpful:

- Be aware of ethical standards developed by the American Counseling Association, the National Board of Certified Counselors, and other organizations to help you use the Internet and other technologies for counseling services in appropriate ways.
- Stay abreast of professional trends and legal rulings about using new technology for providing counseling services.
- Maintain security for confidential and privileged communications.
- Screen assessment programs carefully, and use those that demonstrate the same level of validity, reliability, and cultural sensitivity you expect from traditional assessment instruments.
- Ensure that information you post online and on your school's home page for the counseling program is up-to-date. See Figure 3-5 for an example of a school counseling Web site.
- Use traditional forms of communication and dissemination of information to ensure that students and families without ready access to computer technology remain informed of counseling services.
- Help students, parents, and teachers learn about the wealth of information on the Internet and how to discern the accuracy and usefulness of Web sites they enter.
- Remember, this new technology is to *assist* with services that you provide and is not intended to *replace* you, the essential human element, in helping students, parents, and teachers find and use information for educational, personal, and career development.

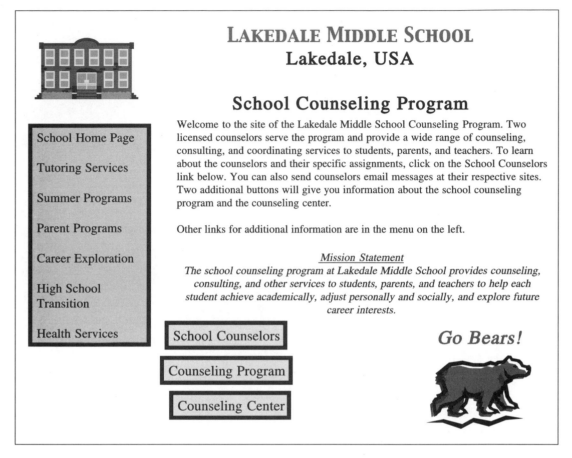

FIGURE 3-5

Sample Web Page

There are countless ways beyond those mentioned here that can help you and your teachers plan and coordinate services and activities in the school counseling program. You may not use them all, but with input from teachers and administrators you should be able to choose ones that fit your program and school. By planning and coordinating services, you are able to focus on the other major functions that you provide in your counseling role. These functions—counseling, consulting, and student appraising—are the core services of a comprehensive program.

IDENTIFYING ESSENTIAL SERVICES

By planning, organizing, and coordinating your services in the elementary or middle school, you give structure and meaning to a comprehensive counseling program. Within this structure, you provide specific functions and services that are essential to the overall educational program. These services—counseling, consulting, and appraisal services—identify the unique role of a school counselor. Each of these three functions is important in a comprehensive school counseling program, and each consists of specific helping skills that identify school counselors as professional helpers who practice in elementary or middle schools.

You have learned about theories and techniques of counseling, consultation, and student appraisal in your preparation as a school counselor. I will not repeat these important lessons here but will explain how these three processes fit into a comprehensive school counseling program. No matter which of the helping approaches you choose and the counseling theories you embrace, you want to structure your theories and practices in a way that establishes a broad program of services. Individual and group counseling, student, parent, and teacher consultation, and educational assessment each have a vital role in elementary and middle school programs. Chapter Four reviews each of these processes and their practical application in elementary and middle schools. It begins with the namesake of our profession, the process of counseling.

COUNSELING

When speaking of counseling as an essential process in a comprehensive school counseling program, we mean any helping relationship that includes the following qualities and characteristics:

- An individual or group process focusing on specific personal, social, educational, and career objectives for the purpose of beneficial development or for remediation of existing concerns
- A process of helping a person or group move in positive directions toward specific goals
- A confidential relationship
- A high level of professional skill, which allows a counselor to choose from a wide range of personal, behavioral, and therapeutic approaches to assist other people

As you can see, these qualities and characteristics define counseling as a goal-directed helping process, requiring confidentiality and a high level of professional skill. In your elementary or middle school, you probably use counseling skills in three types of services: individual counseling with students, group counseling with students, and parent and teacher counseling. How you use each of these services and the amount of attention each one receives within the total program will define and describe in large part your role as a counselor in the school. Let us now consider each of these counseling services.

Individual Counseling

Many elementary and middle school students are assisted by counselors through individual relationships in a series of one-on-one sessions, typically twenty or more minutes in length depending on the age and maturity of the child, and usually scheduled once or twice a week. During these contacts, you guide the child through the introduction, exploration, action, and closure stages of a helping relationship. Individual counseling relationships are most beneficial with elementary and middle school children when you consider the child's

- Language development
- Behavioral development
- Cognitive development
- Understanding of helping relationships

The above conditions are not unique to counseling with children. They also apply to individual helping relationships with older people. In most cases, and particularly with elementary and middle school students, these conditions have a significant impact on the success of individual counseling. Students who do not have adequate language development will benefit little from "talking" relationships. Similarly, children who cannot yet conceptualize their role and responsibility in forming relationships with others will struggle to accept the goals put forth in individual counseling. This is not to say that children with weak language and conceptual development cannot be helped through individual relationships, but in choosing individual approaches with these students you should carefully select the activities and techniques to use.

Since the early years of elementary school counseling, experts in child counseling have debated whether individual counseling can help young children. In an early report, the American Personnel and Guidance Association (now the American Counseling Association) took the position that individual child counseling offered opportunities to

- Help children establish relationships to see themselves as worthwhile persons, learn about their development, and use this knowledge in setting goals for themselves
- Communicate with children by listening to what they have to say about themselves, others, and the world in which they live

The position of this early APGA report remains true for counseling children in schools today. Individual counseling is a beneficial service when you adequately assess the developmental level of the child and choose approaches accordingly. The content of the relationship and the techniques you choose are guided by the developmental level and needs of the individual child. With young children, for example, play activities often take the place of introductory verbal exchanges.

Once you decide to see a child for individual counseling, it is important to set clear goals. In their book *Counseling Children,* Thompson and Rudolph (2003) suggested that we first obtain three pieces of information by asking the following questions:

- What does the child identify as the primary problem?
- How does the child feel about this problem?
- What does the child expect the counselor to do about this problem?

By answering these questions during the introductory phase of the counseling relationship, you and the student will be able to set goals for the sessions, which will give the direction and structure essential in counseling children, especially in elementary and middle schools.

After you gather this information, you are ready to consider the other developmental conditions, mentioned earlier, that enable you and the student to move the relationship in a beneficial direction. When counseling elementary and middle school students, this means deciding whether a strictly talking relationship is feasible, or whether other avenues of interaction are more appropriate. There are limitless techniques and resources that counselors apply in individual helping relationships with children. They include role play, bibliocounseling, drawing, listening to music, playing, storytelling, and other methods of establishing relationships and communicating concerns. You can learn about these techniques by reading professional journals, attending conferences, and participating in workshops.

When counseling very young children, there are some practical factors to consider. Due to their egocentric perceptions, children have difficulty focusing during personal relationships, such as in counseling. It is a challenge to help children focus on specific issues related to their own development and behavior. Their attention is short. In an individual session, a child can frequently be distracted and wander off the subject. For this reason, it is appropriate to avoid wearing clothing, jewelry, and other accessories that distract a child's attention and to limit sessions to a reasonable time span of approximately twenty to thirty minutes.

Sometimes children's perceptions inhibit their ability to focus on the concerns raised by counselors. They fail to see the identified issues and concerns as problems. At these times, you can create exercises and adopt innovative techniques that deviate from the more popular talking approaches to counseling, for example, the use of therapeutic stories to work with reluctant and resistant children. Stories provide an entertaining avenue by which children can creatively deal with problems and concerns.

When beginning counseling with young children and pre-adolescents, a structured interview may help. In this interview, you will want to avoid too many closed questions that elicit limited, one-word responses, such as "yes," "no," "sometimes," and "maybe." Use open-ended questions that encourage children to elaborate on their answers. As noted earlier, a student's language development will influence your success in using a structured interview. Exhibit 4-1 presents a sample list of statements and questions to use in an initial interview with children. Do not use all these statements and questions in a single interview, but rather be selective in the beginning. Invite the child to expand on them by following a child's responses with phrases such as, "Tell me more about . . . ," "That sounds as though . . . ," and "You seem pleased to talk about . . . ."

Another aspect of counseling young children that differs from counseling older clients is how termination (closure) is handled. You might make the decision to end a counseling relationship jointly, involving the child's parents and teachers. Prepare children for ending their counseling relationships with you by reviewing their thoughts and feelings about you as their counselor, reinforcing their successes and the progress they have made during the relationship, encouraging them to express their feelings about the sessions coming to an end, and teaching them about other sources of support and assistance.

EXHIBIT 4-1

Interviewing Children

1. Tell me about the people in your family. What are the names and ages of your brothers and sisters? Tell me what your brothers and sisters are like.
2. Talk about the home you live in. List some things you like and dislike about your home.
3. What about pets in your family? Who takes care of the pets?
4. If you could be an animal, tell me about the animal you would be.
5. Tell me about your favorite things—things you like most to do. What are the things you like least to do?
6. Tell me about sad things that have happened to you. How do you help yourself when you are sad?
7. Do some things scare you? What are they? What is it like to be scared?
8. Tell me what you think about school. Have you gone to other schools? Talk about those other schools.
9. What things do you like to learn about at school? What do you not like to learn about in school?
10. What are some ways to help in your family?
11. Tell me about your best friends. Why are they your friends?
12. If you could be a magician, what would you make disappear?
13. I have asked you many questions. Now you can ask me some! What would you like to know?

Before closing on the topic of individual counseling, a few points about middle school students are noteworthy. If you are a middle school counselor, you have observed that students at this level have higher verbal and conceptual skills than do younger children. For this reason, individual counseling can include more verbal interaction between the counselor and student. Nevertheless, even though a pre-adolescent is more verbal, effective individual relationships will combine verbal counseling with other interactive techniques. Middle school students are action-oriented, and the choices you incorporate into the counseling relationship must be compatible with their development levels, just as they must be with very young children. Artwork, role play, stories, and other activities can better facilitate helping relationships with pre-adolescents when they reflect the developmental needs and levels of these students.

Educational and other types of games are also appropriate for most middle school children and help to establish a relationship and move it toward verbal counseling. One characteristic of the middle school student that is different from the elementary child is the reliance on and interest in group activities. The pre-adolescent is much more aware of his or her peers and wants to belong to the "group." This desire to belong is sometimes contradicted by the student's striving for independence and searching for an identity. Added to these conflicts are the realities of students' changing bodies, the pressures they feel to excel in school, sports, and other ventures, and the uncertainty of interpersonal relationships, particularly those with the opposite sex.

Individual counseling with elementary and middle school students can address all the preceding concerns. Because school counselors typically have large caseloads and are responsible for many services in a comprehensive counseling program, many authorities advocate brief counseling approaches (Schmidt, 2003).

Brief Counseling

As an elementary or middle school counselor, you will find that students bring an array of issues and concerns that you can address through individual counseling. In recent years, many models of brief counseling have appeared in the literature and research, and several aspects of these models have merit for use in elementary and middle school counseling (Bonnington, 1993; Bruce, 1995; Bruce & Hooper, 1997; Davis & Osborn, 2000; de Shazer, 1991; Myrick, 1997). These approaches are helpful in working with students to focus on immediate concerns and make appropriate educational and career plans.

Brief approaches to counseling typically focus on specific concerns and behaviors that block students from making appropriate decisions. Most of these approaches are action-oriented and use a sequence of steps in helping students explore their concerns, review what they have done to resolve the issue, and form action plans to move forward in a constructive manner. Such models of short-term counseling emphasize student independence, self-reliance, and self-responsibility, traits worthy of attention for all elementary and middle school students.

Space does not permit a thorough examination of all the models of brief counseling here. Exhibit 4-2 offers a list of generic steps, gleaned from several different models, that give one illustration of how you might use brief counseling in an elementary or middle school program. This generic model is a sample, but you will need to visit the literature and research to become more familiar with tested models of brief counseling. As you examine and select (or develop) a model that suits your style and program, please keep this caveat in mind: *brief counseling does not mean hasty help.* Although efficiency is admirable with any counseling service, we always keep the best interests and well-being of students in the forefront of what we choose to do as professional counselors. Brief counseling is not a call for unreasonable control, neglectful action, inappropriate manipulation, or other behavior to be used simply to get things done faster. Brief counseling is practiced with all due attention to ethical standards of practice, as is any other service we provide to students, parents, and teachers.

EXHIBIT 4-2

Seven Steps to Brief Counseling

Models of brief counseling frequently use a series of questions to help students process information and make decisions to resolve issues and move forward. Here are sample questions compiled from various models of brief counseling.

1. Ask the student to describe the current problem or situation.
2. How would the student like this situation to change?
3. What has the student already tried to address or resolve this concern or situation?
4. Has the student thought of other behaviors or strategies that might help change this situation?
5. What will be different in the student's life if this problem or situation was resolved?
6. What immediate goal is the student willing to set to help create this difference?
7. What next step is the student willing to take to address this concern and reach this goal?

Although individual counseling is a useful strategy with most students, you eventually want to move toward a group process of helping them focus on developmental issues. Group counseling with both elementary and middle school children is an essential service of a comprehensive school counseling program.

Group Counseling

One of the most important outcomes we can hope for in school counseling is to help children learn about helping others. Group counseling is a vital service because it offers a setting in which you can assist several students and the students, in turn, learn from one another and help each other.

There are two types of group formats: open and closed. An open group has members who come and go and the sessions continue indefinitely. An example is a new student orientation group, where newly enrolled students come into groups as other students, now adjusted to the school, leave the group. In contrast, a closed group consists of a specific number of members who are screened and selected for a particular group and are expected to stay in the group through the final session. The group meets for a designated number of sessions and works through phases of the helping relationship, such as introduction, exploration, action, and closure stages.

With elementary and middle school students, I recommend closed group counseling for most groups. For one reason, students at these levels function better when structure exists, such as a specific number of sessions, and relationships are clear. With open groups, members come and go and there is little certainty about the interactions and relationships formed. A second reason for closed groups is that schools are typically rigid organizations with precise schedules and traditional routines to follow. Counselors who attempt open group programs risk being confronted by teachers who want to know where their students are and by administrators who do not like having frustrated teachers. Closed groups require certainty in scheduling and are more palatable to teachers and administrators. In summary, you should choose a structure that is favorable to your staff so you have a fair chance of selling them on the usefulness of group counseling with students. To be successful with groups, you first need to convince your colleagues of the importance of these services.

Selling Group Counseling

In some schools, any type of group counseling program is suspect. The emphasis on accountability in education has put great pressure on teachers to ensure that all students achieve sufficiently in their academic development. For this reason, teachers are understandably reluctant to excuse students from class. Teachers believe that it is more important for students to remain in class and receive the necessary instruction. No one disputes this point. Indeed, your challenge as counselor is to demonstrate that counseling services can enhance student achievement by helping students improve their perceptions, attitudes, and behaviors toward learning. You can complement student learning through services such as group counseling. Self-awareness, coping skills, career decisions, and other developmental tasks learned in group guidance and counseling contribute to student achievement in academic areas. To persuade your teachers of this, you first need to convince your administration of the value of group processes in the school counseling program. Once you are successful with some students in groups, teachers will be more inclined to allow other students to participate.

Your advisory committee can help you "sell" group counseling to your administrators and teachers. Ask members to help you design a survey for teachers to assess the types of concerns that are blocking student learning. Once you identify these concerns, establish your groups to focus on these issues. For example, one focus with middle graders might be to have students learn to use their time better and improve their study skills. If group sessions help students with these types of teacher concerns, the overall outcome should improve learning in the classroom. Worksheet 4-1 shows a sample survey that you could use to begin acquainting teachers with group services.

WORKSHEET 4-1

Teacher Survey for Group Counseling

Teachers:

I would like to help with some of the children who are having difficulty learning and completing their assignments in your classes. Group counseling can be effective in helping children focus on their behaviors and make appropriate changes.

Please take a minute to complete this survey if you have students who might benefit from counseling services. Check the items that describe students in your class. Your input will help us decide what types of groups are most needed. Thank you!

Teacher's Name: _____

I have students who

____ Do not pay attention in class   ____ Talk out of turn

____ Waste time   ____ Are underachievers

____ Do not hand in their work   ____ Are disinterested

____ Put themselves down   ____ Put others down

____ Do not cooperate with others   ____ Disrupt the class

____ Do poorly on tests   ____ Give up easily

Specific students I am concerned about are: _____

_____

The concern teachers have about students missing instruction is a legitimate one. Therefore, it is wise to design a schedule so students do not miss the same class period for all their group sessions. As one example, if you schedule a group to work on peer relationships, you might begin the group on a Monday at 9:00 A.M. The second session would be held the following week on Tuesday at 10:00 A.M., the third on Wednesday of the next week, and so forth until the group ends. By staggering the days and times of the group meetings, students will miss different classroom activities, and no single subject area will be unduly affected.

Once you have a schedule and the teachers agree to let students participate in groups, you will need a system of keeping track of your groups and identifying which students belong in what group. In elementary schools, it may be helpful to give teachers a copy of your group schedule each month. With very young children, you may need to go to classes and get group members (or use a peer helper who can escort the children to the counseling center). At the middle school level, you might use a pass system. Fill the passes out a day prior to the meetings and put them in teachers' mail boxes. Exhibit 4-3 shows a sample pass.

Organizing Group Counseling

For group sessions, you need a room that is comfortable and private. Group counseling is a confidential relationship for all members, so the room or space you choose for these sessions should be appropriate for private, personal conversation.

Some elementary counselors like to work sitting with young children on the floor when they hold groups. Others prefer to have chairs so children can have a special space in the group, and the chairs provide structure for that space. If chairs are not available, you might consider using pillows or marking a spot with tape on the floor for each group member. Without a specific spot or chair for each child, you may spend more time keeping the students in the group than you do counseling them. It is important for group management that each child has his or her own space.

The developmental concerns discussed earlier for individual counseling also apply to groups. Select group members according to their developmental levels, areas of concerns, willingness to commit to group goals, and understanding of why they are in the group. This screening process is an essential procedure guided by ethical standards of the American School Counselor

---

EXHIBIT 4-3

Group Pass

For: _____Day: _____Time: _____

Teacher: Please give this pass to the student named above for the time shown. If the student is absent, please notify the counselor. When the group session is over, the student will return to class with this pass signed by the counselor.

Thank you!

Time Session Ended _____ Counselor _____

Time:_____

Association (ASCA). When choosing group members, you also should consider factors such as sex, age, cultural differences, intellectual ability, and socioeconomic background. When the diversity of any one of these factors is too wide, it may inhibit group communication and progress.

One vital point about forming groups is that you, the counselor, should be in control of which students are in what group. Assessment and selection of potential group members involve a professional decision that can make or break the success of a group. Several factors must be considered: verbal skills, cognitive development, attitude toward being in a group, willingness to work on one's concerns, commitment to helping others, severity of the individual student's problems, and agreement to follow the group rules.

Group counseling can be a strong part of your school counseling program if you plan and schedule properly. Input from teachers and administrators is vital in helping you be successful. By way of summarizing, the following checklist will help you stay on target with your group program:

1. Introduce group counseling to your administration and faculty by explaining how groups will help children achieve in school.
2. Ask your advisory committee to help you plan a schedule for group counseling.
3. Introduce group counseling to students during your classroom visits at the beginning of the year, and survey student needs and concerns at the same time.
4. Find an appropriate room with adequate furnishings and privacy.
5. Establish specific ground rules for group members to follow.
6. Interview and screen prospective group members, and select members for appropriate groups.
7. Design evaluation methods for each group.

Parent and Teacher Counseling

Individual and group counseling services also are useful with parents and teachers. Although there is not unanimous agreement among school counselors about their role in parent and teacher counseling, many counselors find that individual parents and teachers request their services as well. You probably have faced the question of whether to provide this service as part of your program.

In most cases when parents and teachers approach you about helping them with personal concerns, you should establish an initial relationship with them and eventually direct them toward appropriate professional services outside the school. In doing so, your role is one of a referral agent. Although this is the best role for you to assume in most cases, there may be times when you need to provide direct services yourself. In some communities where there is not an abundance of service agencies and professionals, the school counselor is one of the few trained helpers available. If this is true in your community, you have to decide how much counseling assistance you are able to offer parents and teachers. Can you provide these services without jeopardizing services to students?

The question of providing counseling for teachers raises ethical issues because you are their professional colleague. If no reasonable avenue exists for referring teachers to agencies in the community, you may want to consult with another counselor in your school district who can assist you and the teacher by providing services. Or check with your personnel office to see whether an employee assistance program (EAP) is available. In any event, the initial counseling you provide teachers and parents should be guided by a few basic considerations:

- Are appropriate referral sources available in the community for this teacher or parent?
- Do you have the competencies to assist this person in short-term counseling?
- If you counsel with this person, will children benefit from the outcome of this relationship?
- Is time available to provide counseling so it does not disrupt other services in the program?

School counselors serve three populations: students, parents, and teachers. If you can assist parents and teachers in your school with brief counseling, and this service helps them to make positive choices, the outcome can be beneficial to the children who relate daily with these adults. By helping one parent or teacher, you might indirectly improve the learning situation for many students.

In most situations with parents and teachers, the services you provide will be of a consulting nature. Sometimes when a parent or teacher approaches you for assistance it is difficult to determine whether you are counseling or consulting with this individual. Although many of the helping skills you use in both processes are similar, there are distinct differences between the two.

CONSULTING

The counseling literature emphasizes a consulting role for school counselors (Schmidt, 2003). This guide also highlights the importance of the consulting function in a comprehensive school counseling program. Typically, consulting is as a process that

- Helps teachers learn about the needs of individual students, adjust instructional strategies to benefit classes of students, and identify resources to improve student learning

- Teams counselors and teachers in an effort to examine the curriculum and make instructional plans to increase learning opportunities for all children
- Provides instruction for all students about developmental issues, personal growth, peer relationships, learning, and other important topics
- Assists parents with information about their children and ways to support learning and development
- Collaborates with other school and community professionals to design strategies to enhance student development
- Offers information to students to help them with educational and career decisions

As you can see from the list above, consulting, like counseling, is used with several different populations. To understand how to use consulting skills effectively in your program, it is helpful to examine three basic forms of consulting processes. The first of these is situational consultation.

Situational Consulting

When students, parents, and teachers approach you about a particular concern, the helping relationship that you form is triangular in nature. In this triangle, you are the consultant, the student, parent, or teacher becomes the consultee, and the concern is the situation. In the eyes (and mind) of the consultee, the situation is the problem. For example, Figure 4-1 shows a consulting relationship between a counselor and teacher regarding poor behavior of a few students in class. The role of the counselor (consultant) in this process is to explore the situation with the consultee (teacher), examine alternatives, facilitate decision making, and arrive at a strategy with which the consultee can improve the situation.

Several models for situational consultation are found in the literature. I use a model based on the notion that an effective consultant is like a magician (see Schmidt & Medl, 1983). Accordingly, a successful consultation is

FIGURE 4-1

Counselor-Teacher Consulting Relationship

the result of well-planned, carefully timed steps that allow solutions to be skillfully disclosed and accepted by all parties. This model includes six steps:

1. *The BIG Decision.* When we receive requests for consultation, we often respond by asking ourselves, Why me? This initial, internal response is an anxious reaction to what appears to be a difficult situation. When you recognize your skill and ability to help others find reasonable solutions, you will readily answer this question and move on to the more important issue: Who needs what? When people ask for assistance, the information they share with you frequently indicates that both counseling and consulting services may be needed. If so, you have to determine who needs which services.

2. *The Gathering.* After you answer the initial questions (Why me? Who needs what?) the next step is to gather information. This is a process of collecting data and information from the consultee and other sources, such as cumulative records, test results, observations, and interviews. This gathering of information is a nonjudgmental process; all evidence is accepted as presented by the consultee.

3. *Clarifying.* You and the consultee examine the information gathered in Step 2, and identify and discuss the primary concern. The process must identify and clarify exactly what the problem is. Once you reach agreement on the problem, you clarify your role in the relationship. This clarification is essential because at times consultees (students, parents, teachers) may look toward you, the consultant, to *solve* the problem. In a consulting relationship, the consultee actively chooses a strategy and moves toward a solution for the identified problem. You want to avoid becoming a "magician" who makes all problems disappear.

4. *Exploring.* After clarifying the problem and agreeing on each person's role in the solution, alternative strategies are explored. This step includes brainstorming processes, exploring strategies that have already been attempted, and seeking suggestions from other resources. The immediate goal here is to generate as many reasonable solutions as possible and prioritize them according to the consultee's perceptions of what might work best. Which strategies are most likely to work, and which are most reasonable to implement?

5. *Decision Time.* Once you make a list of possible solutions, the next step is to make a decision about which strategy to use. In addition, you will again clarify everyone's role and obtain agreement about who will do what to carry out the chosen strategy. This agreement and commitment are critical if a consultation is to be successful. If you do not achieve agreement, you must return to step 3 above.

6. *Making the Rounds.* The consultee assumes major responsibility for carrying out the strategy, but you accept responsibility for monitoring progress and evaluating the outcome of the consultation. To assure that services have been beneficial, you will want to follow up on the consultations you have with students, parents, and teachers. A visit to the classroom, a note

to a student, or a phone call home can quickly collect information that will tell you whether the consultee carried out his or her responsibilities and what the outcomes were.

These "Six Magic Steps" offer one model to address situational consultations. In working with students, parents, and teachers and focusing on situational issues, you should design an approach that best fits your style and the needs of your school community.

Another type of consulting that school counselors do is informational in nature. Sometimes when students, parents, and teachers ask for assistance, what they are seeking is essentially information.

Informational Consulting

To make educational, career, and personal decisions, students need access to accurate and up-to-date information. In guiding their children, parents search for information about medical care, special education programs, child-rearing strategies, summer educational and recreational programs, and other resources that will help children develop. Teachers request information about student learning styles, school system policies, community programs, test results, student behavior, and much more. Your school uses and disseminates a vast amount of information, and you are a vital part of that network.

Being a main source of information is a great responsibility because people will use the information you provide to make important life decisions about themselves and others. It is also a critical position because some of the information you process about people is, by nature, confidential, and you must respect that relationship. In schools, administrators, teachers, and parents are frequently concerned about students and children and want information to help them look after the students' best interests. When information is requested, be sure you follow federal and state laws, local school policy, and your own professional code of ethics. Ethical and legal issues are discussed in more detail in Chapter Twelve. Here let us consider practical ideas about handling these information requests.

To handle requests efficiently and accurately, you will need up-to-date and accessible information. Design a file and storage system from which you can retrieve materials and resources easily to assist students, parents, and teachers. Any computer knowledge and capability you have will come in handy. Access to a current community resource guide would also be helpful. Sometimes community agencies such as the United Way and Chamber of Commerce publish guides that are available free or for a nominal cost. Today much of this information is on the Internet through Web sites of state and local agencies. If there is no such resource in your community, you may want to start one for your school system.

Keeping up-to-date files and disseminating information can become a time-consuming task. Parent and student volunteers can assist in maintaining resource files and other stored information so that services consist of current and accurate materials and listings. As one counselor, you cannot have access to all the information needed or know all there is to know about community resources. Relying on the input of others to create a comprehensive information file is the hallmark of an efficient and effective consultant.

To facilitate the handling of information requests, design a short form for students, parents, and teachers to fill out and return to your mailbox. Completed forms are passed on to student or parent volunteers who "fill the order" if the information is readily available. Worksheet 4-2 is one sample of an information request.

Another type of informational consultation by school counselors is any presentation to groups of students, parents, and teachers. The orientation you do at the beginning of each school year, going from class to class to introduce yourself and the counseling program to students, is one such example. Presenting test results to groups of parents or teachers is another. Classroom guidance is also a form of information consultation.

Sometimes the activities counselors use to disseminate information have the look and flavor of teaching. When you design a group activity to teach students concepts and skills to enhance their development or to help parents and teachers learn skills to facilitate student growth and learning, you use a third type of consulting process, which I call instructional consultation.

WORKSHEET 4-2

Information Request

Name _____ Date _____

If you are a student, your teacher's name: _____

If you are a parent, your home phone: _____

Information you need: _____

_____

_____

Please return to the school counselor's mailbox. Thank you!

Instructional Consulting

Keeping in mind that elementary and middle school counselors work in schools to help *all* children in their development, you will understand the important role that instructional consultation plays in a comprehensive school counseling program. If you plan to work with all the children in your school, large group instructional presentations are essential.

The ideal role for a school counselor in instructional consultation is to work closely with classroom teachers in identifying the developmental needs of students, planning appropriate classroom activities to address these needs, and presenting these instructional activities with the teachers. The most common term for these activities is *classroom guidance,* and the most effective delivery system incorporates guidance lessons into daily classroom instruction, which becomes a dual responsibility for you and the classroom teachers. Chapter Five explores in more detail the integration of guidance into classroom instruction and examines the roles of the teacher and counselor in classroom guidance.

Instructional consultation also includes group presentations to parents and teachers. As part of your counseling program, you can take an active role in parent education programs and teacher in-service. Parent education programs are presented in Chapter Eleven. For teacher in-service, the place to start is by seeking input from your colleagues. This might be done informally by asking teachers and administrators what types of information they want to receive during the year, or you might use a formal survey with the faculty. Worksheet 4-3 offers some survey ideas.

A key element in being successful with group consultation, whether in classroom guidance, parent education programs, or teacher workshops, is your ability to plan, organize, and use effective group leadership skills. Many school counselors who have experience as classroom teachers are able to use that background in making a transition to classroom guidance activities.

The processes and skills used to teach are similar to those required in effective classroom guidance. At the same time, these skills and processes are useful in presenting sessions to parents and teachers. According to Good and Brophy (1994), instruction consists of four types: (1) information processing, (2) social interaction, (3) individualized education, and (4) behavior modification. At different times and with different forms of instructional consultation, you might use one or all four of these approaches in various activities with students, parents, and teachers.

You might use information processing to present and distribute educational and career materials to students and parents. For example, presenting high school course information to eighth grade parents and students or sharing community resources at a PTA or PTO meeting are two ways you use informational consultation.

WORKSHEET 4-3

Teacher In-service Survey

Teachers:

The advisory committee of the school counseling program is seeking your suggestions for in-service programs this year. Please take a few minutes to complete the form below and return it to the school counselor's mailbox by the end of the week. Thank you for your input!

In-service topics for the coming year:

____ Classroom management strategies	____ Strategies for resistant learners
____ Classroom guidance ideas	____ Conflict resolution strategies
____ Enhancing self-concept	____ Child abuse and the law
____ Communication skills	____ Parent conference skills
____ Legal issues in school	____ Volunteers in the classroom
____ Sexual harassment in school	____ Effective homework
____ Using test results for instruction	____ Controlling your time

Other topics of interest to you: _____

Please indicate what you prefer for in-service:

____ After school, one-hour programs

____ Evening programs

____ Half or full-day workshops

____ Continuing education credits

Would you like to plan and present a workshop? If so, what topic(s)? _____

_____

Thank you! Please return to the school counselor.

By using social interaction in group guidance with students, teacher workshops, and parent education sessions, you become a facilitator rather than an expert. This is usually a good position to take when consulting, particularly with parents and teachers. Social interaction approaches encourage group members to interact with each other and draw upon each participant's expertise. Such combined knowledge allows group members to rely on each other rather than only the counselor to explore options and decide on plans of action.

In the Six Magic Steps model and the notion of the triangular relationship presented earlier, you learned about some concepts of individualized consultation. Through these relationships, you are able to provide information or instruction in brief contacts with students, parents, and teachers. In them, you take the role of a facilitator and enabler helping people to make decisions, find useful resources, learn a new skill, or reach some other educational goal. As an example of this type of consultation, you might assist a parent in locating community services to help a child become more active in drama, athletics, or other activity. In doing so, you might share resources you have on hand, make some contacts in the community, or suggest Web sites for the parent to explore.

As a professional counselor, you are aware of how behavior modification might be useful with individuals or group work. Behavioral strategies can help students learn a new social or educational skill or might help them learn to cope with difficult situations. Counselors also use behavioral approaches to instruct parents and teachers in behavior management skills for home and school.

These instructional and informational approaches require certain behaviors on your part as the consultant. I group them into four related processes and skills (Schmidt, 2003).

Preparation

To be successful with your instructional and informational sessions, you must do adequate preparation. Scheduling your time and organizing materials are essential to this process. Your success with classroom guidance, teacher workshops, and parent education events will be in direct proportion to the time and planning you put into identifying instructional goals, selecting appropriate strategies and activities, and scheduling time wisely. For example, if you are going to present a classroom guidance lesson, you will want to choose activities that are developmentally appropriate for all the students in the class. This means choosing and using concepts and vocabulary that elementary or middle school students will understand. You will also provide sufficient time for the lesson. Elementary students and middle graders present a wide variance of the types of lessons and lengths of time they can attend to new information or instruction. Because you know this, you plan accordingly.

Presentation

As noted earlier, the skills and processes you use in presenting instruction or information are similar to the art and science of teaching. Research indicates that some of the behaviors related to effective instruction and learning are

- Letting students or other participants know what teachers expect of them and what they can expect to learn
- Providing regular feedback to participants and giving them task-oriented assignments
- Using a well-paced style of instruction or information sharing
- Asking high-level questions that require students or other participants to analyze, synthesize, and evaluate the information presented
- Having high expectations for all involved
- Managing groups with careful skill, encouragement, and attention to achieving the objectives of the lesson (session)

Of course, many other teacher behaviors relate to student success in school. The list above presents processes and skills that are particularly useful in the types of consultation that you will use to convey information or instruct about a developmental task. When presenting these types of activities, you might consider the list in Exhibit 4-4, which provides ideas in addition to the teaching behaviors already mentioned.

EXHIBIT 4-4

Ten Ideas for Leading Successful Presentations

1. Start your presentation promptly and use time efficiently.
2. State the purpose clearly and ask for understanding from the group.
3. Give clear instructions and directions.
4. Encourage all group members to be active participants.
5. Use your group leadership skills.
6. Facilitate each session by listening, questioning, reflecting, clarifying, and summarizing for the group.
7. Respect the individuality and differences of group members.
8. Affirm group members' willingness to contribute to the session.
9. Give effective feedback to group members' comments and suggestions.
10. Evaluate the outcome of every presentation.

As a successful presenter, you will be involved in every activity, facilitate exchanges between you and your audience, encourage useful interaction among group members, maintain order without inhibiting participation, and briskly pace your presentations without moving so quickly that some members get confused.

Feedback

In creating environments and group relationships in which people receive information or attain skills, seek ongoing feedback from all participants. By encouraging and accepting feedback, you invite a free exchange of ideas and opinions about the material presented. Classroom guidance often teaches character traits and other values revered in U.S. society. Still, as a counselor, you will want to remain open to different and sometimes opposing views. Such a stance encourages a healthy exchange, demonstrates acceptance, and instills democratic principles embraced by our society and schools.

Evaluation

You will want to measure the effectiveness of your presentations. Some questions to pose to participants are

1. Was the information presented helpful to you?
2. Were you satisfied with the presentation?
3. What have you learned from this presentation?
4. How will you use the information?

In addition, you will want to ask about how time was used, activities that were useful, and other aspects of the overall presentation. In Chapter Nine you will find a workshop evaluation form (Worksheet 9-1). You might adapt that form for presentations given to teachers and parents. Worksheet 4-4 illustrates a sample evaluation form to use with eighth grade students for a presentation about transition to high school. Use this form to create your own evaluations of classroom guidance. Through periodic evaluation of your instructional information presentations, you will be able to adjust program goals and services. By using this type of feedback, you are better able to ascertain whether services are meeting the needs of students, parents, and teachers.

As a counselor, you have knowledge and training in many areas of human development and learning. For this reason, you are able to make presentations on a number of different topics of interest to parents and teachers. Being an instructional consultant, however, does not mean that you must always be the primary presenter. Sometimes the best role you can play is to coordinate in-service by locating presenters for different workshops. In this way, the most effective consultation you can give is to call on your talents as a coordinator.

WORKSHEET 4-4

Sample Classroom Guidance Evaluation Form

Please complete this questionnaire about the classroom presentation, "Getting Ready for School." Circle your answers and return the form to your teacher, who will give them to the counselor. Thank you!

1. The presentation about going to high school was interesting and helpful.	Yes	No	Unsure
2. The counselor used all the time available.	Yes	No	Unsure
3. The counselor encouraged students to ask questions.	Yes	No	Unsure
4. I will be able to use this information in planning for ninth grade.	Yes	No	Unsure
5. The counselor was able to answer our questions.	Yes	No	Unsure
6. The counselor listened to students' views.	Yes	No	Unsure
7. The counselor came prepared for the presentation.	Yes	No	Unsure

Additional comments: _____

As noted in Chapter Two, coordination requires an effective use of time and an accurate assessment of people's needs. Effective counseling and consulting have this same requirement. To be successful in your counseling, consulting, and coordinating relationships, take time to assess and appraise the people and situations referred to you. This process of appraising is the third essential service in a comprehensive school counseling program.

APPRAISING

Most people who refer themselves or others to you do so because of a need or concern they have. To provide the most effective and efficient service, you first want to gather as much information as possible. The process of gathering information about students, families, and instructional approaches is one of appraisal. You use the information gathered in the appraisal process to decide *who* needs *what* services.

A common error made by beginning counselors is deciding what service to offer students, parents, and teachers before making a thorough appraisal of the situation. Usually when this happens, the decision is to "counsel" the student. A more complete evaluation of the problem might lead to a decision that a teacher needs assistance with classroom management techniques, that parents should be invited to consult with the teacher, or that the child's instructional program needs adjustment. While counseling processes help with many cases, they do not always provide the most effective or efficient service for elementary and middle school children.

A thorough appraisal helps you diagnose problems accurately and prescribe appropriate strategies. *Diagnosis* and *prescription* are sometimes uncomfortable terms for school counselors because of their customary medical implications, but in practice, this is what effective counselors do. They collect data and other information, make professional judgments about what the data mean, and help persons choose appropriate actions to address the identified concerns. To make accurate appraisals of referrals made to you, rely on a few basic methods of data collection: testing, observing, interviewing, and reviewing records. Each method, when used skillfully, adds to the appraisal process and provides information with which to make appropriate decisions.

Testing

Most school counselors have knowledge of educational assessment and are competent in administering and interpreting standardized tests. If this is true for you, you probably use these instruments to help students, parents, and teachers identify achievement levels or ability levels to make decisions about academic placement. Many schools use standardized tests to appraise the achievement of all students at the end of the year. Schools usually give these tests in groups during spring with the results returned by the end of the year. Your role as counselor might include both coordinating the school testing program to assure that the tests are administered according to published practices and interpreting results to parents and teachers. At the middle grades, you also share the test results with students, so they understand the progress they are making and are more aware of their strengths and weaknesses.

Another role you could take in using test results is to help your faculty review schoolwide test summaries. These reports show teachers the strengths and weaknesses in the instructional program. Comparisons of current test results with those of previous years, across grade levels, and for specific classes in successive years can reveal patterns of student achievement that may help evaluate present instructional goals and objectives. For example, individual classroom teachers could use a form such as illustrated in Worksheet 4-5 to identify those learning objectives for which performance was below the school standard. By identifying these objectives, teachers can give more emphasis to mastery of those skills. Using schoolwide test data in this way enables you to become involved with administrators and teachers in curriculum planning and instructional improvement for all students. To accept this role, you must have a high level of competency and knowledge in testing.

WORKSHEET 4-5

Learning Objectives Summary

Teacher: _____ Grade level: _____

Test: _____ Subtest area: _____ Year: _____

INSTRUCTIONS: List the learning objectives reported on the test summary sheet and write the percentage of your students who mastered each objective under the heading "Class." Then write the percentage of students in the entire grade who mastered the objective under the heading "School." Subtract the two and write a (–) or (+) response under the "Difference" column. A (–) response means your class scored lower than the grade level percentage, and a (+) response means it scored higher. Rank all the objectives from the highest (+) difference to the highest (–) difference to show you the class strengths and weaknesses.

LEARNING OBJECTIVE	CLASS %	SCHOOL %	DIFFERENCE	RANK
_____	_____	_____	_____	_____
_____	_____	_____	_____	_____
_____	_____	_____	_____	_____
_____	_____	_____	_____	_____
_____	_____	_____	_____	_____
_____	_____	_____	_____	_____
_____	_____	_____	_____	_____

Individual and group inventories, such as self-concept scales and career questionnaires, can gather data about students. These instruments supplement the results gathered on individual or group tests. When using these instruments, be careful to note that each result is only one piece of the appraisal process and should not be the sole guiding force in making decisions. One single ability test score, for example, is not a valid assessment with which to make educational placement decisions. Much more information is required. For this reason, counselors use other appraisal methods beyond testing. Another example of collecting information is by observing students in the school.

Observing

In most cases, the referrals you receive are a result of countless observations by students, parents, teachers, and administrators. Part of your appraisal process is to validate these perceptions, and you do that by observing the situation yourself. When a teacher refers a middle school student because of "daydreaming" in class, you verify this behavior by observing the student in the classroom at a time when the teacher says daydreaming is most likely to occur. In the same way, you observe on the playground an elementary child who has been bullying other children during recess.

Effective observation is one skill that is not taught consistently in counselor education programs. If you agree that classroom and other observations are a part of the appraisal process, you will want to be competent in this process so that your observations are productive. To begin, here are a few suggestions:

1. In your faculty orientations at the beginning of the year, let the teachers know that observations are an important part of your assessment process. Tell them that you need their help in identifying where and when to observe students they refer.
2. When you and a teacher have agreed to a classroom observation, be *on time* and go directly to the desk that the teacher has designated for you. Normally, it is good for you to have a prearranged seat at a rear desk in a corner of the room. Ask the teacher to mention to the students before you arrive: "The counselor will be visiting our class today and has work to do. Please be courteous and try not to disturb the counselor."
3. Bring a record sheet to write down your observations. A legal pad with margins on both sides provides a simple format to use. In the left margin, record the time every two to three minutes. This will help you keep track of the time when events occurred. In the right-hand margin, record notes of significant observations to ask the teacher about, or events you are unsure about. On the legal pad, record your observations objectively without judgment. Judgments can come later when you and the teacher review the observation. Worksheet 4-6 illustrates the format of your notepad.

Student Observation Notes

Student:_____Classroom: _____Date: _____

TIME	OBSERVATIONS	NOTES TO SELF
_____	_____	_____
_____	_____	_____
_____	_____	_____
_____	_____	_____
_____	_____	_____
_____	_____	_____
_____	_____	_____
_____	_____	_____
_____	_____	_____
_____	_____	_____
_____	_____	_____
_____	_____	_____
_____	_____	_____
_____	_____	_____
_____	_____	_____
_____	_____	_____
_____	_____	_____
_____	_____	_____
_____	_____	_____
_____	_____	_____
_____	_____	_____
_____	_____	_____

4. When you finish the observation (usually a class period of about forty-five to fifty minutes), leave the class quietly and thank the teacher on your way out. Later, at a time agreed on by the teacher, report your observations and give feedback to the teacher about what you saw.

At the feedback conference with the teacher, you will want to ask, "Was the class I observed typical of how it usually goes? If not, what was different?" Often the student you observe is never quite as "good" or "bad" as reports have indicated. This is acceptable, because a trained observer can usually see enough to make appropriate recommendations to the teacher. If the teacher says, "Oh, he didn't do anything like he usually does!" take a positive approach and support the teacher by responding, "He did seem to do quite well. Which tells us he can do it when he wants to, and that is good to know!"

Let the teacher know that you appreciate the opportunity to visit the class, and be sure to share positive observations about the class in general. Most teachers take pride in their students and classrooms. Tell the teacher that you would like to read your observations, exactly the way you saw them, and then let the teacher give reactions. When you read the observations, remember to report them back exactly as you *saw* them, without judgment on your part. Your report might sound like this:

At 9:00, the teacher said, "Open your books to page ten." Billy got up and went to pencil sharpener. The teacher said, "Billy, what are you doing?" He replied loudly, "Sharpening my pencil, what does it look like?" The teacher answered, "Please hurry, we're about to begin the lesson." Mark giggled and Billy hit him on the head on his way back to the desk. At 9:03, the teacher continued with instructions to the class about the lesson.

Continue reporting to the teacher without judging what was good or bad about the class and lesson. If the teacher volunteers a judgment, accept it. The purpose of sharing this observation is to see whether you and the teacher can find clues that will guide you in making a decision about how to help the student. By observing classes in this way and reporting to teachers, you are more able to determine what direct services to provide students and which approaches to use in helping teachers.

Interviewing

Counselors also collect information by interviewing students, parents, teachers, and others who can shed light on identified problems. When teachers are interviewed, the information they provide often complements the findings you observed in the classroom. Parent interviews are valuable because they give you a glimpse of the total family and the child's position in that frame of reference. Depending on the counseling approach you use, information about birth order and family constellation may be valuable in making decisions.

Initial interviews with students allow you to gather yet another perception (perhaps the most important one!) about the situation at hand. The listening, attending, questioning, clarifying, and other skills used in establishing counseling relationships are essential in these initial interviews. By adding student observations to those with parents and teachers, you complete a full picture of the situation in question. Data collected through these interviews help construct the various perceptions of the major players: students, parents, and teachers. This construction gives additional evidence to help you decide *who* needs *what*. In some instances, you might want to interview other key players such as other students, siblings, and grandparents who might share significant recollections and observations to assist you in the appraisal process.

Reviewing Records

Some information revealed during interviews relates to past events such as prior school years. One source to confirm what people have told you about past events is the student's school record. Cumulative records include report cards from previous years, medical histories, family data, and test results that can confirm or contradict current observations and findings of the appraisal process. Occasionally, it is helpful to share this information with the student and teacher because they may be unaware of it. For example, a middle school student who self-deprecates because he is "stupid" or "dumb" might be helped by learning that his test results indicate that he is as capable as most students in his class. Sometimes information in cumulative folders can destroy negative myths perpetuated by students and others. Likewise, it may be helpful for a teacher to know that a student who is inattentive in class is not wearing glasses prescribed by the ophthalmologist.

All the procedures described above can help you design a complete appraisal system for evaluating each of the referrals you receive from students, parents, and teachers. You do not need to adopt all these procedures for every referral, but it is important to collect information from as many sources as possible. Testing, observing, interviewing, and reviewing records give you a sound framework to make reliable decisions about which services to provide in a comprehensive school counseling program. Sometimes the data you collect will lead you and the teachers to conclude that what is needed is instruction and guidance for *all* the students in the school, not simply counseling for a few children. The next chapter focuses on the relationships among the school curriculum, the counseling program, and guidance.

chapter 5

INTEGRATING *the* CURRICULUM *and the* PROGRAM

A half century ago, the Association for Supervision and Curriculum Development (ASCD, 1955) published *Guidance in the Curriculum* as its annual yearbook. In it, the authors presented the view that guidance is not a separate, supplementary service to a school curriculum but rather an essential part of the curriculum, integrated into daily instruction by teachers and counselors. At the time, however, this was generally not the case because, as the authors noted, guidance was treated nationwide as a separate entity and as the primary responsibility of guidance specialists.

In the years after the publication of *Guidance in the Curriculum,* the situation remained relatively unchanged. Labels that identified guidance professionals and services effectively isolated them from the school's curriculum by giving ownership to a single professional group, namely school counselors. Many of these labels still exist today, not only in schools but also in the counseling literature. They include *guidance counselor, guidance personnel, guidance program,* and *guidance office.* These terms separate guidance from the curriculum because they neglect the role of *teachers* in providing guidance activities, and they fail to recognize the importance of guidance in daily instruction and student-teacher relationships.

Fortunately, the counseling movement in elementary and middle schools began in the 1960s to emphasize cooperative relationships between counselors and teachers and the important role that classroom teachers and other school specialists have in providing guidance to all students. As a result, many states and numerous school systems have developed *guidance curriculums* comprising developmental goals, objectives, and strategies. These curriculums assure that all students are exposed to appropriate developmental activities in all their daily instruction. Today, advocates of developmental counseling programs promote the concept of teacher-counselor cooperation first put forth by the Association for Supervision and Curriculum Development in 1955.

As an elementary or middle school counselor, you can take advantage of this trend toward collaboration with teachers and give your program a clear identity by winning support from your teaching colleagues. This chapter presents several suggestions to help with this goal. Your first step is to introduce teachers to the idea of integrating and infusing guidance into their daily instruction and to persuade them that a marriage of teaching and guidance is the highest form of effective education. As such, successful learning results to the degree that schools incorporate affective education into the instructional program.

AFFECTIVE EDUCATION: INTEGRATION AND INFUSION

Successful schools teach *every* child and teach the *whole* child. This is not a simplistic notion or an easy challenge. It requires commitment of the entire school staff to the philosophy that every child can learn and that teaching in isolation without relating subject matter to the overall development of students is an ineffective approach to education. Because this is so, the teaching of math, science, language arts, and other subjects to elementary and middle school students includes application of these bases of knowledge to the acquisition of life skills. Teaching the whole child is in essence the incorporation of guidance into the school curriculum.

Guidance does not occur at ten o'clock on a Tuesday morning when the teacher tells students, "Put your books away, the counselor is here for guidance." Quite the opposite is true. Successful guidance occurs as all subjects are taught, and it relates subject matter to everyday life situations. In this way, teachers integrate guidance goals and objectives with science, math, language, and other learning objectives of the day. They also infuse guidance into every aspect of their student-teacher relationships.

Your role as a school counselor is to help teachers with this challenge. To start, you will want to consider some of the points highlighted by ASCD in its 1955 yearbook. They remain applicable in the twenty-first century. In

Guidance in the Curriculum, ASCD suggested that teachers who effectively integrate guidance with their classroom instruction endeavor to

• *Realize that all children face an array of problems in the process of growing up, and for this reason all students will benefit from guidance.* Excellent teachers have always taught the whole child and have incorporated guidance into their daily instruction. This was true for teachers in the single-room schoolhouse of the nineteenth century and will be true of effective teachers of the twenty-first century and beyond. How you convey this message to your faculty, showing them that guidance in the curriculum is not an additional burden for them but is simply good teaching, is critical to your success as a counselor.

• *Know that children of the same age are often at different levels of readiness regarding specific learning experiences.* When schools treat all students "the same," without regard for individual uniqueness and differences, they fail to infuse guidance into the curriculum. Help your school understand that equity in education means equal opportunity, not uniformity of instruction.

• *Be skilled in gathering and using information to determine student readiness.* Chapter Four describes the role counselors have in gathering data to help teachers make appropriate decisions for optimal student development. Your expertise in student appraisal can assist teachers so they, too, can assess, observe, interview, and relate with students to produce accurate information and make sound educational plans.

• *Know that school success is positively related to student self-concept and the positive beliefs that students hold about themselves.* In his classic book, *Self-Concept and School Achievement,* William Purkey (1970) made a clear case for self-perceptions as a guiding force in all human endeavors. Teachers who accept this view incorporate a guidance philosophy into all their relationships with students. They make every effort to support each student and instill confidence to succeed in school and life. (See also Purkey & Novak's *Inviting School Success* [1996].)

• *Plan lessons with the whole child in mind.* Effective teachers are concerned about helping students learn basic knowledge and skills while also helping them form healthy attitudes toward education, an appreciation for learning. You can assist when teachers identify students who are not responding to their guidance and instruction. At these times, students may benefit from individual and group counseling, or the teacher may profit from consultations with you and the parents.

• *Accept the diversity of students and recognize the social and cultural uniqueness each student brings to class.* Counselors can help teachers through in-service activities that explain cultural differences and by support that helps them cope with an ever-expanding and challenging student population that is entering our schools. Celebrate the cultural, ethnic, familial, and other differences among students.

Teaching is a challenging vocation, and it becomes more so every day. Your understanding of human development and helping relationships is essential to support the efforts of all teachers, recognizing their teaching "expertise" and inviting them to join a guidance-oriented approach to learning for all students. As the preceding concepts illustrate, guidance permeates an entire school program. There is a vital role for everyone.

Guidance: Everyone's Responsibility

If teachers assume a central role in guidance by integrating affective education into daily instruction, what is the role of a school counselor? Everything we know about elementary and middle schools suggests that the best educational programs depend on cooperation among administrators, teachers, and specialists. As one of the specialists in your school, you have an obligation and responsibility to assist teachers in their guidance efforts.

There are countless ways to provide this assistance, but for the purpose of "survival," I will discuss three major avenues for assisting the school with guidance activities. These avenues are (1) helping teachers integrate guidance into the curriculum, (2) providing in-service for teachers, and (3) coordinating schoolwide guidance activities. You can help teachers plan the integration of guidance in classrooms and throughout the school, locate guidance resources and materials to use in the classroom, and co-present special guidance lessons and activities with teachers in their classes. Let us briefly consider each of these approaches.

Planning

By working with your teachers to plan specific guidance topics, you assist them in designing lessons to fit a variety of subject areas. In elementary schools, meeting with grade level teachers to talk about ways to incorporate affective education into language arts, reading, and other subjects could do this. In middle schools, counselors can meet with block teachers to determine how to reinforce specific guidance concepts across units of learning. Whatever means you try, the important point is that the integration of guidance with classroom instruction occurs when someone intends it to happen.

In middle schools, the integration of guidance sometimes takes place as part of the Teacher Advisement Program (TAP). Myrick (1997) suggested that guidance units for TAP be designed with topics that are presented sequentially according to the annual guidance program and important school events during the year. He presented the following topics for developmental guidance units for Teacher Advisement Programs:

1. Getting acquainted
2. Study skills
3. Self-assessment

4. Communication skills
5. Decision-making skills
6. Peer relationships
7. Self-motivation
8. Conflict resolution
9. Wellness
10. Career development
11. Educational planning
12. Community involvement

Encourage teachers to select a few major topics during the year, such as career choices, substance abuse, and friendship, and design guidance activities in every class to focus on each topic for a specific period. Offer your assistance and ideas; search for materials, kits, videos, and other resources to help teachers in presenting their activities.

Locating Resources

Your training in school counseling has exposed you to numerous resources and ideas that will be helpful in designing guidance activities. Because teachers have much to do in preparing academic lessons, they will appreciate any assistance you give them in locating appropriate resources and materials. Recruit your school's media coordinator (librarian) to help with the task of developing guidance resources for each grade level. Some counselors develop resource guides, listing activities and materials such as learning kits, videos, music CDs, and other media that are useful in classroom guidance activities. You can design a guide by grade level and align activities with the annual guidance goals chosen by the faculty. Ask teachers to devise activities and include these in the manual. Loose-leaf binders make excellent resource guides for each grade level because teachers can update activities as they share new ideas and find additional resource materials.

Presenting

One way to share responsibility for guidance in your school is to present classroom guidance activities with your teachers. This is an excellent process for winning the support of your teachers and, at the same time, for learning good instructional techniques from effective teachers in your school. By observing teachers, you hone and perfect your own large group skills and the presentations you make to students, parents, and teachers.

Sometimes teachers prefer to have a counselor lead certain guidance lessons because of the sensitive nature of the subject matter. Ask teachers which topics they would feel comfortable having you lead with their classes, and plan these presentations together. In these team-teaching efforts, teachers should remain in class to observe and assist as needed. From their observations, teachers will be able to plan follow-up instruction. These team efforts also allow teachers and counselors an opportunity to exchange constructive feedback that is helpful in planning future guidance activities and in targeting services for students.

Another avenue for you to present guidance information is through in-service with teachers during the year. Teacher in-service was discussed earlier in Chapter Four under the consulting function. By providing staff development for your teachers on topics of interest to them, you help them learn about learning styles, developmental stages, student needs, and other factors related to guiding the whole child. You may not be able to do all these in-service programs yourself, but by coordinating them with the administration and bringing presenters into the school, you can have a significant influence on the messages your teachers hear.

A third approach to guidance is through planning and coordinating activities and events that foster healthy relationships and enrich school life. Schools can be difficult places in which to work. A guidance-minded counselor is a catalyst for positive ideas and events to highlight student and teacher accomplishments and encourage a spirit of cooperation and togetherness in the school. In addition to encouraging and planning classroom guidance, you should take an active role in designing schoolwide guidance programs, such as Career Day, Good Citizen of the Week, Guidance Teacher of the Month, Teacher Advisement Services, Peer Helper Programs, and other worthwhile events. These kinds of activities help the entire school focus on total development for all students.

Character Education

Since the 1990s, a movement called character education has been encouraged in our schools. In the twenty-first century, it has gained popularity, if measured by the number of Web sites found on the Internet that market programs or provide information about character education. In preparing this revision of the *Survival Guide,* I searched the Internet and found nearly two million Web sites when I entered "character education" as a search identifier.

The basic concepts of character education are essentially healthy ways to help students develop citizenship, self-responsibility, ethical behavior, and other virtues valued by our society. Many of these same qualities were incorporated into guidance programs of past years. Still, some of the current character education information and material available to teachers and counselors are worthy of adoption by schools as part of today's guidance curriculum.

You can take an active role in helping your school identify aspects of character education to use for schoolwide guidance activities as well as through the guidance curriculum as integrated by classroom teachers. As with other guidance initiatives, you might want to enlist the assistance of your school's media specialist to locate appropriate materials, videos, kits, and other information to help teachers with character education. Some form of evaluation is appropriate and may help you and the school determine whether the emphasis on character education was effective in helping children learn concepts, alter behavior, develop healthy relationships, and succeed in school. The ideas for evaluating services presented in Chapter Two can also be used to assess the effects of character education initiatives in your school.

Your involvement in the school's curriculum includes the direct counseling and consulting services you provide to students, parents, and teachers. These services interact with the guidance activities you coordinate with classroom teachers. For example, by communicating and consulting with teachers about their observations of student development, you facilitate educational planning and appropriate placement for each student. When teachers and counselors cooperate for the sake of student guidance, they are more inclined to work together for the educational benefit of all children.

EDUCATIONAL PLANNING AND PLACEMENT

In U.S. schools, with their diverse student populations, it is difficult to address the needs of every individual child. Yet research tells us to consider individual learning styles, abilities, and needs if we want our educational programs to be successful with divergent and multicultural populations.

You share the responsibility for assuring that every child is given adequate attention in planning his or her educational development. Granted, there will be many social and personal concerns brought to you, and at times, educational development may appear secondary to some of the critical human and humane issues you face with students. Nevertheless, when we lose sight of our fundamental purpose as counselors in schools, our overall effectiveness with students, parents, and teachers is diminished. For this reason, every case you handle, regardless of the nature of the problem or concern, should tie into the student's educational development.

Several of the activities and ideas presented in this and earlier chapters foster a relationship with your students and teachers that will keep the educational mission of the school in the forefront of the counseling program. Here are a few additional suggestions:

• Meet with grade level teachers periodically to ask them about the educational progress of individual students, particularly those who are receiving counseling services.

• Form a child study committee or a student assistance team consisting of teachers and other student services personnel to examine cases of students who are not progressing in school, yet do not qualify for special education or other support programs. When a group of professionals looks at a situation, it generates more ideas and solutions than if a single teacher or counselor tackles the same problem. Encourage team building as a process for effective educational decision making.

• Plan study skills groups for students who are not doing their homework or not performing well on tests. Work with the parents of these students to help them structure a study time at home.

• Meet with every student in small guidance groups during the year to give each one an opportunity to talk about educational goals, what he or she wants out of school, and needs for academic success. Bring in guest speakers, parents, and other volunteers who can share views of what an education has meant in their lives.

• Organize field trips to local high schools, community colleges, and trade universities. For students to aspire to higher educational goals, they need to visualize what these goals will mean with respect to where and what they will be doing in the future. Many elementary and middle school students will never have the opportunity to see a college or university unless someone takes them for a visit. Young boys and girls discover heroes and heroines in athletes, movie stars, and entertainers because these are the models seen on television, through the Internet, and in the movies. In a similar fashion, educational role models can be identified. We need only to show students where to look for them.

• Use peer tutors. You will find some of the most powerful resources in schools among students who are willing to tutor peers and younger students. Ask teachers what training these tutors will need, and see whether any are willing to work with you in forming and training this group of helpers.

• Encourage teachers to "Teach to Pass." William Purkey, a professor, friend, and mentor, once said that all teachers, regardless of the level at which they instruct, should be motivated by the desire to see *all* students progress satisfactorily in their studies (see Purkey & Novak, 1996). Sadly, some teachers delight at the prospect of failing their students. This is tragic, but it usually happens when teachers become frustrated and feel unsupported by the school, parents, and counselors.

Help your school and colleagues avoid this debilitating posture. Give out awards for teachers to boost their morale. Organize an appreciation luncheon with the help of parent volunteers. Tap your business community to donate merchandise that can be given as rewards for teachers who go the extra mile and who "teach to pass" every student. One middle school counselor established a "Teachers Are Terrific" monthly drawing at staff meetings to introduce some fun and togetherness to the faculty (see Satz, 1989). This is one of limitless ideas you can create to encourage and support your teaching colleagues.

To help students, start a secret "Red Alert" team for those in danger of failing and a "Code Blue" club for students who make significant progress. Help your school establish programs for students in academic distress who

EXHIBIT 5-1

The Edinburgh Middle School Continuing Progress Award

Felicia Ramos is hereby recognized and highly commended for her superb progress in Mr. Hatchback's Math Class at Edinburgh Middle School on this date, January 4, 2005.

Principal _____ Teacher _____

do not qualify for special services, and create awards for students who overcome odds, make significant gains, and greatly improve their position in their class and school. Although it is appropriate to recognize and honor students who are "high fliers," it is equally important to reward those who survive in spite of insurmountable obstacles. Exhibit 5-1 illustrates an award for continuing progress.

Another way that the curriculum and the school counseling program interact is through your role as counselor both to help teachers interpret and use achievement test results and to help students perform at optimal levels on standardized tests. Student achievement in school is related to the adequacy and appropriateness of the curriculum and student placement within the instructional program. These two factors are often related to teacher understanding and use of test data.

TEST RESULTS AND IMPROVED INSTRUCTION

One outcome of the studies and reports on the status of education in the United States has been increased attention on school testing programs and student results. In every grade, including kindergarten, schools are testing students to evaluate their readiness to learn or to assess the progress they are making in school. Whether or not you agree with this proliferation of standardized testing, it is the reality in many of our schools and all signs indicate it will remain so for years to come. Citizens and elected officials want schools to be accountable and, rightly or wrongly, one expectation is that effective schools will have improved test scores.

Capitalize on this testing movement by helping teachers and students use the results to improve instruction and increase learning. To do so, you must first help teachers and students understand what standardized achievement tests really are. They are merely tools with which to gather information about student learning that can be compared with results of other students in the same grade, at the same age, and in the same areas of the curriculum. In addition, summary school data of student performance schoolwide can be analyzed with respect to the specific learning objectives addressed by the test items. In this way, teachers can examine how the present instructional program relates to the learning objectives assessed on the standardized tests. Worksheet 4-5 in Chapter Four illustrates one way to do an analysis of class summaries of annual test results.

Teachers and Testing

An understanding of how test results relate to instruction may relieve teachers of the pressure of student performance as a reflection of teaching effectiveness. At the same time, teachers will be able to learn what impact they can have on student achievement scores by tailoring their instructional objectives to match the published objectives measured by the tests. Of course, this raises other issues: who chooses the test, and do the objectives match the school's curriculum? You can provide in-service information for teachers about the school district testing program, the test selection process, and the specific objectives addressed on the tests administered to students. In most cases, the results that schools receive on achievement batteries include classroom summaries to show how well students perform on specific learning objectives. Sometimes these results are reported as percentages of students who mastered a particular objective. In-service with the teachers about these school summaries is valuable in two ways:

1. It allows teachers the opportunity to examine the objectives stressed on the standardized test, and determine whether these are the same objectives stressed in the instructional program. If discrepancies exist, teachers have the right (and perhaps the obligation) to question the selection of the achievement test or change their instructional focus. Changing instructional objectives is *not* the same as "teaching the test." By adjusting instructional objectives, teachers bring the subject matter and learning goals of the classroom in line with the content of the test chosen to measure student progress. If these two elements do not match, teachers should question the validity of using the test to assess student achievement. The fundamental question is do the results reliably measure student achievement of the learning objectives taught during the school year.

2. In-service about school summaries removes the mystery of testing and test results by allowing teachers to take an active role in learning about the instruments used to measure student achievement. People tend to be afraid of what they do not understand. The same is true with testing. When teachers learn more about the testing program, the specific tests administered, and the method of reporting student results, they are better informed and less likely to be intimidated by the process. They also have more control over the assessment process.

You can help teachers by providing adequate staff development about the testing program and the annual student results. In large school systems, counselors can be spokespersons for their schools when teachers and administrators conclude that the tests, chosen by central office specialists or other personnel, are not in line with the school's instructional program. To be a competent spokesperson, you need to be informed about curriculum matters in your school and about the standardized testing program of your school system.

Students and Testing

Student attitudes and feelings about taking tests also influence the results. To achieve optimal scores, students need to feel as comfortable as the teachers do with the testing program. Naturally, there are few people, adults included, who view test taking as a positive experience. No one enjoys being compared to other people, on tests or in other ways. You can help students and teachers by designing guidance activities that focus on test-taking skills, relaxation techniques, and other test preparation procedures.

One program used in elementary and middle schools is Bowman's popular *Test Buster Pep Rally* (1987). The kit provides material for a half-hour assembly program and pep rally to focus on student performance on standardized achievement tests. The pep rally includes skits, cheers, and songs that encourage students to do their best on the test. A cassette tape of *Test Buster* cheers and songs is used as background during the assembly skits. The kit also contains preparation worksheets, practice tests, games, songs, and exercises for teachers and counselors to use in classrooms during the school year.

In middle schools, students are aware of the importance of tests and as a result may feel more anxiety. By including group sessions on test-taking skills in your counseling program, students will benefit from basic helpful hints about answering questions on standardized tests. Some students will benefit from learning relaxation techniques to control their testing anxiety. These skills and techniques also are helpful when students take teacher-made exams in class.

Many strategies for helping students relieve stress, such as guided fantasies, relaxation techniques, and thermal biofeedback are in the counseling literature. In addition, behavioral approaches, such as systematic desensitization, reduce anxiety related to test taking. Not all of these approaches fit every elementary or middle school counseling program or are right for every child, but you should have a few strategies from which to choose. Some guidelines for choosing and applying these strategies in your school are

1. *Know the approach well.* Study and learn each of the techniques you plan to use with children in your school. Read the professional journals, study textbooks, attend workshops, and enroll in seminars to become proficient in these strategies. It is particularly helpful to experience the

technique yourself. If you want to use systematic desensitization, for example, you should learn it from a competent counselor or therapist who can walk you through the process to focus on concerns of your own.

2. *Eliminate the mystery and magic of these techniques.* Inform administrators, teachers, and parents about the approaches you use with children. The more secretive you are about what you do, the more suspicious people will be of your practices. Most stress reduction approaches used by counselors in schools are simply educational exercises that anyone can learn when taught by people who have sufficient training. Educate your school about these approaches. For example, if you use relaxation techniques, demonstrate the approaches at a PTA meeting with student volunteers. Invite your faculty to the counseling center on a Friday afternoon for snacks and beverages, and take them on a guided fantasy to the Bahamas! The point is to show people that these techniques are strategies for learning new behaviors and coping with everyday stresses.

3. *Inform parents about the approaches you plan to use with their children, and invite them to discuss these strategies with you.* Elementary and middle school children can make significant progress with assistance from an effective counselor, and parent commitment and support will increase counselor ability to facilitate student development and resolve identified concerns.

4. *Know your local school policies regarding the use of particular counseling and learning techniques.* If there are no specific policies, discuss your ideas with the principal and teachers whose opinions you value. These professionals know the community and can guide your decisions appropriately.

5. *When using new approaches, begin with individuals and small groups of students.* Some techniques can be helpful to students in classes and large groups, but you should begin small. After you have practiced and honed your skills with individuals, you will be able to move into larger settings.

6. *Always practice with the best interest of the student (or other client) in mind.* Sometimes, new techniques and strategies interest and intrigue us so much that we just want to try them! Monitor your enthusiasm about new ideas and, in addition to the guidelines mentioned, always choose them primarily to help students and other clients.

Parents and Testing

The national emphasis on accountability and standardized testing to measure student progress and school effectiveness has left some parents confused, anxious, and angry while others express approval and even delight. As a counselor, you will want to assess, perhaps formally and informally, parents' attitudes about the school's testing program. From this assessment, you will be better prepared to guide administrators and teachers in delivering information to parents about the testing program and how the results are used to improve instruction. Worksheet 5-1 is a sample survey you might use to design an assessment of your parents. The survey could be posted on the school's Web site or sent home in paper form.

WORKSHEET 5-1

Parent Survey of School's Testing Program

INSTRUCTIONS: Our school gives several tests during the year to different grade levels. If your child's grade level is scheduled to take one or more of these tests this year, please complete the survey below by circling your response. The information we collect from this survey will help us work with parents to provide information and make the testing program work for all children in our school. Thank you for your help!

1.	I know about the tests my child will take this year.	Yes	No	Unsure
2.	I usually understand the scores my child receives on standardized tests.	Yes	No	Unsure
3.	I believe the testing program is helpful to my child.	Yes	No	Unsure
4.	I want information about how to prepare my child for taking tests and performing well.	Yes	No	Unsure
5.	I wish parents had more say about the testing program.	Yes	No	Unsure
6.	I feel the school does a good job reporting my child's testing results to me.	Yes	No	Unsure
7.	I think the school spends too much time and emphasis on the testing program.	Yes	No	Unsure
8.	I would like my child to receive services from the school so he or she is more relaxed and ready for the tests.	Yes	No	Unsure

---

Test interpretation with parents is an important function. Understanding the results is frequently challenging to parents, and help from school counselors, teachers, and administrators enables parents to convey the results accurately to their children. Without services to help parents and students understand the purpose of the testing program and the results of testing, the tests and their outcomes are meaningless. As a counselor, you can help your school establish an open dialogue with parents about the testing program and plan individual and group services to inform parents about their child's performance and how the school uses the results to improve or alter instruction.

All the ideas in this chapter—integrating guidance into the curriculum, achieving results to improve learning, teaching to pass, planning educational goals, and coordinating schoolwide guidance activities—have a common purpose. They each contribute to the development of the whole student. This, in brief, is the essence of a comprehensive school counseling program:

to assure that each student has every possible opportunity to develop to his or her potential. One final area of learning that completes this wide-angle focus on the whole child is career development.

CAREER DEVELOPMENT

In some elementary and middle schools the focus on learning basic skills and personal growth is so intense that attention to career development is neglected. At best, this area of learning may receive a cursory glance with a unit on career exploration taught in some grades or a "Career Week" planned for students to learn about occupations in their community. Although these activities are excellent learning opportunities, they do not by themselves give sufficient emphasis to the process of career development and decision making.

Frequently in schools, career decisions are delayed until the last years of high school or several years later. It is common to hear adults joke about their own lack of career awareness with comments such as, "Now that I am thirty-five, I wonder what I'll be when I grow up!" Made in jest, these comments often reflect a degree of truth. Although society continues its rapid technological advancement, we have not become adept at planning our careers or life goals. Students at every level of learning—elementary, middle school, high school, and college—are placed in educational tracks or choose their courses with little thought or guidance for lifelong planning.

It is ironic that career and vocational guidance, which played such an important role in the emergence of the school counseling profession, is often neglected in our schools today. Help your school maintain a balanced focus on career development by encouraging teachers to include career information in the integration of guidance activities. Plan schoolwide career exploration activities and incorporate decision-making skills into your counseling groups.

At the elementary level, students should have frequent opportunities to receive information about different occupations and changing male-female roles in the world of work. Classroom activities and group counseling can also explore personal interests, develop group cooperation skills, and teach how school work relates to career development and future life plans. Ask your advisory committee or another school committee to evaluate how well the instructional program and counseling services address the career needs and aspirations of elementary children. Although elementary students are young and career choices seem years away, it is not too early to begin setting a foundation upon which vocational decisions eventually will be made.

Career awareness is equally important at the middle school level. Decision-making skills become vital as students learn to cope with family, personal, and social transitions in their lives. The relationship between educational success and career advancement becomes more apparent at this level, yet other developmental issues need to be addressed at the same time. Personal career interests are now related to broad occupational areas, and the spectrum of possibilities sometimes is overwhelming and confusing to the preadolescent.

Middle school counselors and teachers who integrate this vast area of learning into the everyday tragedies and conquests of middle school life will be successful in helping students with their career development. To do this, you and your teachers can plan schoolwide, classroom, and small group experiences that focus on

- Decision-making processes
- Conflict resolution skills
- Communications with peers and adults
- The relationship between education and career success
- The changing job market
- An examination of personal interest
- Information about alternative educational and vocational choices
- Sex-role stereotyping, discrimination, and other conditions that limit educational and vocational opportunities

As with other areas of student development, there are countless ways to integrate career learning into the curriculum. You alone do not own this responsibility, but you can facilitate this effort among the teachers, parent volunteers, business groups, and others who wish to make a difference in the choices available to children. At both the elementary and middle school level, everything teachers and counselors do to foster learning, promote healthy development, and master basic skills will contribute to career development. Nevertheless, a conscientious effort to include specific career activities in the school curriculum and the counseling program is required in effective schools. Such an effort also contributes to the value of lifelong learning.

A LIFETIME OF LEARNING

A by-product of integrating affective education into the instructional programs is student appreciation of the power of learning and the impact it has throughout life. Teachers who instill this notion in all aspects of school life can have a tremendous influence on student development. They create schools and programs that promote *success* as an essential ingredient for learning and living. This may seem like a simplistic notion, but many schools fail to educate students because they rely on punitive regulations and requirements rather than *optimistic* opportunities and possibilities.

Successful schools consistently strive to establish places, policies, and programs that treat students as capable, responsible, and valuable human beings. Teachers and counselors who embrace these ideals are in a strong position to help students accept the value of an education and maintain that value throughout their lives. You can apply these principles of learning to a wide spectrum of helping relationships. Whatever ways you choose to include these values of lifelong learning and positive environments into your counseling program and the school curriculum, a few starter ideas may be helpful:

1. *Give students responsibility to care for their school building.* Elementary and middle school students take pride in their education when they are proud of their schools. Ask the PTA to sponsor a tree planting or landscaping outing during a weekend. Invite students to help plan the event and become involved. Spruce up the school entrance with carpets, plants, and comfortable chairs for visitors. Ask local businesses to donate furniture, plants, carpet, paint, and other materials.

2. *Provide in-service for teachers to emphasize positive methods of student evaluation.* Help teachers focus on what students are able to do rather than what students are unable to do. Ask teachers to share both the methods of reinforcement they use to encourage student learning and their evaluation methods. Persuade faculty to replicate these successful approaches. Examples of topics to consider for teacher in-service are

- Emphasize what is right. Help teachers focus on what students do correctly when grading their students' homework, tests, and essays. For example, saying a student got 75 percent correct sounds much better than 25 percent wrong. Help teachers emphasize what children do well, not what they do poorly.
- Use positive reinforcement. Show teachers how to structure positive reinforcement systems and choose appropriate rewards. Search for teachers in your school who use reinforcement wisely and successfully, and ask them to be co-presenters with you.
- Observe and listen. Teachers are the best "scouts" in the school because they are with students daily and many students confide in teachers they trust. Help teachers know what to look and listen for when interacting with students. Often, students who are in need of help, depressed, lonely, or feeling otherwise disconnected send signals that an observant teacher will notice.

3. *Advocate for positive discipline in your school.* Educational research has verified the impact of appropriate classroom management and positive discipline strategies on student learning. With this knowledge, it is bewildering why so many schools cling to archaic and brutal methods of punishment

as a means of controlling student behavior. If your school does not have a consistent model for positive discipline for students and teachers to follow, ask your advisory committee to review some of the approaches that have been successful elsewhere. Some of the approaches found in educational and counseling literature are

- Quality schools (Glasser, 1992). Website: www.qualityschools.com.
- Assertive discipline (Canter & Canter, 1992). Website: www.canter.net.
- Logical consequences. (There are many resources in book stores, libraries, and over the Internet. One popular book is *New Approach to Discipline: Logical Consequences,* by Dreikurs and Grey, 1993.)
- Invitational education (Purkey & Strahan, 2002).

Take a proactive stance by showing teachers you want to be involved in school discipline and want to help them develop positive approaches that work. Plan in-service sessions to examine different discipline models and strategies. Organize support groups for teachers to share successful approaches and encourage their colleagues who are experiencing difficulties with students or classes. Promote parent involvement in the school (see Chapter Ten). Help teachers develop a schoolwide plan for positive discipline, as suggested in Chapter Nine.

4. *Communicate with your teachers by using as many avenues as possible to learn about students who are struggling in class.* Although integrating guidance activities into the curriculum will help many children, some will need additional attention. Develop strategies to obtain this information from teachers on a continuous basis. Visit classrooms, eat lunch with students, drop notes in teachers' mailboxes to ask about particular students, and send thank-you notes when teachers give feedback about student progress. Remember, all of us need reinforcement at times—teachers, too!

This chapter describes several ways in which a school counseling program cooperates with the instructional program to focus on the development of the whole child. The suggestions and ideas advocated here will benefit most students in elementary and middle schools. Because today's schools include divergent student populations, some children will need special assistance and more intense counseling than their peers will. Careful coordination of counseling, consulting, and guidance services is required in these cases. Chapter Six considers your role in reaching out to exceptional children and other students who require your services.

chapter 6

REACHING OUT *to* DIVERSE POPULATIONS

Elementary and middle school students are a diverse population of learners, and each year U.S. schools see an increased diversity within the communities they serve. An ever-changing society contributes to emerging differences among students, which in turn introduce a variety of challenges to elementary and middle school counselors and teachers.

This chapter considers diverse populations in elementary and middle schools and how you can reach out to these students. Among them are students with learning difficulties and exceptionalities, social and behavioral problems, the challenge of learning a new language, and cultural differences. For these students, counselors make a special effort to assure optimal development, prevent long-term difficulties, remedy existing concerns, and include them in all school programs.

School counselors have a responsibility and obligation to intervene on behalf of students who have unique needs not always met by the regular school program. Some of these children receive services from specialists such as exceptional children's teachers, school nurses, social workers, English language teachers, and psychologists. Because they receive particular attention from these services, students with diverse needs are sometimes overlooked by school counselors. This is unfortunate because, as emphasized in this guide, comprehensive school counseling programs serve all students. To be effective, counselors provide a wide range of services to meet the needs of a broad spectrum of students. At the very least, they should be knowledgeable of other specialized services and coordinate these with the guidance and counseling provided in schools.

Students with unique needs enrich a school population and challenge each of its programs to provide services in an equitable manner. Before focusing on specific students with diverse needs, this section considers a few general guidelines.

GENERAL GUIDELINES

As an elementary or middle school counselor, you work with many specialists who have responsibility for students with particular needs. How you relate to these professionals, cooperate with them, and include them in a comprehensive school counseling program will determine to a large degree the success you have with exceptional or other students and the educational progress these students make in school. The following guidelines outline some areas to consider:

1. *Know the specialists who serve your school and keep them informed about your role as the counselor.* Invite specialists who serve the children in your school to meet with you and share information. Learn about their programs of services and about their professional backgrounds. Give them information about your program and ask them for suggestions about how you can work together for the benefit of all children.

2. *Check for duplication of services.* Part of your role as a school counselor is to coordinate various student services. Because so much goes on in schools, we occasionally lose track of which students are receiving what services. When this happens, students may receive the same or similar services from different professionals. For example, a school social worker may be working with a student who also is receiving services from you. When duplicate professional relationships occur without the knowledge of each specialist, confusion results and progress is inhibited. Design a system of tracking and monitoring the services you render to the students in the school. Worksheet 6-1 shows a student services record to use when many school specialists serve the same students. This record should be kept in a separate, confidential file, accessible only to student services professionals: school counselor, social worker, nurse, and psychologist. Individual records are an accounting of services provided to students, parents, and classroom teachers.

WORKSHEET 6-1

Student Services Record

Student: _____ Grade: _____

Teacher: _____

DATE	SERVICE OR ACTIVITY	STUDENT SERVICES STAFF
_____	_____	_____
_____	_____	_____
_____	_____	_____
_____	_____	_____
_____	_____	_____
_____	_____	_____

3. *Encourage communication among all the student services specialists who serve the school.* Set aside time to meet on a regular basis, say monthly, to share cases. Regular meetings facilitate communications among staff members and provide professional support for each specialist. The previous chapter stresses the importance of focusing on the whole child. Student services teams, which frequently comprise school counselors, social workers, nurses, psychologists, exceptional teachers, English language teachers, and others, bring together a variety of professional perspectives with which to consider the whole child.

4. *Know your competencies.* Serving a wide range of students, you may find that in certain instances your knowledge and skills are limited. Search for professional allies who are highly skilled and can assist with critical cases. If such professionals are not available in your school system or community, you may want to become competent to handle, at least at an initial level of service, some of these critical situations. Worksheet 6-2 can be helpful in listing professionals in your school system and community and identifying their areas of specialty. Keep this list in an easy-to-locate area of your office. If you have a computer, create a community specialists' file with the information listed.

WORKSHEET 6-2

School and Community Specialists

NAME	SPECIALTY	LOCATION	PHONE NUMBER
_____	_____	_____	_____
_____	_____	_____	_____
_____	_____	_____	_____
_____	_____	_____	_____
_____	_____	_____	_____
_____	_____	_____	_____

5. *Be knowledgeable and skilled with the strategies you choose.* Many techniques and strategies for assisting special students and students in crises are in the counseling literature. Choose carefully and caringly by doing your homework. Read journals, attend workshops, discuss strategies with colleagues, and become proficient in the services you provide. In most cases, your learning will never end. Everyday medical science, educational research, and psychological discoveries lead to new information that enables professional helpers, such as counselors, to design effective ways of assisting students and others in need.

6. *Learn about yourself: your feelings and prejudices.* Working with children who are different due to exceptionality, handicap, or cultural background takes a high level of caring and respect. Examine your own values and beliefs about handicapped people, minorities, gender stereotypes, sexual preferences, divorce, substance abuse, and other conditions that can identify students as different from the norm. If your beliefs prevent you from forming beneficial relationships with students, reflect on these values and see how you might alter or change them before proceeding.

In the professional counseling literature that teaches us about working with culturally diverse clients, one of the caveats often mentioned is the counselor's cultural encapsulation. It is difficult if not impossible to help people who have different worldviews and experiences from ours when we hold tightly to our perceptions of the world, unable to understand fully and empathize with theirs. Worksheet 6-3 illustrates a brief self-assessment checklist to evaluate your cultural encapsulation. If you find yourself weak in some

WORKSHEET 6-3

Assessing Your Cultural Encapsulation

Sometimes I find myself

· Measuring all persons according to the same "normal" standards of behavior, notwithstanding their cultural differences
· Presuming individuals to be more important than the collective group in most settings and situations
· Presuming the collective group to be more appropriate than individuals in most settings and situations
· Defining professional boundaries narrowly, and discouraging interdisciplinary cooperation
· Describing psychological health in mostly abstract terms (for example, functioning normally), with little or no attention to unique expressions of cultural differences
· Always viewing dependency as an undesirable trait or condition
· Ignoring the relevance of a client's support system to her or his overall psychological health
· Maintaining a narrow view of scientific process by accepting only linear, cause-and-effect thinking
· Expecting individuals to adjust and fit the system all the time
· Disregarding or devaluing the historical roots of a client's background and heritage
· Presuming to be free of racial, social, and cultural bias
· Believing that all people can make changes in their lives through counseling if they are only willing to try

Worksheet 6-3 is adapted from P. Pedersen (2002), "Ethics, Competence, and Other Professional Issues in Culture-Centered Counseling" in *Counseling Across Cultures,* 5th Edition. Thousand Oaks: California, Sage Publications (pp. 3–27).

of the areas assessed by these statements, consider attending a diversity workshop, reading more about counseling diverse populations, or attending a university course on social and cultural issues in counseling.

The preceding guidelines apply to all relationships that counselors form with students and parents who face special challenges in learning, or who have language or cultural differences that present particular hurdles in adjusting to classroom and school environments. The next three sections examine specific aspects of each of these groups of students and present ideas for working with them, their families, and their teachers. Let us begin with students who present exceptional challenges related to learning and behavior.

CHILDREN AND CHALLENGES

The Education for All Handicapped Children Act of 1975, commonly known as Public Law 94–142, changed our schools and the lives of millions of children across the country. This law, and its subsequent revisions, has had significant impact both on the role of school counselors, particularly elementary and middle school counselors, and their professional preparation. Prior to this law, few mildly to severely handicapped students attended our public schools. Now these young people are an integral part of our educational programs and they, like other students, face an array of developmental challenges. They also benefit from the services of a comprehensive school counseling program.

Counseling texts, journals, and other resources list various approaches to assist exceptional students. From these resources, general guidelines for counseling challenged children can be summarized. You will increase your likelihood of being effective with these and other students if you

1. Achieve a basic understanding and knowledge of the child's exceptionality; learn about the characteristics of each exceptional condition and the limitations and strengths of the child.
2. Work closely with special education teachers to choose and plan appropriate counseling strategies. By coordinating services with special education and classroom teachers, your counseling services will be on target and the teachers, in turn, will provide supportive activities in the classroom.
3. Focus on the personal and social development of students and allow teachers to focus on appropriate instructional services. Choose counseling activities that focus on self-concept development, acceptance of the identified exceptionality, and acquisition of coping skills.
4. Emphasize the possibilities and potential that exist for every child; encourage students to look beyond their disabilities and find positive

ways to manage, overcome, and compensate in their lives; choose counseling activities that teach specific social and personal skills.

5. Use group approaches when possible and, if appropriate, include nonexceptional children in these groups. Select group members carefully, being sure to include students who are sensitive to the differences of others and willing to form relationships with students of diverse backgrounds. Group activities are not the time or the place to "sensitize" antisocial and prejudiced students to the challenges of being an exceptional or handicapped person.

6. Become aware of community agencies and services that cater to the needs of people with different challenges. Coordinate your services with professional helpers in the community.

7. Support exceptional teachers and parents of these students. Teaching special children, including gifted and talented youngsters, is an exceptional challenge, and parenting them has its own unique set of concerns and difficulties. Meet with teachers and parents on a regular basis. Form parent discussion and support groups.

8. Include awareness activities in the guidance curriculum to educate all students in the school about the exceptionalities of some children and what these unique challenges mean in terms of educational and career opportunities.

9. Provide information to teachers and parents to help them understand how cultural differences interact with certain exceptionalities, such as retardation and giftedness.

10. Offer services that assist students with the numerous transitions that occur within the school, from one school to another, and from school to adult life in the community. In most elementary and middle schools, changes and transitions occur regularly, and sometimes children have difficulty with change. Design strategies to help children who have difficulty coping with adjusted schedules, changing programs, and newly adopted policies.

11. Include siblings in counseling services. Brothers and sisters of the exceptional student are often affected by, or contribute to, the challenges faced by the entire family. Help siblings by providing them with information about the exceptionality. Offer a safe environment in which children can explore their feelings of guilt, fear, and anger, establish their own self-identity, and learn coping behaviors.

These guidelines offer a framework with which to develop specific services for students in your school. Given the range of intellectual, emotional, and physical disabilities that children bring to elementary and middle schools, a wide selection of guidance and counseling approaches is reasonable to expect. The next section presents a few starter suggestions that cut across various counseling, guidance, and consulting activities.

Approaches with Exceptional Students

Many approaches are useful with a variety of exceptionalities including learning disabled, emotionally handicapped, educable handicapped, and physically challenged youngsters. Individual and group counseling, social skills learning, behavioral contracting, career guidance, and parent education are among those recommended. The following sections consider a few of these approaches, starting with cognitive interventions.

Cognitive Counseling Strategies

Some approaches to individual and group counseling encourage the incorporation of cognitive goals into instructional programs for students and into interventions planned by school counselors. Cognitive instructional goals enable students to

- Evaluate present skills and abilities
- Assess the nature and difficulty of a specific task before attempting to do it
- Design a clear plan of action for approaching tasks
- Explore all reasonable alternatives

Instructional goals also help students internalize their responsibility for achieving and succeeding in class. A cognitive focus helps students alter beliefs and attitudes that inhibit their learning while encouraging their confidence and self-reliance.

Individual and group counseling have a similar focus. The goals of these helping relationships are to improve understanding of individual differences, attack irrational beliefs, increase self-acceptance, design decision-making and problem-solving strategies, and encourage student participation in classes and schoolwide activities. In counseling these students, try a structured group counseling approach that introduces basic cognitive principles of self-acceptance, self-talk, and rational-irrational thinking to the helping relationship. In these groups, instruct students about self-talk and its positive and negative influence on their behaviors. Post positive self-statements around the room and ask students to add to these sayings (Bello, 1989). Some examples are

- I can do this task.
- Math is tough, but it can be done.
- It is all right to make mistakes.

After sharing and adding to these self-statements, students begin to learn the skill of positive self-talk. As an example, a middle grade student is given a sentence with a grammatical error to correct on the blackboard while other group members gently provide encouraging, helpful statements. Then the same student attempts another problem while this time saying positive self-instructions aloud. Finally, the student works on other sentences using self-talk quietly. This instructional process helps students internalize responsibility for their progress and enhances self-appreciation for academic success.

When students have learned about self-statements, the group moves to a discussion of individual differences and the process of being identified as an exceptional student. In this phase of group counseling, students explore their notions of "differences" and are given accurate information by the counselor about special education and placement in the program.

Successive stages of this kind of group process include examining and debunking irrational beliefs, teaching problem-solving strategies, and encouraging mainstreaming experiences. Each of these stages extends and supports the learning begun in the earlier sessions of the group. The goal is to help students establish rational views of their abilities and capabilities and choose behaviors that reflect these views.

Using another cognitive approach, you can help middle school students by teaching them to check the rationality of their thoughts using five basic questions:

1. Are my thoughts based on obvious facts?
2. Do these thoughts help me protect my life and health?
3. Will these thoughts help me achieve my short-term and long-term goals?
4. Do these thoughts help me prevent unwanted conflicts with other people?
5. Do these thoughts help me feel the emotions I want to feel without using drugs or alcohol? (Maultsby, 1986)

When students honestly answer "no" to three or more of these questions, they identify irrational thoughts that they might want to alter. Developing new rational thinking requires at least three honest "yes" answers to these questions and a willingness on the part of the student to use this new thinking in place of old irrational thoughts. Exceptional children can learn to use these rational questions to check their thinking, particularly the thoughts they have about their abilities and disabilities.

Token Economy Systems

For some students, behavioral strategies are helpful in establishing productive counseling relationships. One such strategy, a token economy system, can help elementary and middle school students stay on target when learning new behaviors, changing behaviors, or adjusting to new situations. When you use token economy strategies, close communication between home and school is essential. To maximize parent involvement, try these steps:

1. *Identify concerns.* Ask the teacher (or other referral source) for specific behaviors he or she would like to see increased, decreased, or extinguished.

2. *Gather additional data.* In addition to the teacher's referral, gather information from your observations of the student and cumulative records. Student interviews may be desirable.

3. *Collect baseline data.* The teacher collects baseline data on the identified behaviors. This involves gathering data on the frequency with which the behavior occurs during a specified time (that is, a class period, in the morning, during a day, or all week).

4. *Meet with parents.* In a parent conference, the teacher shares the concern, the strategies that already have been attempted, and the results of collecting baseline data. The token economy system is explained, and if the parents agree, you, the teacher, and parents design a plan, agree on responsibilities, choose an appropriate reinforcement and schedule, and design follow-up procedures. You might design an agreement form, such as that shown in Worksheet 6-4, and give a copy to all participants. Usually follow-up is done by phone unless there is an immediate need to reconvene with the parents.

5. *Implement the plan.* Each adult—the parent, teacher, and you—takes responsibility and has a role in implementing the plan. All responsibilities and roles must be carried out as agreed if the plan is to be successful.

6. *Evaluate the outcome.* At the end of an agreed period, assess the progress made with the teacher and parent.

WORKSHEET 6-4

Token Economy Agreement

Teacher:_____Conference date: _____

Student: _____

Parent (guardian): _____

Teacher assignment: _____

Parent assignment: _____

Counselor assignment: _____

Reinforcement schedule: _____

Follow-up conference date: _____

The goal of a token economy system is to help children experience initial success with external reinforcers so that eventually they transfer this success to handle other concerns and develop new, appropriate behaviors. When successful outcomes are not realized, roles and responsibilities need to be reexamined and reinforcers need to be reevaluated. Sometimes parents and teachers are inconsistent with the agreed reinforcement schedule, or the reinforcers lose their importance over time and no longer hold the power they once had. In these cases, a conference may be appropriate.

Career Guidance

One area that has not received adequate attention with challenged students is career education. School counselors should take advantage of comprehensive competency-based career guidance programs to assist special students. In some instances, curriculum competencies may need to be adjusted to meet their developmental needs and instructional level. The sequence of the career education competencies includes learning activities that focus on career awareness, career exploration, and vocational preparation.

Counseling Strategies

Several counseling approaches offer strategies that you can use with exceptional students in either individual or group sessions. The following are a few strategies that can be adapted and used.

1. *Journal writing.* Have students keep a journal of their actions and thoughts, and ask them to share their journal with you individually or in a small group. Use of journal writing is affected by the students' level of writing ability. Yet many children with limited writing skills enjoy this type of activity and frequently incorporate artistic renditions to illustrate their actions, thoughts, and words or to depict an event that has happened to them.
2. *Bibliocounseling.* Use storytelling and read books with students to facilitate the expression of their own feelings as they identify with story characters. Books and stories also can provide avenues by which students learn helpful problem-solving skills as they give suggestions of how story characters should resolve conflicts.
3. *Imagery.* In individual and group sessions, children can be assisted in fantasizing how they would like to be. At the same time, they can visualize how they are, and how their self-defeating behaviors prevent them from achieving their goals. Once they see these debilitating behaviors in their imagination, it is easier for them to choose more positive actions in relating in healthy ways to themselves and others.

4. *Role playing.* Exceptional children sometimes have difficulty conceptualizing solutions to their problems. They also may struggle with language to express how they view these concerns. Role-play activities offer opportunities for these students to act out how they see their problems, how others behave toward them, and ways to resolve these conflicts. A type of role play used in Transactional Analysis may be helpful with these students. It is called the "Empty Chair" and is a form of role play in which the child sits in one chair and talks to the "person" in the empty chair. Then the child changes positions, sits in the once empty chair, and talks as the person would to the now empty chair. This process is discussed with the child to increase his or her understanding of relationships with others.

Consulting with parents and others is another major area of services for exceptional students. You want to be involved with parents and support professionals who assist these parents and their children. Consulting skills and processes are avenues through which you can increase your involvement and provide indirect services.

Consulting with Parents of Exceptional Children

Consulting with parents of exceptional children begins at the point that the parents are informed of their child's disability. Regardless of the social and educational backgrounds of parents, this is often a difficult task for counselors and teachers of exceptional children. Here are a few guidelines to consider:

1. *Be prepared.* Review all the assessment information carefully before meeting with parents. Have a clear understanding of all aspects of the program for which the child qualifies. Know the legal regulations by which the child is being placed. Anticipate questions the parents might ask, and prepare accurate responses.
2. *Set up a conference.* Establish an agreeable time and choose a private meeting place where the conference will not be interrupted by accidental intrusions or phone calls. Avoid placing barriers, such as a desk or table, between you and the parents. Maintain an open posture. Plan adequate time to cover all the information and answer all questions.
3. *Lead the conference.* One person, either you, a teacher, or an administrator, should be in charge of the meeting and lead the discussion. Others who attend the meeting are there to provide information when requested. Be careful not to overwhelm parents with a legion of professionals, or overcome them with burdensome regulatory processes. Establish rapport, be open, and support one another. You can facilitate group discussions and coordinate action plans. Let the parents be the "experts" in giving support and advice.

Resource brochures and program updates offer two other effective ways to reach out to these parents. You can design and publish an annual resource guide listing community and state agencies that assist families and children. When new parents with exceptional children enroll at your school, place this information in their orientation packet. Program updates can be provided through collaboration with children's teacher(s) and by planning periodic meetings throughout the year for parents to receive information about their child's program of instruction. Also, give parents an update about new regulations or programs related to special education services.

Learning challenges not only affect exceptional students, they also test students who come from other countries. Many students whose families immigrate to the United States enroll in school without any knowledge of English. Programs for English Language Learners (ELL, formerly known as English as a Second Language, ESL) exist in schools across the United States to help these relocated students.

ENGLISH LANGUAGE LEARNERS (ELL)

Some authorities estimate that there are over 180 languages represented by students in our schools, and programs for English Language Learners (ELL) serve about three million of these students. Furthermore, some predict that the population of ELL students is growing at a rate nearly two and half times faster than the English-speaking population. Among these students, the Latino-Latina population is the fastest-growing ethnic group in the country. According to Clemente and Collison (2000), "the United States has the fifth largest Latino population in the world" (p. 339). It seems clear that schools, teachers, and counselors in the future will need to serve this growing population.

The challenge of coming to school without command of the primary language makes school adjustment and academic achievement unreachable goals. In addition to the general guidelines and strategies mentioned for exceptional students in the previous sections, your support of ELL students in your school may include the following:

• *Accurate assessment of students' understanding and proficiency in speaking, reading, and writing English.* This is essential for proper placement of students in the academic program and in the ELL program. In addition, this assessment will help with decisions about using interpreters.

• *Nontraditional methods of academic assessment.* Students who are not proficient in English will not produce reliable or valid results on regular academic and psychological instruments. If you are unfamiliar with alternative methods of assessment, consult with professionals who can assist you and the school with these procedures.

- *Sense of belonging.* All students perform better in school when they feel as though they belong. ELL students need special attention and empathy. Design strategies with classroom teachers and students to help all students feel welcomed as an important part of the school.

- *Bilingualism versus foreign languages.* Help your school soften the stance against bilingualism. Encourage students and staff members to embrace the concept of learning another language, which can become a goal of the entire school, not only the ELL students!

- *Team-building.* Form close working relationships with ELL teachers and learn techniques that will help you and the students establish rapport. Keep in regular touch with the ELL teachers in your school to be sure that you and the school are meeting the needs of students.

- *Buddy-up.* Assign new ELL students a buddy from their grade level or class. English-speaking students you choose for this important responsibility should be selected carefully and prepared for the role. They could be some of your peer helpers. You might use more than one buddy for each new student so that a number of students benefit from this experience. Buddies can help their new friends learn their way around the school, understand school regulations, find out who the counselor is and what the counselor does, and generally welcome and support the ELL student.

- *Interpreters and translators.* Find out who the interpreters and translators are in your community and learn how to use interpreters appropriately. Select interpreters carefully to be certain they have the language competencies and personal qualities that fit with the goals of the counseling program. Avoid using family members or other relatives as interpreters, and do not use students to interpret for their parents. Translators might also be needed by the school to translate documents from the family to the school and vice versa.

- *Student empowerment and family involvement.* One of the most important roles you will play as a counselor to ELL students is that of an advocate. While ELL students are learning a new language and adjusting to a new society and culture, it is especially important that you allow them to retain and express pride in their native language and culture. At the same time, you must invite their families to become an integral part of the community. For example, a starting point may be to find out what special skills or talents family members have to share with the school and enrich the curriculum.

- *Cultural acceptance and sensitivity.* As you select interventions to use with ELL students, be sensitive to cultural nuances of ELL students. Likewise, encourage your school administrators and teachers to examine school policies, programs, and processes to ensure that traditions of the school do not hinder the adjustment of students from different cultures. Most important, actively search for ways to help your school celebrate diversity all through the year. By making an effort to appreciate and celebrate diversity through the school year, you demonstrate understanding and acceptance of students and families from varied backgrounds.

CULTURALLY DIVERSE POPULATIONS

In addition to learning challenges, exceptionalities, and different languages, children bring their divergent ethnic and cultural backgrounds to school. Across the United States, it is difficult to find schools that are untouched by our shrinking world and uninfluenced by children of Native American, Asian, African American, Latino, Indian, or other heritage. With constant social and political changes taking place in Europe, Africa, Asia, and other continents, inevitable multicultural exchanges will continue to have an impact on American education.

As an advocate for all children in the school, you accept responsibility for assuring that issues of equity, appropriate services, and adequate educational planning are addressed for students across cultures. Equally important is your role in helping the school to increase its multicultural awareness, including the knowledge and skills of teachers and other professionals. Multicultural awareness begins with an acceptance of the belief that cultural differences influence the needs, learning styles, and behaviors that contribute to student development. Paul Pedersen (2000) noted that culture is not outside but rather inside the individual and therefore integrated with other learned experiences. For this reason, effective schools design educational programs that accept the cultural diversity of students, and this acceptance is visible in all school procedures and activities, including counseling services.

All counselors have an obligation to see that counseling programs—and, in a larger sense, schools—strive toward a high level of multicultural awareness and acceptance. To do this, you need knowledge of the school population and the cultural subgroups within it. You also need to acquire counseling skills appropriate for children of different cultures and information about community resources to assist culturally different and disadvantaged families.

The first step is to become aware of your own perceptions and attitudes about different cultures. In a now classic article, Derald Sue (1978) identified several characteristics related to effective multicultural counseling. Worksheet 6-5 is an adaptation and expansion of these characteristics. Use it as a checklist to rate yourself and identify areas to strengthen so you can work effectively with children from different backgrounds.

An analysis of your values and beliefs helps you identify areas of concern for your school as well. Identification of these concerns will help you design a program of services with a broad perspective on multicultural counseling. Multicultural counseling is not limited to specific individual or group counseling skills, but rather is concerned with all the services you offer in your school. Multiculturalism is also illustrated by how your school celebrates its many cultures.

WORKSHEET 6-5

Multicultural Checklist

_____ I am aware of my own values and attitudes regarding the nature of people, and realize that some people differ in these views.

_____ I am knowledgeable of basic counseling skills that span different classes, cultures, and ethnic groups.

_____ I am aware of social and political influences in my community, the country, and world that have prejudiced cultural differences and attitudes toward people of different groups.

_____ I choose from different theoretical orientations and approaches when selecting counseling strategies and tailor services to the culture and needs of students, parents, and teachers.

_____ I am comfortable forming helping relationships with people who are different from me.

_____ I believe that all students are capable of learning.

_____ I include students from all groups in services of the school counseling program.

_____ I help identify areas of discrimination and inequity that exist in our school and in the educational program.

_____ I encourage my school to establish programs and services that reflect the school's population (for example, the cultural makeup of the exceptional children's program, student council, and peer helper program).

Celebration of Cultures

Many services and programs can be offered in your school to celebrate culturally diverse populations. These programs and services are educational and appropriate in small group guidance, classroom guidance (integrated into daily instruction), and schoolwide activities. Such activities with elementary and middle school students begin with instruction about cultural differences. This information should be incorporated into the school curriculum across all subject areas, including social studies, language arts, math, science, and health. Schools that recognize and celebrate cultural differences are more effective in establishing healthy learning environments.

Cultural celebrations include activities in the school that focus on cultural traditions, festivities, and historic events. Allowing students of different cultures to perform dances at assemblies, hang students' art in the hallways, write columns in the school newspaper, read literature to classes, teach classmates popular phrases in their native language (or cultural differences within the English language), and share other aspects of their cultural heritage invites these students to become part of the school. These activities initiate a feeling of belonging among students. Invitations that encourage cultural sharing encourage all students to come to school and continue their educational careers. By asking students to share a part of themselves with their peers, the school says, "We want to be with you."

Schools can design guidance units for students from diverse cultural backgrounds to encourage them to set educational goals, adjust to school customs and expectations without abandoning their own cultural traditions, and continue to attend school. Although these types of activities are important to helping students celebrate their differences, some of the counseling services you and your teachers design for students of different cultures will focus on developmental needs of these students.

Guidance and Counseling Services

Students from different cultures who enter your elementary or middle school require the same attention to developmental concerns as do other students. In some instances, they may need more attention, particularly when language difficulties must be overcome. Differing attitudes and beliefs associated with class and culture need to be considered as you plan services for these students.

Activities you design should enhance the personal, educational, and career development of culturally diverse students. Use group counseling services and group guidance programs to help students develop essential skills and become successful in their educational and vocational careers. Specific group processes can focus on student self-confidence, career goals, human relationship skills, problem-solving skills, study skills, and test-taking skills.

The following are guidelines for establishing relationships and counseling services across cultures in your school:

1. Learn about and appreciate your own culture. Such learning facilitates understanding and acceptance of other cultures.
2. Be open and honest in your relationships with children, parents, and teachers of other cultures. Be receptive to different cultural attitudes and encourage students to be honest and open with you about cultural issues.
3. Demonstrate genuine respect for culturally different attitudes and behaviors. Cultural differences, such as how people dress, eat, or worship, sometimes can be surprising when first observed. Remain open and receptive to learning about these customs and beliefs.
4. Become involved and participate in cultural opportunities and activities in your community. Invite representatives from different cultures to your school.
5. View all people as unique individuals and as members of a cultural group. Respect their individuality and encourage their group heritage.

6. Examine and eliminate prejudicial and racist behaviors. This begins with your own self-examination and extends to staff development and educational activities you plan for your school.

7. Reduce stereotypical behaviors. Help teachers and students become more aware of their beliefs about race, gender, age, religion, and other aspects related to ethnicity and culture.

8. Help your school plan ongoing cultural exhibits and exchanges throughout the year. Whereas some nationally sponsored and celebrated events highlight cultural differences (for example, Black History Month in February), it may be better to plan a variety of activities during the year so students of different cultures do not become associated with an obligatory calendar. If we truly accept peoples from all cultures, there is no need to limit our awareness and appreciation to a few designated weeks or months of the school year.

9. Plan schoolwide programs to integrate with the curriculum. Choose curriculum materials that represent a divergence of cultural heritage.

10. Encourage your colleagues and parents to set high expectations for all students. Too often, a child's educational legacy is diminished due to an inaccurate assessment of ability, based on biased perceptions of cultural differences. Help teachers and parents set high-water marks for student achievement that are determined by accurate assessments and reasonable expectations.

11. Become involved with students from culturally different backgrounds. Invite them to visit the counseling center. Go to lunch with them. Ask about their cultures, and share your culture with them.

Your objectives in designing the counseling services are to help culturally different students remain in school, advance academically, and form friendships. These overlap with the educational, social, and career development goals of these students. Likewise, some of these aspects also relate to counseling services you offer to help students correct situations, change behaviors, or overcome obstacles to learning and development. In all these instances, it is imperative to be mindful of the difference between the processes of accommodating and assimilating students of different cultures in your school. On the one hand, accommodating activities and services help students adjust to the school and encourage the school community to make adjustments for these students. Assimilation, on the other hand, is a process of absorbing the student into the majority culture while risking the loss of his or her own cultural identity. It diminishes the celebration of cultural differences and detracts from the developmental goals of your counseling services. The approaches you choose should strike a balance between helping students adopt new behaviors that will facilitate their adjustment to school and allowing them to have pride and respect for their heritage.

While group processes are effective with culturally mixed groups to help them alter behaviors, you want to screen members carefully to assure that differences will not impede group progress or individual development. Explain why the student is being invited to join a group and describe the group's purpose. Students should understand that being part of a group means focusing on making changes in their lives. For culturally diverse students, you will want to examine these potential changes in relationship to their unique cultures. The consequences of changing their behavior could affect their relationships with their community and family. These possibilities and consequences must be fully and openly explored.

Counseling culturally diverse students, either individually or in groups, requires an accurate assessment of their present situation and level of functioning. This means avoiding assessment instruments and processes that have socioeconomic and cultural bias. In addition, guard against making educational decisions for any student based on data from a single assessment instrument or process.

Individual and group counseling relationships with culturally different students place high importance on the development of self-esteem and worth of the individual. With the exception of destructive, disruptive, and violent behaviors, the goal of altering behaviors should be a secondary consideration to one of fostering a feeling of self-worth, value, and belonging for the student. At the same time, these helping relationships should elevate the individual's cultural identity by giving value to membership within a particular ethnic or cultural group.

This chapter explores ways for you to reach out to diverse student populations and children with special concerns. In doing so, you are encouraged to plan counseling services that satisfy preventive, developmental, and remedial needs of all students and to include as many professionals as possible in assessing needs, planning strategies, and delivering services. Having a broad program allows you to intervene accurately and effectively when crises occur in the school. Sometimes events happen that threaten the welfare of students, teachers, and the school as a community. When such crises occur, you must be prepared to assist. Chapter Seven presents ideas and strategies for intervening in critical situations.

chapter 7

PREPARING *for* CRISIS INTERVENTION

Schools face many challenges, and sometimes these challenges present themselves in critical situations. Similarly, parents confront a variety of pressures and stresses that, at times, can magnify into potentially explosive circumstances. Added to these commonplace emergencies are a multitude of social, economic, and environmental events that have an impact on schools, students, families, and the learning process. Family deaths, destructive tornadoes, war, factory closings, automobile accidents, substance abuse, and other trauma and tragedy contribute to crises that students, parents, and teachers face daily.

You have an important role, both as an individual helper and as a team member, in assisting students and schools when crises occur. This chapter examines some key points to determine your role in crisis intervention. Among the suggestions in the chapter, one point is clearly emphasized: *be prepared.* Successful resolution of crises in the school will depend on your readiness to act in a direct and purposeful manner by

- Gathering necessary information
- Involving appropriate personnel
- Seeking supportive resources

- Formulating a plan of action
- Following the plan to its conclusion

This chapter includes suggestions for developing a crisis intervention team, designing a plan of action, implementing preventive in-service, and providing direct intervention for students and others who are in crisis. The ideas in this chapter suggest a framework within which you can work with your principal and teaching colleagues to design and implement crisis intervention strategies. In preparing for your role in crisis intervention, consider these preliminary suggestions:

- *Be informed.* Because we live in an ever-changing society with an ever-increasing storage house of information and knowledge, it is essential that you stay abreast of the latest techniques and procedures to use in critical situations. To stay informed. To avoid becoming outmoded, attend workshops, read professional journals, and visit with other counselors to learn how to approach these high-pressure roles.
- *Seek assistance.* In most crises, if you use the services and resources of other professionals, you will be more successful than single-handedly attempting to save the day on every occasion. Schools and communities often have professionals and resources that they can pool to resolve crises efficiently and effectively. A capable counselor is one who seeks collaborative relationships with other professional helpers.
- *Know your limits.* Regardless of the knowledge that you possess and the level of skill you have attained, there will be times when your knowledge and skills are insufficient to help people who have critical needs. It is imperative in all helping relationships to monitor your level of competence and refer cases when you have reached the limit of your expertise.

By staying informed, seeking assistance, and knowing your limitations, you can establish effective helping relationships and formulate precise plans to meet most crisis situations head on. The first step is to achieve an understanding of what a crisis is. A clear definition helps you distinguish between emergency intervention processes and other types of helping relationships and enables you to choose appropriate strategies and techniques accordingly.

DEFINITION AND DESCRIPTION OF A CRISIS

A crisis is an intolerable situation, an unstable condition, or a sudden change in routine that disrupts the normal functioning of a person, group, or organization and requires immediate attention and resolution. For persons who are in a crisis, the surrounding events can be so emotionally or physically threatening that they believe that they have lost control and are unable to cope.

Students and teachers are affected by crises that occur in the school and the community at large. Tragic deaths, violent assaults, chemical accidents, and natural disasters, among other events, can have serious impact on student behavior and the learning process in schools.

Characteristics of Crises

Although individual crises have their own unique traits, they also have some common characteristics. For example, in all crises the immediate needs of people must be identified and addressed to resolve the situation. Usually, these needs involve physical welfare, emotional stability, and personal security. Generally, crises consist of abnormal, uncommon, and extraordinary conditions that bring forth strong emotional reactions from affected populations. These reactions include high levels of fear, stress, and anger. Frequently, victims of crises become preoccupied with their situation and function in a state of disequilibria. Because of this high stress level, confrontations are common.

Many crises have the potential to upset entire school communities. Some are so traumatic that they alter the consciousness of schools and communities for years to come. Americans will remember for decades the shock of the World Trade Towers in New York City being hit by hijacked planes and crumbling to the ground, killing thousands of innocent people. When we see old news videos or pictures of this devastation, we remember where we were and our reactions to this attack and national tragedy. The explosion of the Challenger spacecraft in 1986 and the sudden breakup of the Columbia Shuttle in 2003, witnessed by school children across the country, are other examples of how tragic events disrupt the educational process. School counselors, social workers, psychologists, and teachers at all levels of education assisted in the wake of these disasters, as they did after the World Trade Towers were attacked.

In similar ways, the premature death of students, teachers, or community leaders can have a significant impact on a school. Suicides, homicides, and tragic accidents result in feelings of loss, hurt, and anger that extend beyond the immediate family and close friends. Classmates and teachers who have had relationships with the victims also experience these feelings. In such crises, the welfare of all involved is an important consideration for counselors and other helping professionals.

Types of Crises

Situations we define as crises occasionally happen in our schools. At times, these crises are sudden and traumatic, such as accidents and suicides; others, such as illnesses that are terminal, long-term, or contagious, tend to be chronic events that disrupt the school setting. Sometimes the illnesses themselves are not as critical to the school as are the fears raised among the school and community populations. Uncertainty about AIDS, herpes, and infectious hepatitis, for example, can feed unfounded rumors and exaggerate the threat to personal safety and well-being. Instances of irrational fears can create a crisis.

Social and economic events also can be disruptive to schools. Such events include violent crimes, imprisonments, sexual deviance, substance abuse, sudden unemployment, industrial closings, and bank failures. Likewise, natural disasters such as hurricanes, tornadoes, floods, and fires, can have a debilitating effect on students, parents, and teachers. In some cases, the aftermath of a major disaster requires long-term intervention and counseling to help students and others regain their momentum and stability. In our high-tech world, we are also at risk of environmental disasters such as industrial accidents, chemical leaks, and nuclear incidents that place large segments of our population in jeopardy.

In all these situations, you are a central figure in helping to plan, assess, coordinate, and intervene on behalf of students, parents, and teachers. However, you cannot do it alone. For this reason, it is more beneficial and effective if your school uses a team approach in designing and implementing a crisis intervention plan.

A CRISIS TEAM AND PLAN

Because each crisis has its own unique characteristics, as well as traits that are common with other crises, many different types of expertise are needed to assist in handling tragic and traumatic events in schools. Crisis teams can meet these needs. Establishing a team and choosing team members are explored later in this chapter. Here are some factors that you should consider when assisting your school in designing a crisis intervention plan.

Factors to Consider

To help your school design a crisis intervention plan, you will want to focus on a few factors that facilitate the successful handling of critical situations. Some of these factors are

- Safety
- Media
- Communication
- Stress
- Authority

Let us examine each of these briefly.

Safety

During a crisis and its aftermath, your school must ensure the safety of students and staff. The exact steps taken to protect people and secure the building will vary from crisis to crisis, but one essential point is that the basic needs of security, shelter, and safety from physical harm must be met in all critical situations.

Media

When tragedies occur in schools and communities, the media—press, television, and radio—want information to broadcast and distribute to the public. In most instances, the media takes this "need to know" stance with the best interest of the public welfare in mind. The media want to keep people informed as a public service. Furthermore, in some crises schools may rely on media to seek relief and assistance for students and teachers. For example, if a rare blood type were needed for transfusions, the media would be most valuable in broadcasting this emergency. Or if there were a serious chemical spill in the neighborhood and people needed to evacuate, the media would announce appropriate procedures.

Although the media can provide beneficial services to your school, they also can be a hindrance during crises. Sometimes a reporter's aggressiveness in creating a newsworthy story might impede the school's progress toward calming an explosive situation and resolving the crisis at hand. The public right to know must be balanced with an individual's right to privacy and protection. An appropriate plan for handling crises in your school will address this need for a balanced perspective. Write specific guidelines for the dissemination of information and media access to school personnel and present them to the school staff and local media.

Communication

Specific procedures for disseminating information depend on the nature of the crisis, but schools should establish general guidelines. Appropriate guidelines will address how to distribute information, in what form, and by whom. The most important reason for controlling the flow of information in a systematic and reasonable way is to assure that all announcements and requests are accurate. Misleading and inaccurate information has the potential to exaggerate a crisis, hinder attempts to help, and fuel an already volatile situation.

Emotional and Psychological Stress

Estimating how much the overall impact of a crisis will heighten the emotional and psychological stress of students, teachers, and others is another factor to consider. Factors such as the seriousness of the crisis, the number of people directly involved, and people's initial reactions to the event will serve as indicators by which you and other professional helpers will be able to estimate the scope of the problem and begin taking steps to provide assistance.

A school bus accident that kills several students is one example of a crisis that touches everyone in a community. Helping a large number of people deal with loss in circumstances such as this is challenging to everyone involved. At the same time, a tragic bus accident may raise other divergent issues during the peak of emotional stress. Extraneous issues such as competent and qualified bus drivers ("this never would have happened if the system hired better drivers") could become emotional topics that, if not contained, might fuel an already critical situation and, more important, hamper the assistance being offered to students, parents, and teachers. The emergence of such issues presents an additional challenge for school administrators and community leaders to handle. With a comprehensive crisis plan, your school and community are prepared for all possibilities when crises occur, including the expression of a wide range of emotional responses.

Authority

A fifth factor to consider in a crisis is authority. During a crisis in your school, who will be in charge? This is not simply a question of who runs the school or school system. It is a statement that strikes at fundamental issues, such as parents' rights and legal jurisdiction of the police department and other agencies. For example, in a crisis such as an explosion in a school, fire marshals, police officers, medical personnel, and the school administrators want to coordinate their decisions and recognize the parameters of their authority in dealing effectively and efficiently with the situation.

It makes sense that we should establish cooperative channels of communication and authority between schools and communities before crises occur. A well-publicized crisis intervention plan helps make strides in this direction. The first lines of authority for crises in schools must be established among school personnel who will be coordinating services. For this reason, a team approach, which is examined in the next section, can be helpful in dealing with most critical situations.

The Team

When determining crisis team members, your school should consider three areas of crisis management and intervention:

1. Management of the situation
2. Direct intervention strategies
3. Post-crisis procedures

Successful outcomes in each of these three areas will require appropriately trained and competent professionals. Management, communication, intervention, and other skills are organized and used to facilitate the most beneficial solution and assistance for individuals, the school, and the community.

The first area, crisis management, requires people to make organizational decisions, handle communications, and arrange hospitalities if needed. Management personnel include people who will

- Be in charge of the overall operation
- Notify other team members of their responsibilities
- Respond to the news media
- Manage the crisis headquarters
- Notify the appropriate authorities
- Keep logs of incoming and outgoing phone calls
- Prepare news releases for publication and broadcast
- Arrange for refreshments and appropriate facilities if a prolonged crisis is expected

Some people on the crisis team have the primary function of intervening and assisting students, parents, and teachers. These team members are counselors, nurses, social workers, rescue technicians, and other available professionals. They are responsible for

- Assessing immediate needs of the people in crisis
- Determining what services to deliver and who will deliver these services
- Identifying and referring cases to appropriate agencies and professionals
- Establishing an assistance center in the school or community
- Deciding about classroom interventions, services, and strategies

After a crisis has ended, the team assesses the post-crisis environment and makes decisions about

- Returning to a normal school schedule and routine
- Continuing assistance for people in need of services
- Determining the appropriateness of special events; for example, memorial services, fund raisers, and recognitions of valor and heroism
- Examining causal and contributing factors
- Evaluating management and intervention strategies
- Planning preventive measures to avoid or deal with future crises of this nature

As you can see from these considerations, a crisis team consists of several professionals and support staff. Your school may have a large crisis team designated each year, but each crisis will dictate which team members need to be involved. Possible crisis team members include the principal, assistant principals, counselors, nurses, social workers, psychologists, campus security, staff trained in CPR, staff to handle communications, and one or more teachers. In addition, crisis teams might include local police officers, mental health counselors, medical personnel, rescue squads, and others. Because of the emotional and psychological stress associated with most crises, it is reasonable to assume that you would be involved during and after the event in providing necessary counseling services.

When many team members are involved, leadership is essential. For example, if school counselors, social workers, and psychologists provide assistance during a crisis, one of these professionals needs to lead this team of helpers and coordinate services to students, parents, and teachers. Adequate coordination avoids confusion and duplication of services. Because you work daily with students and coordinate student services in your school, you are probably in position to provide team leadership during crises.

The Plan

In addition to designating a team, a crisis intervention plan should include general guidelines and specific procedures to follow. The school should evaluate the plan each year and revise it as needed. After appropriate revisions, staff in-service should be planned for the beginning of the school year to include an overview of the crisis plan and designated responsibilities of each team member.

Schools can design individual crisis plans, but they should coordinate their efforts with plans developed at the school system level. This is particularly true in large school systems where several elementary schools feed into each middle school, and the middle schools feed to one or more high schools. In such systems, consistent crisis procedures would be necessary to facilitate communications among all the schools and community agencies.

General Guidelines

In helping your elementary or middle school develop crisis plans, you may want to present general guidelines as an initial step in the process. The following guidelines offer ten starter steps for handling crises:

1. Define the type and extent of the crisis as soon as possible. Be cautious about the information you collect and release. Accurate information is essential.
2. Contact the superintendent or designee and inform that person of the current situation. Let the superintendent know the specific steps taken thus far.

3. Notify the school staff about the situation as soon as possible and inform them of appropriate actions to take. Depending on the crisis, it may not be necessary to notify all staff. Only those with an immediate need to know should be notified.

4. Contact person(s) affected by the crisis. For example, call parents and guardians of students involved in the incident.

5. Identify a central location as a communications center. Appropriate personnel who coordinate all communications in and out of the school will staff this location. All school personnel should be instructed to refer information and questions regarding the crisis to the communications center. Assign staff members to answer phones and to call for additional information and assistance.

6. When appropriate, contact the news media, and provide accurate information about what is known about the crisis. Release information when facts are verified and the school's position regarding the crisis is clear. Read all news releases from prepared statements. Avoid speaking "off the cuff." In critical situations with emotions high, statements can sometimes be misinterpreted and misunderstood. A prepared text is a safeguard against miscommunication.

7. Maintain a record of all incoming and outgoing phone calls and personal contacts regarding the crisis. This guideline is particularly important in crises that involve criminal activity, but it also is helpful in other situations to demonstrate that staff acted responsibly and reasonably during a difficult incident.

8. Relieve key people from their normal duties. Design strategies to allow crisis team members and the communications center staff to delegate their normal duties to other staff members. Use all available personnel.

9. Provide refreshments for employees, rescue workers, media, and others if the crisis is prolonged. Hunger, fatigue, and similar conditions add to an already difficult circumstance. Having nourishment and adequate facilities available will help keep emotions in check.

10. After the crisis has ended, express appreciation to all persons and agencies that helped resolve the problem.

Specific Procedures

In a crisis plan or manual, step-by-step procedures, such as the following, specify for all school staff ways to respond to a crisis in the school:

- The first individual who observes the crisis alerts the principal or designee.
- The principal notifies appropriate crisis team members and gives the location to which they report. Schools might consider a crisis signal

that indicates the nature of the crisis, such as the following example of a color coded signal:

> Blue: sudden illness (heart attack, severe fall, seizure)
> Red: suicide threat
> Yellow: hostage taking, kidnapping
> Brown: physical attack or abuse
> Green: evacuation needed
> Orange: social disturbance
> Black: accident
> White: hostile intruder on campus

(Note: a caution about crisis codes and signals is appropriate here. If your school chooses to use a signal, such as the color code suggested above, consistent staff in-service is necessary. Train staff members at least once a year to inform them about the code. Teacher transfers and retirements will make crisis signals obsolete unless you share regular updated information with the staff.)

- One member of the crisis team supervises the communications center. This center is usually in the principal's office with phone and other communication capabilities.
- The coordinator of the communication center relays a message to the superintendent's office immediately (see Exhibit 7-1). The coordinator contacts appropriate persons affected by the crises (for example, parents, spouses).
- Outline specific procedures for the crisis team to follow in each type of crisis. You might develop these procedures in a handbook for crisis interventions.

EXHIBIT 7-1

Communication with Superintendent's Office

Instructions for sending a crisis message to the central office:

1. Identify who you are and your school.
2. Identify the type of crisis.
3. Give pertinent facts regarding any individual or service that has been called, for example, fire department, rescue squad, and police.
4. Give facts regarding individuals involved in the crisis; for example, names of students, parents, and teachers.
5. Follow the instructions of the superintendent or designee regarding
   a. information to be released to parents and family members
   b. information to be given to others (media, neighbors, concerned citizens)

In preparing general and specific procedures to follow during crises, the school staff will need adequate in-service training. You can assist in planning, coordinating, and delivering in-service opportunities to teachers and other staff members in your school.

IN-SERVICE

In-service opportunities for teachers and other school personnel regarding crises can be categorized as prevention and intervention strategies. This section explores topics for you and your teachers to consider when planning in-service for the school year. To begin, it examines some general information related to crises in schools and a few procedures that could influence staff development plans.

General Information

At the beginning of the school year, it is appropriate to assemble the staff and have the faculty openly discuss the types of crises that have occurred in the school and community in recent years. During this discussion, as crises are identified, you, the principal, or other leader could ask the staff to determine how the school should respond to similar crises in the future. This discussion can help identify the essential elements of an annual crisis plan for the school. It can also highlight potential topics for staff development.

One such topic that could come from a discussion of past crises in the school is the need for emergency medical intervention. For example, teachers may decide that they need training in CPR procedures. If so, a representative of the American Red Cross or similar organization could provide this in-service. Similarly, the staff may want to learn basic procedures for responding to other medical crises such as seizures, fainting spells, and lacerations that occur in schools. Medical organizations in most communities will cooperate in providing schools with basic information about how to respond to these types of crises until professional medical assistance arrives. You can help by determining how many staff members want this type of training and by locating appropriate professionals to present the workshop. A quick survey such as illustrated in Worksheet 7-1 can provide teacher input.

Another area related to crises in schools is information about legal and ethical implications surrounding crisis intervention. Principals, teachers, counselors, and other school personnel frequently are concerned about their personal liability when assisting in critical situations. A school board attorney or other local law practitioner can assist with information. In addition, you probably are concerned about *confidentiality* in your school practice and how you handle privileged communications in crises. If you have these concerns, you should first become familiar with local and state policies and statutes

WORKSHEET 7-1

Crisis In-service Survey

Teachers:

At our faculty meeting, we discussed many different ways for us to be prepared for and ready to handle various crises that could occur in our school. As a follow-up to that discussion, we are asking for your ideas about specific in-service and training you would like to have regarding skills for dealing with critical situations.

Please give us your suggestions and return this form to the counselor.

Thank you for your input!

First aid: _____

Group management: _____

Handling the media: _____

Dealing with specific crises: _____

Natural disasters: _____

Other skill areas: _____

Name:_____ Date: _____

regarding privileged communications for school counselors. You also should be knowledgeable about the code of ethics of the American School Counselor Association, which is the code followed by most professional school counselors. Last, you do not maintain confidentiality when clients threaten themselves or others, or when students are in imminent danger. Additional information about this topic is in Chapter Eleven, which presents legal and ethical issues.

Learning about procedures for contacting rescue squads, the fire department, or other agencies is another area you can address through staff in-service. What may appear to be simple procedures sometimes become major ordeals during a crisis because people have not received the necessary training and information beforehand. Gather important phone numbers and post emergency numbers in suitable locations around your school. Coordinate with your principal to invite agency representatives to present at faculty meetings about procedures for including these organizations in crisis interventions. In addition to this information, teachers and staff members may want to review the general and specific procedures outlined in your school's annual crisis plan.

Learning ways to respond to the news media and other inquiries into the school during and after a crisis is another topic for staff development. When crises occur, it is difficult to think of what to say, how to say it, and to whom. If teachers receive this information and training at the beginning of the year and practice these procedures in mock situations, they are better prepared to handle communications appropriately in the heat of a crisis.

Preventive Activities and Programs

Many activities that you organize and deliver in the school counseling program help prevent crises or limit the impact of inevitable and uncontrollable crises. In most cases, prevention takes the form of instructional services; yet these activities require all the helping skills used in counseling relationships. One such activity is classroom guidance, which, as noted in this guide, is an ongoing component of the school curriculum.

Classroom guidance activities help students learn about their development, their relationships with peers and others, and the personal, educational, and career decisions they will make during a lifetime. You and your teachers can plan classroom guidance to help students identify indicators of stress and danger in their lives and the lives of their friends. At the same time, children can be encouraged to help their friends by referring them to you or a teacher for assistance. Children often notice changes in their peers before problems become apparent to teachers and counselors. Encourage them to share these observations through appropriate channels so that their friends and classmates can be helped.

A by-product of classroom guidance activities is the ability of teachers and you to identify students who need special attention. Sometimes students who are quiet and withdrawn are not identified by teachers as needing counselor assistance. Through classroom guidance, teachers and you are able to determine whether a particular behavior warrants referral for counseling or contact with the student's family.

You also use developmental counseling as a preventive measure. In some respects, developmental counseling is similar to guidance activities because it frequently uses instructional processes. Its purpose is to help students explore developmental concerns and issues and learn appropriate ways of handling them. In other ways, developmental counseling is different from classroom guidance: it is practiced in individual and small group settings; it establishes a confidential relationship; and it incorporates a specific helping process of beginning with an introduction, moving through exploration and action phases, and ending with closure.

Developmental counseling helps students learn about a variety of issues, including peer relationships, feelings, assertiveness training, decision-making skills, loss and grief, educational planning, and stress management. Through developmental counseling, in groups and individually, you help students acquire skills to cope with normal, everyday problems before these concerns become overwhelming crises.

Peer helper programs combine some of the aspects of guidance and developmental counseling into a variety of helping processes. Typically, counselors or teachers or both organize and supervise peer helper programs. They select and train students in basic helping skills. In middle schools, students become peer helpers to tutor fellow students, act as a "buddy" for new students, present guidance activities with teachers and counselors in the classroom, or be listeners for classmates who need a friend. Middle school students who are trained peer helpers also assist in elementary schools by tutoring younger students, reading to kindergarten and first grade groups, and assisting teachers and counselors with classroom guidance.

Training in basic helping skills is essential for peer programs to be successful. In particular, peer helpers need to learn how to refer to you for counseling students who are in critical need. In this way, peer helpers are the "meteorologists" in your school, helping the staff stay informed about school climate and critical issues affecting students.

Parent education programs presented in large sessions, such as PTA meetings, or in small, ongoing parent groups are another example of instructional and informational services that you can use to prevent crises. In these programs, you assist parents with communication skills and help them identify early warning signs in the behaviors and developmental patterns of their children. More detailed information about setting up parent education programs is presented in Chapter Ten.

Safety education offers another area of prevention topics that you and teachers can plan and present to students and parents. Safety lessons can be planned at all grade levels, but they are particularly important in the elementary grades, where young children are curious yet unknowing about the world around them. Safety issues that you can present include information about riding the bus, walking to and from school, talking to strangers, walking in the hallways, and playing on the playground. In some communities, the local police department has a special program on safety, and officers come to school and present to classes of students. You can assist by contacting community agencies and locating these services for teachers to use as resources for classroom guidance activities or school assembly programs.

Student safety also relates to adequate supervision of student behavior. Elementary and middle schools can prevent accidents if faculty and staff adequately supervise students. This is not always an easy task, particularly on campuses with several buildings and expansive grounds, but even so, close supervision is necessary. Small elementary children can sometimes disappear before a teacher realizes it. Their curiosity and enthusiasm frequently lead them astray and into areas of the classroom or school yard that could be hazardous.

In-service to help teachers learn strategies and techniques to increase their supervisory abilities will prevent some crises from occurring. One way to plan this type of in-service is to ask experienced teachers to share ideas and suggestions they have found to be successful in student supervision. A related skill is that of observing and referring students who are in need of services beyond classroom guidance and instruction. Offer your teachers in-service on observable, behavioral indicators that, if left untreated, could evolve into major crises. This topic is of particular importance at the middle school level where students are entering transition years, which present limitless challenges to their physical, social, emotional, and educational development. Helping teachers learn about crisis indicators places your school in a stronger position to plan prevention activities and strategies.

The observational skills of teachers relate to their listening and communication skills. For this reason staff development activities on student supervision for crisis prevention might also address topics such as active listening, reflection of feelings, and effective attending skills. When teachers acquire these basic helping skills, they accurately respond to the needs and concerns of students in crisis. By effectively handling crises during the initial stages, teachers become better informed to make referrals to you or other student services professionals.

You may occasionally receive referrals of crises from students, parents, and teachers, and need to determine whether you should provide direct counseling services in these instances. In the next section, I will consider factors and processes related to crisis counseling in elementary and middle schools.

CRISIS COUNSELING

There is no clear and easy formula for you to decide what crisis cases you should or should not handle. Sometimes this question is answered simply by the fact of whether there is, or is not, a more qualified professional to serve the student. For example, in large urban areas where we find a wealth of mental health practitioners in both the public and private sectors, a counselor may decide to refer all crisis cases. But in rural areas with few services for students and families, a school counselor may be the only professional helper available. Whatever the decision, you always provide services within the scope of your professional competencies and abilities. At times, this may mean going back to school or attending seminars to learn new information and skills.

When you receive a referral for crisis counseling, the following questions may help you explore the situation and make an appropriate decision:

1. *Is the situation such that the school crisis team needs to be informed?* In all critical situations, you should inform the school principal. Together you

and the principal will be able to determine whether other team members should be involved.

2. *What steps do you take immediately?* Depending on the nature the case, you and the principal will make decisions regarding the safety of the child, notification of parents or guardians, and referral to other community agencies such as the health department or social services.

3. *Do you have the training and knowledge needed to counsel effectively in this case?* If you have the skill, will you have the time necessary to see this case through to a successful resolution? If you do not have the skill or time, what other agencies or professionals are available to accept this case?

4. *If another agency accepts the case, are there support services you and the teachers should provide in the school setting?* You will want to keep in contact with the outside agency as the case progresses to learn the best approaches for the school to take with the child and family.

When you receive a referral and decide to handle a critical situation, taking a few clear steps will help in establishing a counseling relationship. These steps involve assessing the nature and severity of the crisis, establishing and implementing a plan of action, and following up by evaluating the outcome of the counseling process.

Assessment

In assessing crisis referrals, you first determine the "degree of risk" for the student's welfare and safety that enables you to then decide who needs to be contacted about the situation and whether or not you have the skills to intervene. When possible, include other professionals in the assessment process.

Use assessment procedures that include interviewing the student, parents, teachers, and peers, observing behaviors of the person in crisis, screening the individual by using standardized and informal measurement instruments, and gathering data from other available sources. In making accurate decisions in crisis, the axiom "leave no stone unturned" applies. There is no such thing as too much information in these cases.

Of course, some crises do not permit enough time to do a thorough assessment. When a student is having a seizure is not the time to go check the health record. First, you must handle the immediate medical emergency. Later, when the student is stabilized, a more thorough gathering of data might be done.

If you determine that a student is at high risk to harm himself or herself, or is at risk of doing imminent harm to another, you must bring in all resources and appropriate authorities on the case. You should inform the principal and notify the parents. The last section of this chapter discusses specific instances of crisis counseling and presents additional information about assessment. Much information about assessment in critical situations is in the literature, and you should be familiar with these procedures.

In addition to assessing the scope and severity of the situation, you eventually will want to assess causal and contributing factors. When the case is referred to another professional or agency, such as a mental health center, it is still appropriate for the school to be involved in this assessment process and informed about factors that may have contributed to the crisis. School-related factors need to be examined and altered if found to be detrimental to a healthy learning environment.

Whatever assessment procedures you use to determine the extent of the crisis and contributing factors, they are simply the first steps in the crisis counseling process. Once you have decided to intervene through a counseling relationship, the next step is to determine an appropriate plan of action.

Plan of Action

Crisis counseling in most situations is direct and action-oriented. This is not the time for self-reflection and exploration on the part of the student. For the same reason, in critical situations you will not have the luxury to sit back and allow the counselee much freedom to make decisions, particularly in life-threatening situations. Typically, students in crises want direction, and it is only after they are stabilized and secure that they are able to assume some decision-making responsibilities. This responsibility comes gradually, after an initial plan of action has been established and the student has experienced preliminary success.

A sample plan of action for crisis counseling is

1. Identify the problem
2. Narrow the focus
3. Formulate specific steps for action
4. Agree on a plan or contract
5. Refer the student for other services

Identifying the problem means helping the student recognize and verbalize what his or her concerns are. The essential question for the students is, *What do you want to have happen?* Sometimes the answer to this question may be broad and difficult to pinpoint. When this is so, help the student narrow his or her focus. For example, the student might respond, "I'm not happy." By helping the student narrow the focus and clue in on specific factors, you might learn that the student's best friend has moved away, he or she just failed a test, or the student shows indications of abuse in the home. It is these facts, rather than global feelings, that enable you and your students to decide on precise plans of action.

A plan of action in crisis counseling includes a commitment to what the student will and will not do, and what you will do in the helping relationship. Sometimes in crisis counseling it is helpful for the student and counselor to write a contract and sign it to seal their agreement. If the contract is broken, the relationship continues, but a new contract is negotiated. As mentioned earlier, when a counseling relationship is not improving or you have reached the limits of your expertise, it is time to refer to other agencies and professionals. Students may balk at this prospect, particularly in elementary and middle schools, because they fear forming new helping relationships. Assist them through this referral process by going with the students for their first visit and by continuing to see them at school by agreement and with the approval of the other mental health professionals. Be honest with students about the reason for the referral: "We need to find someone who has more knowledge about this and is better able to help you than I am."

Whether you provide services or refer to another professional, you have responsibility to follow up and evaluate the outcomes. In this way, your school assesses the professionals and programs to whom you refer students and families.

Follow-up and Evaluation

Follow closely the students and families you serve through crisis counseling. This is necessary both to assure that the student continues to receive supervision and is safe from harm and to measure the progress you are making in the counseling relationship. When you have been involved in a crisis relationship for a period of time and little or no progress is seen, it is time to examine the direction and approaches chosen in the helping process and consider the option of referring to another professional or agency.

When referrals are made, you retain responsibility for following the case and making contact with the receiving agency or professional. Following cases takes time, particularly in elementary and middle schools where counselor-student ratios are often quite high. Phoning community agencies, other professionals, and parents ensures that the services you expect are in fact delivered and received. Sometimes all the work you do to refer a student and family to an agency falls through because the family fails to keep the appointment. By staying in touch with referral agencies, you are in a better position to remedy the situation when other people neglect their responsibilities.

By following up with the family, you let parents know that the school cares and is not simply passing the child off to another agency. This demonstration of concern encourages the family to continue therapy and lets students know that the school is looking out for their best interests. In addition, it allows you to gather information about student progress and to evaluate the strategies and approaches chosen to handle critical situations. Through evaluation processes, both informal and formal, you will become better equipped to choose effective approaches efficiently and expeditiously when crises occur.

In this and the preceding chapter, you have learned about general guidelines and approaches to working with students with special needs and diverse cultural backgrounds, as well as for being prepared for crises that occur in schools and communities. Chapter Eight highlights several areas of student concerns and presents ideas and strategies for assisting in particular cases. Some of these concerns, when traumatic and debilitating, place children, the school, and families in crises.

chapter 8

USING ESSENTIAL SERVICES *to* ADDRESS STUDENTS' CONCERNS

This chapter takes the guidelines and framework presented in Chapters Six and Seven and explores strategies for establishing student-counselor relationships to address several issues and concerns of typical elementary and middle school students. Most elementary and middle schools include children who, while not identified with a specific exceptionality, have concerns that require the attention of teachers and counselors. In some respects, these particular concerns place children at risk of school failure, contribute to poor peer relationships, or relate to other conditions that negatively affect student development. At the same time, elementary and middle schools frequently face critical situations with their students.

This chapter comprises two sections. The first presents particular student concerns that, in most instances, do not present critical situations. Of course, this list is not exhaustive, but the examples, ideas, and strategies might be useful in selecting approaches to help students with a wide range of normal, developmental issues. Many of these concerns you undoubtedly have handled or will confront as an elementary or middle school counselor.

The second section of this chapter focuses on critical issues that students and families bring to school or the community presents and that have an impact on the school. Again, the list is not all-inclusive, but by combining the ideas from Chapter Seven with strategies for critical cases in this chapter, you will be better prepared to help students, parents, and teachers with difficult situations.

STUDENT CONCERNS

Due to our complex society with ever-changing norms and divergent populations, elementary and middle school teachers and counselors must be prepared to assist children with a variety of issues. In many instances, these concerns arise because of social forces over which children have little or no control. This section considers the following childhood and preadolescent issues: bullying, divorce, child care, stress, loneliness, underachievement, care taking, relocation, and physical challenges. As noted, it addresses additional and more critical issues in the next section.

Bullying

Bullying is a phenomenon that appears at many levels of schooling. Although considered a significant problem in U.S. schools, bullying is also a noted problem in other countries, such as England, Australia, and Japan, to name a few. Research in the United States indicates that between 30 and 80 percent of students, depending on the region of the country, suffer from bullying at some point in their educational career. About 160,000 students remain home from school everyday to avoid being bullied. These data show that bullying in schools is a persistent problem that requires attention from counselors, teachers, administrators, students, and parents.

The effects of bullying often leave students with long-term physical, emotional, and educational scars. Victims of bullying frequently have problems focusing on their schoolwork, perform below levels of expectation, show symptoms of anxiety, depression, and poor self-confidence, and, as noted earlier, have higher absentee rates. All of these consequences take a tremendous toll on students and, equally important, on the school as a community.

Bullying is a specific type of aggressive behavior used to

- Harm or disturb another person or persons
- Repeatedly and over time willfully expose others to negative behaviors
- Create a harmful relationship in which power is exerted over another person

Bullying comes in many forms from name-calling and verbal put-downs to physical abuse. Between these extremes, we find a range of behaviors that might include blatantly discriminating against or excluding another person; deliberately ignoring someone; taunting, teasing, taking, or damaging property; coercing people to do something they do not want to do; or a combination of hurtful and harmful behaviors. The literature also mentions two main types of bullies as either aggressive or passive. We might expect the aggressive bully to overtly and actively taunt, tease, abuse, and bother others. In contrast, passive bullies usually associate with aggressive bullies but rarely take the initiative to bully others. They are "hangers-on" who support the aggressive bully.

As important as it is to identify types of bullying and design interventions to prevent bullying, it is equally important to know why bullying occurs for those interventions to be effective. Students bully other students for a variety of reasons, and some researchers have noted that understanding these underlying dynamics and the symbiotic relationship between bullies and their victims is important in choosing successful strategies (Roberts & Morotti, 2000). One critical point to remember is that bullying in schools is everyone's problem. These destructive behaviors not only have a negative impact on the victim, they also inhibit the healthy development of the bully and create fearful, disinviting schools.

So, what can you do as an elementary/middle school counselor to help address bullying? The first step is to recognize the problem when it exists. Too often, adults dismiss bullying as a "normal" part of child development. Be proactive. Let your administration and teachers know when you observe children in bullying relationships and offer specific suggestions to address the situation.

Another early step is to help your school develop a clear code of conduct that spells out appropriate behavior and what to do when faced with repeated inappropriate behavior. This code needs to be available and easily understood by everyone in the school. Simply publishing the code without a systematic procedure for introducing and explaining it to the student body is insufficient. As counselor, you can help develop and explain this code of conduct.

Schools need to assess their physical environment to diminish opportunities for bullying. Search areas of your school where inappropriate behavior is likely to take place, and help teachers and administrators address and change these sanctuaries of hostility. At the same time, look for ways to increase student supervision without needlessly burdening teachers. Consider using volunteers, such as parents or retired citizens, to help with this initiative.

Incorporate information about bullying into the school's guidance curriculum and assist teachers in delivering this content. Also, teach students what to do when faced with bullying situations. Help them learn appropriate coping skills as well as where to turn for assistance when they become frustrated or fear for their safety. Establish small groups in the counseling program to give added attention to victims who need it.

Finally, address the concerns of the bully. Encourage teachers and administrators to make contact with bullies in nonthreatening ways. Provide individual and group counseling so bullies can have a safe place to speak openly about their concerns. Listen carefully and be sure you understand the full dynamics of what the bully is saying. Create guidance and counseling services to help these students learn ways to make changes in their behavior, become more tolerant of others, and use their power in constructive ways to help others. Let bullies know that you are there for them just as you are for all other students, and you will be there for the long haul whenever they need you.

Divorce

Divorce continues to affect a high number of children and families. It is stressful and painful for all involved, and teachers and counselors usually see the effects acted out by children in school. Divorce results in the collapse of a supportive and protective structure, and without this protection and support a child feels alone, frightened, and insecure in an uncertain, often terrifying world. With some children, the effects of divorce are readily apparent whereas others may not exhibit developmental reactions for several years after the breakup.

Very young children of preschool age have limited understanding of divorce and, as a result, often feel insecure and frightened, experiencing nightmares and behaving in an infantile manner. Elementary children with advanced cognitive development frequently view the divorce as their fault and hope the family will reunite. As children approach their middle school years, they experience feelings of loss, shame, rejection, and anger over the divorce, yet they strive to adjust to the change and usually cope satisfactorily. Judith Wallerstein studied children from divorced families for ten years and, based her research, established six tasks that children of divorce must resolve to achieve healthy development in their lives. Counselors and teachers who understand these tasks are able to design intervention strategies—preventive, developmental, and remedial—to assist elementary and middle school children of divorced families. Here are Wallerstein's (1983) six psychological tasks and some ways in which you can intervene as a counselor:

1. *Acknowledging the reality of the marital rupture.* It is essential that the child move from a state of fantasy, fear, abandonment, and denial to an acceptance of the divorce. The sooner the child is confronted with the reality of the breakup and assisted with his or her feelings, the earlier a resolution of concerns is possible. Relationship-building skills, such as listening, clarifying, and reflecting, combined with stress reduction and relaxation techniques, may be helpful when counseling children of divorced families.

2. *Disengaging from parental conflict and distress and resuming customary pursuits.* Withdrawal from normal activities and neglect of school work are common concerns with children of divorce. They have difficulty distancing

themselves from the stress and conflict between their parents and as a result tend to lose interest in school and other activities. Counselors and teachers need to be understanding and respectful of children's desire to be concerned and involved with their parents during this stressful time. At the same time, services should be available to assist students so they can eventually distance themselves from the conflict and resume normal childhood activities. Group counseling is one approach that has been found to be a successful intervention strategy in helping children of divorce confront these issues and learn coping behaviors.

3. *Resolving loss.* This task requires children of divorce to resolve several factors related to loss. These factors include the obvious departure of one parent, often felt as rejection and worthlessness, as well as the possible loss of neighborhood, school, friends, and place of worship if the divorce precipitates a family move. In addition, abstract characteristics such as status, security, and family traditions may diminish or disappear in the eyes of the child. Individual and group counseling sessions to focus on self-esteem and the value and worth of the individual child will be helpful. When children of divorce become consumed with irrational thoughts of how the divorce is "catastrophic" to their life and lifestyle, cognitive behavior modification and restructuring techniques are helpful.

4. *Resolving anger and self-blame.* Children and adolescents sometimes resort to anger and blame in their search for answers to the family divorce. They might blame one or both parents, themselves, or their siblings. Very young children fault their own "badness" for the breakup, whereas older children blame themselves for an inability to keep their parents together. Older children also might direct intense anger toward one or both parents for "wanting" or "causing" the divorce. These feelings of blame, guilt, and anger must be resolved, and children must forgive themselves and their parents for the family breakup. Bibliocounseling in groups or individual sessions can help children come to terms with these feelings. Books can be helpful media in counseling with children.

5. *Accepting the permanence of the divorce.* In dealing with this tremendous feeling of loss, children will hold on to the fantasy that their mother and father will eventually reunite and the family will again be together. These feelings persist even in the face of remarriage by one or both of the parents. Children will benefit from counseling and guidance activities that encourage them to test the reality of the situation, accept their parents' decision to divorce, and continue forward with their lives. In counseling, children can make choices that will enable them to accept the permanence of the divorce and move ahead with their own development.

6. *Achieving realistic hope regarding relationships.* For middle school children who are entering their adolescent years, a divorce can influence how they view their own relationships, their ability to love and be loved, and their

willingness to take risks in establishing relationships. Teachers and counselors can encourage these children to take the risk of becoming involved, realizing that not all relationships will succeed. When relationships end, it may be painful but nevertheless all right. When relationships are never attempted, however, they have absolutely no chance of succeeding.

As with any special concern, counselors who help children through family divorce must have adequate skills and demonstrate appropriate acceptance and understanding of the situation. The following guidelines will help when working with children who are dealing with divorce:

- Examine your own values and views regarding divorce. Children are perceptive and will identify any negative responses you convey.
- Avoid abstract explanations and sweeping generalizations. Use concrete examples to help children understand their feelings about the divorce.
- Give children time to express their feelings of hate, anger, fear, sadness, and relief. Encourage them to look toward the future and identify their strengths for dealing with challenges that lie ahead.
- Emphasize that the children are blameless for the divorce and avoid labeling anyone as a "bad guy" or "good guy" in the situation.
- Make only the commitments you can keep, and avoid promises you cannot deliver. Further disappointments for divorced children could be devastating.
- Offer children the opportunity to meet in groups with other students experiencing divorce. They can gain strength by identifying and sharing with others.
- Refer children to local practitioners and agencies if more intensive or long-term counseling is necessary.

In addition to these guidelines, you might consult with teachers and administrators about school factors that will aid children and parents of divorced families. As a counselor, you can help the school

1. Review forms and regulations that demonstrate a bias toward traditional families. Such policies discriminate and potentially embarrass single parents and children of divorce.
2. Collaborate with the media coordinator to establish a section of the library for materials on divorce and ask your advisory committee to correlate these materials with grade level curricula.
3. Help teachers plan classroom guidance activities to include information on various family structures in society and integrate these lessons with daily instruction.

4. Coordinate in-service opportunities for teachers to learn effective strategies that assist them in working with divorced parents and help children of divorce in the classroom.
5. Maintain classroom structure and a consistent school routine. Consistency in school schedules and discipline provides security for children whose families are going through a divorce.
6. Be available to children who need to confer with you during periods of severe stress and conflict at home.

When working with parents who are going through a divorce, encourage them to focus on the children's needs rather than on past problems with the former spouse. Reassure parents that although their children may be experiencing some difficulties, most children rebound and overcome the negative aspects of divorce. Provide them with community resource information, and suggest that they be open and honest about the divorce with their children. It is not necessary for parents to burden their children with unnecessary details, but an honest explanation at the child's level of understanding can facilitate the healing process. Other suggestions you may make to the parents are to

1. Avoid using children as messengers between partners or as "investigators" into the life of the other spouse.
2. Permit children to remain children and not become miniature adults. Resist the temptation of having them become "the man of the family" or "the big sister" for everyone else.
3. Respect the parent-child relationship. Do not seek counseling from your child for your own problems.
4. Keep your commitments and promises. Do not make promises you cannot keep.
5. Talk with your children about their future. Include them in plans for the family.
6. Give children appropriate responsibilities and chores to help them feel an essential part of the family. Everyone in the family should have responsibility. Assign chores that are developmentally appropriate and expect children to accept responsibility and follow through.
7. Avoid conflicts and put-downs with your ex-spouse in view of the children.
8. Cooperate with your ex-mate in arranging suitable visitations. Demonstrated love on the part of both parents will overcome most obstacles in difficult situations.

The changing structure of the American family will continue to influence the lives of our children. Elementary and middle school counselors and teachers will want to identify family factors that inhibit learning and development, and they will want to assist children and parents with these hindrances. One factor associated with families of working parents is the issue of child care, particularly after school when many children go home and care for themselves while their mothers and fathers are at work.

Child Care

Many students leave school at the end of the day and go home alone to an empty house, or they are cared for by an underage brother or sister for a significant portion of the day. It is difficult to estimate the number of children who care for themselves and younger siblings after school and at other times when their mothers and fathers are working. The increasing number of women in the workforce, the rise of single-parent households, changing values, and burdensome economic pressures have all contributed to this phenomenon.

These students often experience higher levels of worry, fear, boredom, and loneliness. Children who care for themselves have shown lower academic achievement than those with parental supervision, and children who care for their younger brothers and sisters also show a decrease in school performance.

Schools should develop programs to help children reduce the feeling of isolation, which frequently accompanies self-care. They also can encourage neighborhoods to establish networks of community resources and organizations to assist latchkey children. In addition, schools can sponsor programs to help children learn about self-care and protection, and they can organize after-school activities that allow children to spend additional time at school with adequate adult supervision.

Counselors and teachers could develop guidance units to present to all students about being responsible for self-care. The lessons might include information about arranging systems of communication, establishing home rules, practicing safety, handling emergencies, coping with fears, overcoming boredom, and talking with parents about concerns. In addition, students receive information about how to care for younger children.

Another role for you in assisting children who spend a significant time at home alone without supervision is as a presenter at PTA/PTO meetings and to other parent gatherings. Encourage parents to establish set routines with their children, provide a safety checklist, know their children's friends, and keep open the lines of communication so children feel free to raise their concerns and feelings about staying alone. Also, remind parents of their responsibility to come home immediately after work. Children worry when their parents do not heed family schedules.

Loneliness

Another issue you might face as an elementary/middle school counselor is children's feelings of loneliness. Some estimates of loneliness are as high as

25 percent for the population in general, and there is no reason to expect that it is less for children.

In helping lonely children, you should work jointly and cooperatively with the teacher because often the classroom environment can be altered to facilitate the inclusion of these children in social and learning activities. Classroom structure and size can enhance or inhibit the social isolation of children. When teachers arrange their classrooms and plan activities to encourage student interaction, friendships develop, cooperation increases, and isolation diminishes.

Help children develop social skills by using modeling and role playing to teach them how to approach people, begin conversations, give and receive compliments, send notes, and improve their personal appearance and grooming habits. You might try cognitive approaches to counseling to help students develop positive thought processes about themselves and overcome fears of social interaction.

Shyness sometimes goes hand in hand with loneliness. Shy children will express their feelings more readily when puppets, drawings, storytelling, unfinished sentences, or play therapy techniques are used. A few specific activities that may help when you are working with shy and isolated children are to

1. Involve children in peer helper services and have them assist other students through tutoring or other active means.
2. Invite children to participate in small group activities in the counseling center or as members of other school programs such as student media aids, school spirit committee, or office helper.
3. Locate a "pal" for a shy child and team the two together. The friend you find should not be a domineering and overpowering type of student but will need instruction about the concerns of shy children.
4. Give shy and isolated children responsibilities in the school. Let them run errands for the school secretary, bring supplies to the custodian, hand out materials in class, answer the counselor's telephone, and help the media coordinator by showing other students where to locate books and materials.
5. Use bibliocounseling to help isolated students learn new coping skills and relationship-building techniques. By using books and other media in a non-confrontational approach, you will encourage students to adopt positive methods of gaining acceptance from their peers.

Some children are naturally shy and can be encouraged to become involved and "belong with" others in the school through programs and services such as those listed above. Other children become quiet and withdrawn when they suffer a personal loss. At these times, you and the teachers need to show concern and understanding toward the child by allowing time to grieve and by being available to students when they need support and comfort.

Relocation

Many families move each year, thus affecting millions of children who relocate and must change schools. Elementary and middle school children sometimes have trouble when they transfer to a new school. In most cases, children who move are able to adjust to their new school and establish new friendships when given time. Sometimes family moves are actually beneficial because they offer children a wider perspective and additional challenges in life. Too many moves for individual children, however, are rarely helpful to their educational and social development.

You can ease children through their relocation by helping teachers and parents understand the stress and loss that children can experience when moving away. Teachers and parents also can be instructed about behavioral signals children send when under stress. These signals include withdrawal, aggressiveness, chronic ailments, and infantile behaviors. At times, children will also exhibit irrational fears about their new house or the school they will attend.

The following are some strategies that teachers, parents, and you can use to help children with relocation:

1. *Have classroom discussions to focus on positive aspects of the impending move.* Recognizing the losses is important, but it is equally helpful for the child to focus on the future: new experiences and friends. Class discussions in the school the child is leaving can bridge the old with the new by encouraging children to correspond with their former classmates. Children can send letters about their new surroundings and photographs of their new home and friends.

Similar discussions also are helpful in the new school, where the child should be made to feel welcome. Assist in this process by establishing "peer welcomers" who are trained to meet new students, orient them to the school, and be their "buddy" for the first few weeks or months while they learn their way around. For a new student, having someone your own age "show you the ropes" is much better than being guided through a tour by a counselor, principal, or other adult who cannot possibly see the school in the same way you do.

2. *Meet with parents to prevent a difficult move from becoming catastrophic.* If parents have children who are leaving your school, help them understand the difficulties the child may experience. Do some planning and have discussions so parents can help the child survive the initial examination of new peers. At the same time, parents can encourage their children to maintain links between the old and the new. For example, buying new clothes and

school supplies might seem appropriate for a new start, but some children may feel more comfortable with familiar clothes and a favorite backpack. Students will feel awkward enough just being new to school. They may not want to be "freshly wrapped," announcing their arrival to the whole world! Encourage parents to let their children keep a low profile if they choose to.

If you are a counselor in the receiving school, you can meet with parents to find out about children's interests, the subjects they like, and the activities they pursue in and out of school. At the same time, parents can be informed about the school procedures that may differ from the sending school. With this information, they can guide their children in knowing what to expect from the new school environment.

Help parents become familiar with the community and its resources. Prepare parent orientation sessions periodically during the year to assist new families. Arrange to have community leaders speak about social opportunities, financial assistance, municipal facilities, medical care, and other community resources. The more information and assistance afforded parents, the less stressful the move is for them, and in turn the easier the move is for their children.

3. *Hold individual or group sessions with children whose families are leaving the community or have moved into town.* These preventive relationships can be used to give children accurate information, allow them to express their feelings in a safe setting, and help the counselor identify children who are going to need special attention. Group sessions can provide mutual support for children who will identify with each other's concerns. Bibliocounseling with individuals or groups also will give children information and allow them to identify role models illustrated in the books. Books about relocation can be used in classroom guidance to help all children learn ways to welcome new students to their school.

4. *Call the new school or send a postcard and let the school know a student of yours is coming.* If you have been counseling the student, ask to speak with the school's counselor (or principal if there is no counselor) and let that person know the student may need some special attention and support. Exhibit 8-1 illustrates a sample postcard to send to the new school.

Stress

Stress is widespread among children and adolescents in American society. Advanced technology and increased family mobility have contributed to the erosion of deep, meaningful interactions among people. For school children and adolescents, several stress factors emanate from a number of sources. For example, the freedom resulting from having working parents is often coupled with childhood and adolescent decisions about sexual activity, drugs, and other inappropriate behaviors. Family divorce, relocations, and deaths, as already discussed, also add to the stress experienced by school children.

Postcard for Student Transfers

Dear *Washington Elementary School*:
We understand that one of our students, *Jack Rogers*, a *5th* grader, is transferring to you this month. Please know that we are available to help you with this student's transfer and adjustment to your school. If you need additional information, you may call our counselor, Mr. Robert Hastings, at (020) 555-7000 or write to him at Downtown Middle School, Railroad Street, Anywhere, USA, or e-mail rogersj@downtownmiddle.usa.

Added to these factors are the expectations of the school and the increased emphasis on testing and achievement.

Various strategies are available to help children deal effectively with stressful situations. Systematic desensitization, relaxation, and cognitive behavior therapy, among other approaches, are methods that are effective with young people. In helping children handle stress appropriately and effectively, the following suggestions may be useful:

1. Choose strategies carefully and know whether your school's community is receptive to different types of counseling approaches. Terms such as *systematic desensitization, biofeedback, cognitive behavior modification,* and *guided fantasies* are sometimes suspect because they are mysterious and unknown to most people, including teachers and administrators. Use language that is clear and understandable to children and parents. For example, cognitive behavior modification is translated as "learning to tell yourself to do good things."
2. Learn your techniques well. Obtain the necessary training through coursework, seminars, and readings to be proficient in the approaches you choose. Incorrect use of strategies may result in outcomes quite opposite from what you envisioned. As one example, by using relaxation techniques forcefully and awkwardly you might increase a child's stress rather than reduce it! The same is true for other misused and misguided approaches.
3. Consult with teachers and parents to help them become familiar with stress factors among children. Parent education programs and teacher in-service activities can be planned to educate adults about the indicators of childhood stress and appropriate stress management strategies.
4. Coordinate classroom guidance activities with teachers and health educators in your school to include information about stress reduction. Plan

physical activities schoolwide so children learn the relationship between appropriate exercise and stress management.

5. Learn ways of managing stress in your own life. Counselors face the same frustrations and challenges as others and need to be equipped to handle stress effectively. Take care of yourself. Chapter Ten of this guide emphasizes in more detail the importance of your own personal self-care.

Underachievers

One of the most frequent referrals counselors receive from teachers is about students who "are not doing the work" or "do not complete their assignments." In many cases, these students are not performing up to their capabilities as measured by educational assessments and teacher judgment. In effect, they are underachieving in their school performance.

Although not as alarming as other problems, such as substance abuse, depression, suicidal talk, and physical abuse, student underachievement is a critical problem in American education. Often it is a symptom of more serious dysfunctions in a student's life, but increasingly we are seeing these instances of underachievement as a combination of personal, psychological, intellectual, and social concerns inherent in a large number of our students.

Sometimes underachievers are students who act out in class, disrupt the learning process, and rebel against school and classroom regulations. Other times, however, they are quiet students who simply appear apathetic, disinterested, or lazy. Teachers and parents frequently describe these students as behaving immaturely, giving up easily, being overly critical of themselves, or lacking self-confidence. Whatever the characteristics, the results are the same: poor academic performance in class, lower than expected scores on achievement tests, and increased frustration among teachers and parents.

When underachievers are allowed to continue without intervention, the result is often complete failure and disinterest in school, contributing to school dropout in the upper grades. For this reason, you must place high priority on assisting these students. To do so effectively, it will help to know what strategies and interventions with underachievers have been most successful.

A review of studies that examine the effects of counselor interventions with underachieving and low achieving students in elementary, middle, and high schools shows that

- Group procedures appear to be more effective than individual counseling with these students. In addition, groups that use structured, behaviorally oriented sessions as opposed to unstructured, person-centered approaches tend to be more effective in improving student performance.

- Longer treatment programs, those lasting more than eight weeks, are more effective than short-term interventions. This finding indicates that you should not expect a quick fix to student attitudes and behaviors related to school achievement.
- Voluntary participation is essential to program effectiveness. When students agree to join a group, they are more likely to commit to change than if they are forced into a program.
- Counseling in combination with study skill instruction is effective in helping students raise their school achievement.
- Parent involvement is an additional factor related to improving student performance. Programs that include parent participation tend to show positive results.

In addition to these findings, instructional strategies and counseling approaches to consider when you are working with underachieving students include the following:

1. *Individualize homework assignments.* Underachieving students may need tailor-made homework assignments that gradually increase requirements as earlier assignments are completed successfully. Homework assignments should be clear to students. Teachers might take these students aside and ask each what he or she will complete as a homework assignment: What will be turned in to the teacher the next day?

Some teachers might resist attempts at treating some children differently than others. Through staff development and teacher in-service, teachers might learn about and discuss the importance of uniqueness and individual attention in the educative process. When we refuse to recognize individual qualities and the unique concerns of students, we condemn many children to certain failure. By individualizing educational approaches, you and your teachers offer every child equal opportunity to join other students in realizing academic success.

2. *Focus on success.* Underachieving students will climb the highest mountains, swim the deepest oceans, and take on the most threatening challenges to avoid class assignments or homework that "sets them up" for failure. Encourage teachers to begin with assignments and projects that interest students and offer them a reasonable chance of success. When grading students' work, emphasize the positive and de-emphasize the errors. Teach students to capitalize on their strengths in order to compensate and overcome their weaknesses.

3. *Be consistent and keep your end of the deal.* When students renege on agreements they have made with you, do not give in by lowering your expectations. Gently remind students of the agreement and let them know that you always keep your end of a deal because you care about them. You also

want them to care for themselves, so you expect them to keep their agreements with you. Sometimes you may decide that the agreements made are too stringent or unreasonable. When this happens, it is appropriate to renegotiate with students and draw up a new plan.

4. *Keep the lines of communication open with the home.* Report frequently with parents about the progress of students. Let parents know that their input and opinions are valued. Show parents how to establish a study time at home and identify an area where the child can be alone during this time to complete assignments. Ask parents to join parent groups to share strategies they have found to be successful in their families. In these groups, you can facilitate learning and offer positive approaches to help parents communicate with their children and preadolescents.

5. *Use volunteers, such as retired citizens, to establish study partners for underachieving students.* Schedule times during the week when students and their partners can meet, read together, review assignments, and establish healthy working relationships.

6. *Form a peer tutoring program.* In elementary schools, contact middle schools or high schools to identify student helpers who can offer services to younger children after school. Middle school peer helpers can be trained to tutor in classes, during lunchtime, or after school.

7. *Write behavioral contracts with students.* Let them work toward in-school rewards such as a trip to the Media Center, an extra half-hour on the playground with the counselor, a free ice-cream bar after lunch, or other special events. Exhibit 8-2 illustrates a sample contract.

8. *Share test data.* Students in upper elementary and middle school grades can learn where they stand in academic achievement and ability. Most children do not realize their potential and may not see themselves as capable. Test results explained in understandable language can be a powerful antidote to self-deprecation.

EXHIBIT 8-2

Student Contract

(Student) agrees to complete all assignments in *(class)* for the next *(number)* of days. The teacher will determine whether assignments are complete and will give the student a receipt for each day that work is turned in. At the end of *(number)* days, the student will submit receipts to the counselor. The student and counselor agree that:

(Number of receipts) can be exchanged for *(reward)*.
(Student's signature)   *(Counselor's signature)*

In some cases, students who are not achieving may need additional assessment. Communicate with teachers and, when appropriate, seek the assistance of other student services specialists such as the school nurse or psychologist. By gathering as much information as possible, you are more likely to plan and implement effective helping strategies.

CRITICAL CASES

In many ways, schools reflect the image, concerns, and status of the communities surrounding them. Therefore, students and teachers in the school often feel the impact of crises in the community. Similarly, when critical events occur in the school, the community, as a whole or in part, experiences alarm, grief, anger, and other residual feelings.

This section includes several areas of critical concern that schools and counselors frequently face: child depression and suicide, child abuse, chronic and terminal illness, substance abuse, loss, violence, and school phobia. Each of these areas presents a different set of circumstances and dynamics for you and your counseling program. In assisting individuals and groups with these concerns, you will find the earlier information on crisis intervention to be a helpful framework with which to structure your helping relationships. In addition, specific information and guidelines about these areas of crisis are presented in the following sections.

Child Depression and Suicide

In recent years, reports of teenage suicides in epidemic numbers make it one of the leading causes of death among adolescents. To complicate matters, fatal accidents, usually cited as the prime reason for teen deaths, may frequently be suicides. Added to these tragic statistics are a number of child fatalities of suspicious origins. Young children who attempt suicides are rarely successful because they usually do not choose lethal methods. Nevertheless, some experts believe that suicidal thoughts, attempted suicides, and deaths from suicide are higher than available statistics indicate. If this is true, the dynamics and conditions associated with suicide, particularly depression, should be a major concern in our schools and communities.

In years past, society gave little attention to childhood depression, perhaps because we think of childhood as a carefree, happy period of life. In American society, with its changing conditions and added pressures, the perception of childhood is becoming less favorable. Separated and divorced families, physical and sexual abuse, increased attention to school success, drug usage, violence in the media, and other phenomena have drastically altered the face of childhood. These conditions increase the likelihood that students in our schools will experience depression. Depressed children see much of their problem as related to outside forces that are beyond their control. Their depression may lead to suicidal thoughts and attempts when the pain of rejection and feeling of hopelessness reach unbearable proportions.

The first step in assisting depressed, suicidal children and adolescents is to assess the extent of their despair. Interviews with the child, parents, and teachers will help determine the consistency of the depression and the degree to which a child's behaviors are affected. If a child's unhappy state is pervasive, affecting many aspects of school and home life, the depression is severe.

Assessment also examines causal factors. Sometimes children become depressed due to specific events that have occurred at home or school. The death of a relative or pet, a family relocation, an argument with a friend, a failing grade on a test, or other situation may contribute to feelings of loneliness, worthlessness, and hopelessness. In these cases of temporary feelings of grief and despair, you should examine ways to alter events, teach coping skills, and provide other short-term relief and support for students.

Other times, child depression may be more frequent and not related to any single event. This kind of chronic depression is more severe and requires more in-depth assessment and treatment. On these occasions, it is appropriate to consult with parents about referring the child for a complete medical and psychological examination. At the same time, you may need to confer with other student services team members such as the nurse, social worker, and psychologist about appropriate intervention strategies in the school.

Common indicators of depression include emotional, physical, cognitive, and behavioral characteristics. Emotional traits are sadness, guilt, anxiety, anger, fear, pessimism, mood swings, unhappiness, feelings of worthlessness, and a sense of helplessness. Physical characteristics may be fatigue, eating problems, upset stomachs, headaches, sleep disorders, constipation, high pulse rate, and menstrual irregularities. Cognitive indicators are poor self-concept, pessimism, self-doubt, self-blame, loss of interest, poor concentration, apathy, and indecision. Some behaviors associated with child depression are withdrawal from normal activities, excessive time spent alone, slow speech, soft intonation, group avoidance, lower school achievement, frequent crying, procrastination, preoccupation with death, disinterest in personal appearance, and a demeanor seldom smiling or laughing.

When you find that suicidal indicators are present, parents should be contacted immediately, and the student should be protected and monitored at all times. In these cases, always maintain helpful, protective, caring relationships with students while taking steps to meet your ethical and legal obligations.

The literature reveals several motives associated with child suicide attempts. These include

- Signaling distress, a "cry for help"
- Being angry at another person
- Escaping from an unbearable situation

- Attempting to manipulate others
- Wanting to join a loved one who has died
- Behaving impulsively
- Punishing oneself for misbehavior
- Avoiding punishment for misbehavior
- Seeking revenge
- Hoping to be rescued

In addition to the above list of childhood motives, adolescent factors related to suicide are

- Family problems
- Loss of a relationship
- Sexual and physical abuse
- Financial difficulties
- Despair about one's identity
- Academic competition
- Rejection
- Value conflict
- Decline in communication
- Lack of support

Sometimes people who contemplate suicide give signals that indicate their present state of mind and plans they are making. Some of the verbal clues that teachers, parents, students, and counselors might hear from children and adolescents in schools are

"I am going to kill myself."
"This is so bad, I could just die."
"My family doesn't care about me."
"I won't be seeing you anymore."
"I can't stand it any longer."
"If this doesn't change, I'll kill myself."
"No one needs me anymore."
"Life doesn't mean anything to me anymore."

Behavioral clues are

- A previous, unsuccessful attempt at suicide
- Giving away valued possessions to friends
- Writing a suicide note
- Sudden happiness following a time of despair
- A new interest in guns or other lethal weapons
- Resigning from clubs, teams, and other groups

- Loss of appetite
- Sudden abuse of alcohol or drugs

The preceding clues and indicators are a sample of signals that you may see from children and adolescents who are contemplating suicide. One behavior or verbal clue may not mean anything, but you need to check it out. A combination of indicators is definite reason for concern. When you notice a pattern of these behaviors and traits, or when other students or teachers bring them to your attention, establish a relationship with the child as soon as possible. It may be that the student will not want to talk with you, but do not let that hesitancy dissuade you. Maintain contact with the student and continue to establish rapport. With a young child, you might have lunch together, go for a walk outside, play a game in the counseling center, or read a book. At the same time, you will contact the home and inquire about what the parents or guardians have seen there. When the student becomes more comfortable in sharing concerns with you, he or she may disclose suicidal thoughts. If so, you will want to structure an assessment to determine the severity of the situation and the lethality of the student's plan. It is best to include another professional that has experience in this type of assessment.

Questions for school counselors to ask students who express suicidal intentions might include

- How much do you want to die right now?
- How do you plan to kill yourself? How will you do it?
- How much do you want to live right now?
- How often do you have thoughts about dying or killing yourself?
- When you think these thoughts, how long do they stay with you?
- Have you ever tried to kill yourself? What happened?
- Did you write a suicide note, or do you plan to write a note?
- Has anything happened to make life not worth living?
- Is there anyone or anything that would stop you?
- Do you have close friends? Do you feel alone or isolated?
- On a scale of one to ten, how likely are you to kill yourself?

The student's responses to these and other questions will enable you to assess the seriousness of the student's threats, and with the crisis team you will be able to plan strategies and interventions accordingly. Remember these important steps in handling any level of suicidal threat:

- Notify the school principal.
- Collaborate with another professional in the assessment process.
- Supervise the student.
- Contact the parent or guardian.
- Confer with other student services team members.

When you establish a counseling relationship with a student who is experiencing depression or contemplating suicide, the following approaches will be helpful:

1. Be action-oriented. Students who are self-destructive need more than passive affirmation from you. Let these students know what can and will be done to protect them and help them learn coping behaviors.

2. Focus on self-concept development. Students can be encouraged to discover the power to make good things happen. Although not everything in life can be controlled, they can learn to capitalize on positive events and prevent negative outcomes.

3. Take charge of the helping relationship. A directive process is required in suicidal cases. Students should know that you are going to do everything in your power to keep them safe and help them choose appropriate behaviors, now and in the future.

4. Help students learn the art of compromising with oneself. Sometimes the goals we set for ourselves are unrealistic and unreachable. Students can learn to negotiate with themselves to set attainable goals.

5. Teach the concept of time as related to the past, present, and future to help students de-emphasize their focus on immediate events and crises. Young children and adolescents need assistance in stepping back from critical situations and placing these significant events in a balanced perspective in relation to their entire life span.

6. Demonstrate your trust. While confidentiality about suicidal thoughts and attempts cannot be honored, you can show your faith and trustworthiness in relationships with students by not revealing intimate feelings and thoughts they disclose. Students need someone in whom they can believe and trust.

7. Show your confidence and patience. Be optimistic about the future with these students. Let them know that together, you will overcome obstacles and meet the challenges that lie ahead. At the same time, accept their confusion and inconsistencies by patiently guiding them back on track when they falter. Their own unrealistic expectations do not need to be confounded by the impatience of others.

8. Require a commitment from students that they will not harm themselves or attempt suicide. Stay in contact with suicidal students and give them a systematic plan to handle depressed feelings when they occur. Although there is controversy about the use of no-suicide contracts, they are widely used among counselors and other mental health professionals (Range and others, 2002). See Exhibit 8-3 for a sample of a self-protection agreement. If you decide that a no-suicide or self-protection agreement is appropriate, be sure to design one that is developmentally suitable in language and concepts for the student.

EXHIBIT 8-3

Self-Protection Agreement

While I am in counseling with *(School Counselor's Name)*, I, *(Student's Name)*, will do the following things:

1. I will live a long and happy life.
2. I will come for counseling at my scheduled times to learn how to be happy and understand my feelings.
3. I will not hurt or kill myself while I am seeing my counselor. I know it will take time to learn how to be happy.
4. I will tell _____ immediately when I am feeling sad and wanting to hurt or kill myself. If I cannot find _____ , I will call _____ or tell the nearest adult in my neighborhood or at school.
5. I agree to the bedtime and eating schedule planned by my parents (guardians).
6. I will keep this agreement until _____ , when I see my counselor again.

Student: _____ Counselor: _____ Date: _____

When working with these students, keep in touch with their families, maintain contact with classroom teachers about student progress and behaviors, confer with other student services specialists when progress is stalled, and be prepared to refer the case when you have gone as far as time and competency allow. In summary, the following guidelines will help you and the students' teachers approach and support students who are experiencing severe depression and expressing suicidal thoughts in school:

1. Recognize the clues to depression and suicide. Take these signs seriously and contact appropriate personnel.
2. Trust your judgment. Act on your suspicions and beliefs when you think a student is in danger. Do not ignore the evidence. You may be wrong about the severity of the situation, but it is much better to take action than to hesitate and witness a tragedy.
3. Ensure the short-term safety of the student. If there is immediate danger, stay with the student and send for assistance. Remain with the student until help arrives.
4. Tell the authorities and parents. As mentioned earlier, there is no confidentiality where suicide is concerned.

5. Listen to the student. Encourage the student to talk about the situation. Be nonjudgmental and avoid responding with unsubstantiated assurances such as, "Everything will be all right." Use reflective listening and empathize with the student.

6. Show support. In these situations, the most important ingredient a counselor or teacher can offer is care and understanding. Let students know you are with them and want them to be well. Help them feel worthwhile and valuable. Tell students you are there for them and will stick by them through this rough time.

Child Abuse

Unlike suicide, which is a self-inflicted consequence of being unable to cope with overwhelming feelings of helplessness and worthlessness, child abuse is the tragedy of children and adolescents victimized by adults who are their caretakers. Abuse comes in different forms, including physical harm, sexual attacks, emotional and physical neglect, and psychological torment. As community caretakers of children, schools have a legal, professional, and moral obligation to offer protection and appropriate services to students when they are victimized physically, sexually, or psychologically.

The first step is to learn about local policies and state laws regarding obligations and procedures for reporting abuse cases. In some schools, crisis teams are used to examine initial evidence, make a determination about the suspicion of abuse, and contact the appropriate investigation agency. Reporting abuse can raise the anxiety of a teacher, counselor, or administrator who has to contact the agency. For this reason, a team approach helps by (1) assessing the information observed and obtained from the student, (2) determining appropriate steps to ensure the safety of the child, and (3) delegating responsibility for reporting the suspicion of child abuse to the authorities.

One difficulty for school personnel is defining "suspicion" and determining whether or not there is reason to report a case to the authorities. The question arises, What if we are wrong? The fear of wrongfully reporting suspected child abuse sometimes inhibits teachers, counselors, and administrators in following through on their legal obligations. Crisis teams can help by instructing school staff members about indicators of abuse, reporting procedures, legal and liability protection for reporting in good faith, and the extent of the school's role in the investigation. In any event, the school should always follow the practice, "when in doubt, report." Let the investigation agency have the responsibility of substantiating the case. If there is sufficient doubt about the likelihood of abuse, trained professionals from an appropriate agency are the ones to make that determination.

Another area of in-service for teachers and staff is in the legal process when a case goes to court. Occasionally, school personnel are called to testify about their observations of the child in school. In-service workshops can help teachers and counselors become comfortable with court appearances. You can plan instructional and informational sessions by recruiting the services of a local school board attorney or other lawyer who is willing to share expertise.

The next step you should take as a counselor is to determine your role in assisting the child after the abuse has been discovered and reported. As with other crises, your decisions are guided by your knowledge and skills, the availability of appropriate services in the school and community, and the amount of time you have available to assist the student. Your knowledge and skills will include an understanding of the family dynamics involved, information about traits and characteristics of abusers, an awareness of the child's perceptions and feelings, and a command of effective counseling approaches and techniques.

When the child is referred to another professional or agency, such as a family counseling center, you should maintain contact with this referral source so you and the teachers are able to determine what supportive services, if any, to deliver in the school. Be sure to coordinate these activities with the professional or agency providing the primary care to the child and family. Adequate coordination prevents contradictory and confusing relationships from developing that would thwart the child's progress.

Abused children are not easy clients. Their trust has been shattered and, understandably, they are unwilling to establish close relationships. To be effective, immerse yourself in the helping relationship and show the child that responsible people are trustworthy. At the same time, you should understand that abused children often will stretch the limits of their trust by testing your patience and empathy. You must meet this challenge by consistently demonstrating caring behaviors toward the student and interacting in the most positive manner.

The following guidelines are compiled from various resources and may be helpful if and when you become involved with cases of child abuse:

1. Establish a trusting, empathic relationship with the child. To do this, begin by examining your own feelings and beliefs about the issue of child physical and sexual abuse. If you have difficulty with the subject, your reactions may inhibit the child in freely expressing feelings, and your relationship could be counterproductive by affirming the guilt and shame the child is experiencing. Interview the child in a quiet, safe, and private area. It may be best with young children to hold initial sessions in a playroom rather than an office, which usually has all the trimmings of an "adult world."

2. Use approaches and techniques that help children overcome feelings of worthlessness. Design strategies that focus on improved self-worth. To do this, you must distinguish between an *empathic* relationship and a

sympathetic stance. By empathizing with the child's situation, you increase your understanding, become closer, and gain credibility. Your opinions become valued and accepted. Sympathy, on the other hand, merely expresses sorrow and pity, neither of which elevates the child to a position of capability.

3. For young children and preadolescents, use individual sessions to establish effective helping relationships. Because of ambivalent feelings toward their abusers and their own feelings of guilt and shame, children are usually not ready to share their experiences in group sessions.

4. Be prepared to provide support for the family of the abused child. Teachers, counselors, and other members of the school often feel anger and repulsion over the hurt experienced by the child. Although these reactions are understandable, the school cannot allow such feelings to impair its working relationship with the home. Once the legal process has determined the status of the abuser, the child and remaining family members must be supported if progress is to be realized.

5. Design preventive activities and programs for all students in the school to help them learn about appropriate "touches" and achieve a better understanding of their own bodies. Students in classroom guidance and small group discussions can learn assertiveness skills for saying "no" and handling potentially harmful situations. Classroom guidance can also teach children about their rights, the procedures for reporting abusive situations, and how to seek help when they need it.

Chronic and Terminal Illness

Unfortunately, children are not immune to various chronic or terminal illnesses that can debilitate them or lead to an early death. Children who suffer from chronic conditions or terminal illnesses often experience emotional and psychological adjustment problems that interfere with their schooling. These problems are additional dimensions to their physical illness.

As the counselor in an elementary or middle school, you strive to serve all children, including those suffering from illnesses that may make their school attendance inconsistent and sporadic. Here are some points to consider in providing guidance to these children and their families:

1. Let parents and students know from the beginning of the year that you are available to assist students whose illnesses may prevent regular school attendance.

2. Work with administrators to monitor school policies, such as strict attendance guidelines, that may hinder or interfere with helping particular students.

3. Learn about medical centers, support groups, hospice facilities, and other community services that are referral sources for students and their families.

4. Stay in touch with parents through phone calls, e-mail messages, and home visits to assure them that the school is doing its part to help. Send students friendly notes and greeting cards when they have missed long stretches of school days.
5. Present guidance lessons on illnesses that some children have, so their classmates can understand and empathize with them.
6. Select appropriate counseling approaches to use with chronically or terminally ill children and work closely with parents and other helping professionals in selecting these interventions. For example, play techniques might be appropriate for use in short-term counseling to help children understand, accept, and cope with their illness. Counseling might also help these children deal with loneliness, a common concern for children with chronic and terminal illnesses.

Substance Abuse

The crisis of alcohol and drug abuse in our society is affecting every aspect of our lives. For elementary and middle school children, substance abuse is an issue that is related to their own personal choices as well as to the choices made by their parents. In many families, children are the victims of substance-abusing parents. Estimates are that over 25 million children are raised in families with problem drinkers and the children of these parents are four times more likely to become alcoholics themselves. A significant portion of these children is under eighteen years of age, attending elementary, middle, and high schools across our country.

Children of alcoholics often report strong feelings of hostility and anger toward their parents, have lower self-images, and show a higher incidence of learning disabilities. Children whose mothers drink or use drugs during pregnancy tend to be more likely to become drug dependent and demonstrate lower performance on standardized ability tests. Substance abuse in families is also correlated with child abuse.

Although these children often suffer emotional and physical abuse in their relationships with the parents, they tend to protect their parents by not talking about "the problem." Very few children talk about it with their own parents at home. This unwillingness to discuss the issue makes it difficult for you to identify the nature of the concern and offer assistance. A combination of the following behaviors and characteristics may indicate a family drug or alcohol-related problem. Use caution to avoid making hasty judgments about a single, observed behavior, but when you notice several of these factors in association with a child, you and the school have reason to be concerned:

- Low self-esteem
- Antisocial behaviors

- Withdrawn and isolated demeanor
- Lack of trusting relationships
- Poor eating habits
- Signs of physical abuse
- Feelings of rejection
- Extreme self-criticism
- Overly responsible behavior
- Passiveness
- Frequent school absences
- Poor school achievement
- Missing or incomplete homework assignments

Upper elementary and middle school children who experiment with alcohol and drugs may be reflecting a chemical dependency found in the home. As children of alcoholics grow older, they have a stronger tendency to abuse alcohol themselves. Reports indicate that the use of alcohol and drugs continues to be a concern with elementary and middle school populations.

Intervention

To help children from alcoholic families, schools can provide a wide range of educational experiences and counseling services. As a counselor, you may not be able to invest the time or have the expertise to assist the family in much needed therapy, but you can coordinate services in the school. It is critical that you know what agencies and professionals in the community are best equipped to help alcoholic families. You should be familiar with programs such as Alcoholics Anonymous, Al-Anon, and Alateen as well as centers that provide crisis intervention for alcohol and drug abuse.

Interventions that schools can provide include the following:

1. *A consistent school environment.* In alcoholic families, rules are inconsistent and schedules often are abruptly altered. Schools offer stability by letting children know they can depend on teachers and counselors. By avoiding schedule changes and keeping promises with children, schools minimize disruptions and disappointments that add to children's stress.

2. *Alcohol and drug abuse education.* Children can learn that they are not alone with this problem and that they are not responsible for their parents' drinking. Alcoholism is an addictive condition, which is the reason that some alcoholic parents have such difficulty quitting, even to the point that they lose all control over their lives. When drinking heavily or using other drugs, these people cannot stop themselves. They are out of control.

   On the upside, children also can learn that alcoholics and drug users can be helped to overcome these problems. First, they recognize and admit the problem exists, and then seek help. In the same way, children from alcoholic and drug-abusing families must come to understand the problem and seek assistance for themselves.

3. *An assessment of neglect and abuse in the family.* When children are suspected of being physically or sexually abused, emotionally traumatized or neglected, or deprived in other ways, the school is required to report these findings to proper authorities. Because alcoholism is such an emotional and secretive issue, people are hesitant to report abuse that stems from this disease; however, the school has a primary obligation to protect the child in abusive situations, regardless of the underlying causes.

4. *Instructional and support groups for parents.* Group programs help parents learn appropriate ways to remedy the destruction caused by the alcoholism in the family. You might not be able to run these groups as part of your school program, but you can facilitate their development by cooperating with community agencies such as churches and civic clubs.

5. *Group counseling for children of alcoholics.* Children are more willing to share feelings and discuss family situations in a safe environment where they identify with each other's concerns. When a group is first started, you may want to lead students through several ice-breaking activities to get acquainted before discussing the nature of their concerns. Usually a small, comfortable room for group work is conducive establishing a trustful, secure environment.

Most children will need to see a counselor by themselves before agreeing to join a group. When establishing individual counseling relationships with these children, a few guidelines may be helpful:

1. *Focus on the child first.* Learn about the child's interests, what he or she likes to do and thinks he or she does well. Show genuine interest in the child's accomplishments. Reflection of the content of the child's message and the feelings the child expresses is essential in this stage, especially since young children often struggle to express themselves about difficult situations.

2. *Confront the issue of drinking in the family clearly, but gently.* As noted earlier, children will be protective of their parents. Take it slowly, and consistently show your concern for the child. Look for reflex recognitions and reactions from the child to statements you make. A raised brow, changed body posture, pursed lips, or other behaviors may indicate that a child understands but is unwilling to discuss the issue. Proceed patiently in these instances and take time to develop trust.

3. *Avoid asking questions.* Give the child illustrations and examples of concerns of children in general. Offer specific situations regarding alcoholism and drug abuse. Let the child react, either verbally or nonverbally, to these scenarios. With some children, a book or video may be appropriate as stimulus for further discussion in the counseling relationship.

4. *Inform the child about group counseling.* After the student has become more comfortable and begins sharing concerns with you, introduce information about group counseling and invite the child to join a group. Tell the child about groups you are forming and the types of concern children in the groups have in common.

Some middle school and elementary students will become involved with drugs and alcohol even though no such addiction exists in their families. They may be introduced by a peer, older student, or adult. Help your teachers become aware of changes in children's behavior that point to drug and alcohol usage. Consultation with parents usually will identify additional behaviors of concern when alcohol and drug use are involved. These behaviors include

- School absence and tardiness
- Lower academic performance
- Loss of interest in activities
- Chronic lying
- Stealing
- Sudden change of friends
- Emotional outbursts and mood swings
- Change in dress
- Mysterious and unexplained phone calls
- Preference for staying alone at school and home
- Secrecy about friends and whereabouts
- Apathy, lack of ambition, and general disinterest
- Changes in speech, eye functions, and coordination
- Defensive behaviors and constant denial of wrongdoing

With middle school and upper elementary students who are referred for counseling due to suspected substance abuse, specific procedures should be followed. Here are a few suggested guidelines when counseling students about substance abuse:

1. *Know your school policies regarding reporting substance abuse.* Usually school systems have clear regulations regarding substance abuse and parent notification. Learn about your ethical responsibilities to the counselee and how they relate to local policies.
2. *Assess the case accurately.* Get the facts from the student about actual drug usage. When was the alcohol or drug taken? How was it taken? Who was present? How often has the student done this? Where was the alcohol or drug obtained? Your assessment of the degree of usage will guide you in

determining whether this case should be referred to another professional. Exhibit 8-4 is an interview questionnaire for middle graders about alcohol and drug use.

3. *Be directive.* Cases such as this are not the time for passive listening. Take charge of the relationship. Be respectful and show concern for the student, but at the same time convey the seriousness of the matter and be firm in letting the child know the behavior must stop.

4. *Inform the parents.* When your assessment indicates that the abuse is frequent and substantial, the child's welfare and life are at risk. In this case, the destructive behaviors of the child preclude confidentiality. You must tell the parents. Even in cases of drug and alcohol experimentation, counselors of young children should involve parents. The child needs to understand the seriousness of these types of behaviors, and parent support is essential.

5. *Expect commitment from the student to desist from further abusive behaviors.* If the counseling relationship is to make any progress, the student must show good faith in wanting to stop the drug or alcohol abuse. Without this commitment, the relationship is unfounded and threatened from the start.

6. *Become knowledgeable about the drugs currently being used in the community and learn about expected reactions to these substances.* Attend workshops to acquire effective skills in handling substance abuse cases. Learn about reliable resources in the community to which you can refer children and families.

EXHIBIT 8-4

Middle School Drug and Alcohol Assessment

1. Tell me about the drug/alcohol you took, and how you took it.
2. When did this happen? Where did you do this?
3. Were you alone or with someone?
4. How much of the drug/alcohol did you use?
5. Have you done this before? Tell me about those other times.
6. Where did you get the alcohol/drug?
7. Have you told your parents about this? What have you told them?
8. Have you ever talked with a counselor or other person about drug/alcohol use?
9. Tell me what you think about this drug/alcohol experience?
10. Do you want help with this problem?

Prevention

Because drug and alcohol usage continues to be a destructive force in American society, elementary and middle schools must take an educative role in helping young people understand the dangers. Preventive activities are essential to the school counseling program, and your role includes planning and coordinating educational services.

Help your school establish a broad philosophy and basic premises for drug education and prevention programs. From what we already know about drug and alcohol prevention, the following beliefs will serve as starter points for establishing a comprehensive program in your school to address this concern:

- Community and family involvement are essential. Schools do not exist in isolation. Commitment to drug prevention is a community and family affair.
- Drug information is insufficient for prevention. Awareness programs, information brochures, and "good health" events can supplement comprehensive educational programs, but information alone does little to help people change behaviors.
- Effective drug prevention programs are ongoing components of a healthful living curriculum, community youth activities, public commitment to education, and family involvement. A single focus on drug problems without an emphasis on improving the quality of life for young people is an ineffective approach.
- Drug prevention requires a commitment of time and resources. Effective programs do not take place in one class period, a weeklong community campaign, or a year's instruction. Prevention requires an ongoing program reflected throughout the community and school.
- Drug and alcohol prevention in schools can be best implemented and facilitated by professional educators who care about children, plan effective teaching, create emotionally healthy learning environments, and invite parent involvement in schools.

In addition to these beliefs, we know that drug prevention programs are most successful when they de-emphasize peer pressure and teach students assertiveness skills. This being so, you will want to develop programs that include strategies to help children make important life decisions, expand their alternatives, identify essential information, and act on the choices they make.

Loss

Children in elementary and middle schools sometimes face the death of someone close to them—a grandparent, parent, sibling, or friend. Occasionally, this loss is expected due to a long-term illness; other times it results from unexpected tragedy. In either case, the child needs support and understanding from the school community. Through cooperative and careful communication, you and the teachers can help children come to terms with a death, experience their grief, and move ahead with their development.

When counseling with children who have experienced a loss, you want a clear understanding of how the child perceives death. Children in first grade and younger rarely conceptualize the finality of death when it first occurs. They perceive death as something that happens to others, not to oneself or even to those one is close to. Very young children often take an egocentric view of death that involves magical thinking and fantasies. (Of course, we modify all developmental assumptions as we take diverse cultural backgrounds into consideration.) As children move into middle childhood, they begin to conceptualize specific ways that death occurs. Preadolescents are able to think about death in abstract terms and construct logical causes of death. Helpful counseling techniques in individual and group settings include bibliocounseling, role-playing, puppetry, storytelling, and drawing.

In helping a child cope with a recent death, consider these guidelines:

1. Openly express your sorrow and regret for the loss the child has experienced. Let the child know you are available if he or she would like to talk about it. When a child agrees to discuss the death with you, maintain an open posture and avoid shocking or judgmental responses to the information being shared. Send gentle invitations to the child to become involved, and resist coercing the student into a counseling relationship. Some children need time to themselves before they are able or willing to talk about their loss. In these cases, you may want to have contact with the child by eating lunch together, playing games, or reading a story without forcing the issue by talking about the loss.

2. Accept the child's right to mourn the loss. Some children cope with death by behaving in ways different from the ordinary—behaviors noticed by their peers. When teachers and counselors show understanding and acceptance for these changes, other students will show support for the bereaved child.

3. Maintain as normal a schedule as possible for the child. At the same time allow avenues for the child to cope with the loss—a safe place to go when emotions are high, acceptance of some behavior changes, understanding of lower-quality school work during the grieving period.

4. Avoid surprised or shocked reactions to the child's expression of grief. Children, like people in general, show their grief in a variety of ways. When a child is aggressive, withdrawn, or uncooperative, genuine concern and gentle reminders about class and school behavior may help. You can assist by showing the student appropriate ways to cope with anger, grief, and other feelings.

Classroom guidance lessons can provide preventive measures as well as remedial approaches to helping children cope with death and dying. For example, an instructional unit about death could focus on the following topics, depending on the developmental level of students:

- All living things die.
- People often need help when someone dies.
- People feel different emotions when they suffer a loss such as death.
- Death is final and this makes it sad.
- Certain activities follow a death.
- Life is worth living.
- We all leave things behind when we die.

Children experience loss in many different ways. As noted earlier in this chapter, one common phenomenon that results in feelings of loss by children is a family move from one community to another. It is tragic that another way children experience loss is through the all too prevalent acts of violence in our society.

Violence

Violence is a phenomenon that has significant impact on schools and the learning of students. Physical, sexual, and psychological abuse are characteristics of our society from which students in middle and elementary schools should be diligently protected. At the same time, too many students resort to aggressive and violent behavior when faced with conflict. The number of fights, murders, and suicides among our youth is alarming and frightening. As a school counselor, you have a responsibility to help prevent and remedy the senseless use of violence by students and against students in our schools. Simply passing policies to punish students for possessing weapons and fighting in school is not the full answer. Schools need to be proactive in providing counseling and educational services for students. Here are some starter ideas:

1. Stay abreast of what is taking place in the school and out in the community among students. As noted earlier with bullying, the first step to thwarting violence is to pay attention and not ignore behaviors that will lead to altercations. Be alert—listen to what students are saying and how they are treating each other.
2. Include conflict resolution material in the school's guidance curriculum. Help students handle conflict and hostility in appropriate ways while maintaining an acceptable level of assertiveness. Invite law enforcement officers and other professionals into the school to talk with students about their rights and how to prevent violence in the community.

3. Use your peer helpers to help identify students who are victims of violence or who are threatening to do harm themselves or others. Elementary and middle grade students will frequently confide in their peers before they approach a teacher, counselor, or even their parents.

4. Educate teachers and other staff members to observe indicators and precursors of violent or self-destructive behavior. Suicide attempts and other self-destructive behaviors are a private form of violence, and teachers, counselors, and other school personnel are often the first to recognize when students are in serious distress.

5. Educate parents to identify symptoms and signals their children are sending them. Teach parents to monitor television, movie, music, and computer games that emphasize and glorify violent behavior. At the same time, encourage parents to spend time talking with their children about these media, some of which are inescapable in our society.

School Phobia

Suicide, child abuse, violence, and substance abuse are crises that pose immediate danger to students' physical or emotional welfare. By comparison, school phobia presents a crisis of immediate concern, but without the threat of imminent danger. Children who suffer from school phobia are considered critical cases because of the long-term implications to their personal, social, and educational development. Rational and irrational fears that are allowed to continue will thwart normal student progress. Left untreated, the school-phobic student may develop multiple phobias such as the fear of being alone, fear of the outdoors, and fear of people.

Estimates of the incidence of school phobia range from 1 to 8 percent of the population. It is a critical phenomenon about which teachers and counselors must not only be concerned but also develop approaches and procedures to assist these students. This is particularly true in elementary and middle schools, where school phobia generally occurs.

School phobia is the fear of attending school, often associated with being emotionally upset, complaining of illnesses for which no physical cause is found, and having temper tantrums. Although a number of factors may be involved, school phobia in young children is often associated with fear of separation from a mother who has nurtured an overly dependent relationship. Older children, some of whom have never exhibited fear of school during their first few years, become phobic when they change schools, move from elementary to middle or high school, or begin a new school program.

Most children resist going to school on some occasion or express fears about changes in school schedules and routines, but the school-phobic child experiences a level of fear and anxiety that approaches panic. The problem can be one of incapacitating trauma, and this is why teachers, counselors, and parents should intervene as soon as possible.

Among the intervention strategies you will find in the counseling literature, three schools of thought encompass the major approaches to treating the school-phobic child: psychodynamic, behavioral, and cognitive. If you plan to intervene with phobic students, you should become familiar with different views and approaches, and choose ones that fit your philosophical beliefs and those of your school and community.

Psychodynamic approaches focus on the separation anxiety of the child and the overprotective posture of the parents. By helping parents understand their contribution to the phobia, giving them alternative strategies for handling the separation anxiety, and helping them learn to cope with their own emotional reactions to the child going to school, you and the teachers will be in a stronger position to help the child accept the school experience. Play therapy, conducted individually and in groups, can be used to help young children express their fears about school and discover appropriate ways to handle their anxieties. Older children may benefit from drama techniques, storytelling and story writing, or direct verbal counseling to formulate a plan of action.

Cognitive therapies, such as Rational Emotive Behavior Therapy (REBT), are appropriate with middle school students. In these approaches, you and the student examine the irrational and illogical beliefs about school, explore the student's responsibilities, and plan the best ways to handle the situation so that the student alters his or her thinking about school.

Behavioral approaches call on a variety of techniques that include relaxation, systematic desensitization, implosive therapy, positive reinforcement, and removal of secondary reinforcers. In most cases, behavioral techniques can be combined with other therapeutic approaches. For example, middle school students receiving individual counseling can be taught relaxation strategies to help themselves during times when anxiety is high.

Whatever approaches are used, you should establish guidelines for yourself and for teachers when working with school-phobic students. Here are some suggested guidelines:

1. Give immediate attention to cases of suspected school phobia. The more time that elapses, the more difficult it will be to help the child and family turn around the situation.
2. Insist that the parents take the child for a medical examination if he or she is exhibiting physical symptoms and illnesses. Although the probability of a physical etiology is minimal, it is important to check it out.
3. Include the crisis team in severe cases of school phobia, and make referrals when appropriate.
4. Establish open lines of communication with the parents. Maintain frequent contacts with the parents to check on progress at home and report about progress at school. Individual consultation or parent education groups are appropriate for helping parents examine their feelings, address

their own behaviors, and establish constructive routines for getting their children to school. In extreme cases, family counseling may be necessary.

5. Consult regularly with classroom teachers. A warm, caring, and pleasant environment in school is essential in helping children overcome their fears. Teachers need to be firm, but gentle, when helping a child understand that he or she must remain at school. Schools should avoid placing children in uncertain situations that may cause fear or embarrassment. Children who are prone to anxieties should be carefully guided through and informed about all new experiences. Provide appropriate reinforcements to let children know they are being successful in overcoming their fears and accepting responsibility for attending school.

6. Give the phobic child an avenue to choose when he or she feels extremely anxious and is unable to cope in the classroom. Perhaps the child could go to the counseling center to sit for a few minutes alone or talk to you. Maybe he or she could call home to check on mother and make sure everything is all right.

For all of the concerns addressed in this and the preceding chapters, effective school counselors establish clear guidelines and approaches to helping. There are many other concerns that counselors handle with children, parents, and teachers, and each requires specific knowledge and skills. Beyond the critical and special concerns presented in these chapters, you probably will help children on a regular basis with peer relationships, stealing, cheating, conflict resolution, tattling, lying, school attendance, daydreaming, hyperactivity, inattentiveness, and a host of other behaviors.

To be effective in all helping relationships, establish a resource file of approaches and strategies to handle a wide range of concerns. These resources not only will assist you in your counseling relationships but will also be helpful to classroom teachers who must interact with these students every day. By helping teachers with these interactions and relationships, you establish an essential role for yourself as an elementary or middle school counselor. Equally important, you establish relationships within the school and community that consistently communicate this role. Relating to professional staff is the subject of the next chapter.

chapter 9

BELONGING *and* BEING *with the* SCHOOL

E arlier chapters emphasized the development of strong working relationships with teachers and other personnel in your school. The school counseling program, as implied in its title, belongs to the entire school—the students, parents, teachers, and you. For this reason, it is essential that you become an integral part of the school staff and program. To do so, make a conscious and purposeful effort to relate personally and professionally with your colleagues in the school.

This chapter focuses on the responsibility you have in developing healthy relationships within the school setting. The ultimate success of your program will be influenced by the personal and professional relationships you establish with administrators, teachers, students, parents, and others involved with your elementary or middle school. In turn, developing personal and professional relationships fosters positive public relations, which is essential for any program, particularly one that relies on a high level of trust and respect of the populations it serves. However, maintaining a good public image is not sufficient to establish close personal and professional relationships that are required in effective elementary and middle school counseling programs.

Here, the idea of positive public relations is taken a step further by advocating that counselors are an essential part of the school program, and to function effectively they need to be accepted and sought after by the school community. As counselors, we incorporate proactive behaviors into our daily functioning, telling people that the counseling program belongs with the educational program rather than as a separate, distant, and special service apart from the instructional program of the school. Elementary and middle school counselors who are successful in creating this type of relationship respect the role of parents and teachers in the education and development of all children.

ESTABLISHING RELATIONSHIPS

To be a successful school counselor, you will want to demonstrate equal respect for your profession, the teaching profession, and the role of parents in the education of children. In addition, you will realize that it is through cooperative efforts that school children overcome obstacles to learning and development. The following are some guidelines and principles for you to follow in establishing a proactive and respectful posture as an elementary or middle school counselor.

Counseling services are an extension of the instructional program. School counselors who see themselves as therapists, delving deeply into the realm of unconscious motivations of their clients, tend to distance themselves from other professionals in the school. Counseling and consulting relationships, whether practiced in schools or other settings, are essentially educative and instructive in nature. Delivered by highly trained professionals who understand the importance of facilitative skills in developing effective helping relationships, these processes supplement and complement the school curriculum and classroom instruction. When you successfully help students, parents, and teachers alter behaviors and choose new directions, the approaches and strategies you use ultimately can have a therapeutic effect. This is true for your counseling relationships, consultations, and guidance activities in the classroom.

School counselors, while not necessarily trained as teachers, are an integral part of the school staff. As such, we want to be included in all aspects of the school's program and professional responsibilities. This means sharing responsibilities for student supervision and administration of school services. Classroom teachers perform many duties beyond the realm of instruction and learning. This reality is indigenous to most school environments. Teachers collect book fees, monitor hallways and restrooms, supervise cafeterias, and perform an array of functions that have little to do with language arts, mathematics, physical education, or other curricular areas.

As an elementary or middle school counselor, you enhance your working relationship with teaching colleagues by sharing some of these responsibilities. At the same time, know when to limit your participation so that these ancillary functions do not interfere with direct counseling services to students, parents, and teachers. Work closely with your school administrators to assure that the integrity of the counseling program is not compromised for the sake of administrative efficiency.

School counseling services are most beneficial and accepted by school communities when they relate to the educational progress of students. In some schools, teachers are under tremendous pressure to demonstrate that students are achieving academically. For this reason, teachers are understandably reluctant to allow their students to miss instruction in order to see a counselor. If you accept the important relationship between academic success and positive self-worth, you will be able to convince your teachers of the benefits of counseling. Make a concerted effort to share information about your services and illustrate how these services enable students to study better, attend class, behave appropriately, and achieve academically. When you demonstrate successful helping relationships and subsequently persuade your teaching colleagues of the importance of providing individual and small group services to children, you will have little difficulty getting their permission for students to visit the counseling center and receive your services. Individual and small-group services are especially vital in overcrowded schools where teachers are pressed to provide attention to students who need it most.

Collaborate with teachers and parents. Although you must respect your ethical and legal responsibilities regarding confidentiality and privileged communication, you will be most effective when you establish relationships with the adults who are closest to the children. In elementary and middle schools, children make progress with their personal and educational adjustment when we include teachers, parents, and administrators in the process of helping. By facilitating healthy relationships from the start, you inform teachers and parents about the importance of confidentiality in student-counselor relationships. At the same time, you convey to teachers and parents the necessity of including them in the helping process because their input and involvement are valued.

Teaching is an admirable, vital, demanding, and challenging profession in today's schools with widely diverse student populations. The overwhelming majority of teachers practice at a high level of professional expertise, which is indispensable to helping children succeed in school. Respect the role of your classroom colleagues and accept the professional knowledge and expertise these professionals offer in designing intervention strategies for children. Keep frequent contact with teachers whose children are receiving counseling services and listen to their observations and recommendations.

• *School principals have ultimate authority and responsibility in the school.* For this reason, close communication and cooperation between you and the administrators is essential. Inform your principal about prevalent issues and trends you observe in the school. Particular concerns expressed by a number of students, common family issues experienced in the community, teacher frustrations, and other observations should be shared so the principal can provide appropriate leadership in addressing these issues. In a sense, you are the eyes and ears of the school community, helping the principal stay in tune with the needs of students, parents, and teachers. To accept this role and perform in an ethical and beneficial manner, you and the principal must establish a positive relationship with each other.

• *School counseling services are one of several opportunities to assist students and their families.* Middle and elementary counselors rely on professionals within the school system, such as social workers, nurses, psychologists, and exceptional children teachers, as well as agencies outside the school, to provide additional services. To assure that you refer students and families to competent professionals, become informed about available services and inquire about the effectiveness of professionals in the school system and community. In addition, cultivate professional relationships with other practitioners to facilitate their referral processes. Personal and professional relationships established with other practitioners can have a significant impact on the speed of a referral when students and parents are in need of services. Take time to establish working relationships so that you can expedite referrals to a number of community resources. By doing so, you will be perceived by social workers, physicians, and others as a competent professional.

Each of the preceding guidelines implies the use of competent skills when establishing effective helping relationships. In particular, personal and professional relationship skills are essential. Both types of functioning are necessary to be successful with the many populations you serve. The next two sections consider each of these areas of functioning and how they complement successful staff relationships.

RELATING PERSONALLY

In schools and other settings, beneficial professional relationships are established when you function in helpful and caring ways. By personally demonstrating concern and regard for individuals, you set the stage for your professional invitations and interactions to be accepted. Through these personal contacts, you establish the foundation for your professional helping relationships.

There are many ways to form helpful personal relationships. The approaches we choose and the styles we adopt also affect the level of success we achieve. In most cases, the helping behaviors we choose are either visible or invisible styles of functioning. To be successful in establishing professional relationships you should be able to use either style, appreciate the value of each, and know the rationale and purpose for each. Know when it is appropriate to be visible with your relationships and appreciate the value of discretion and lack of visibility when it is best for others to receive recognition and attention. The following discussion examines ways to be visibly and invisibly helpful in our personal relationships. (An additional resource about these two styles of functioning is *Invitational Counseling*, 1996, by William W. Purkey and myself.)

Being Visible

You want people in the school community to know what you do as a counselor. It makes sense to want the personally helpful relationships you establish with students, parents, and teachers to be beneficial. In many situations, you also want these relationships to be visible. By demonstrating your concern, respect, and regard openly toward people, you enable them to identify you as a caring, helping person. This kind of identity, as you know, is essential for effective counseling.

Consistency is paramount to establishing a genuine identity as a caring person. Some people turn their personal charm off and on depending on the situation at hand or the clientele with whom they are working. Such a discriminate, inconsistent posture is destructive to human relationships and incompatible with professional counseling. As discussed in an earlier chapter about special populations, effective counselors do not determine their level of concern or regard for individuals based on circumstances, values, or other conditions. They view all students, parents, teachers, and others as having value, being capable, and able to be responsible. In this way, you consistently demonstrate respect and trust toward those you serve.

There are limitless ways that you can be visible in your school and reach out personally to others. The first step is to let people see you. This may seem obvious, but many school counselors are unsuccessful with their colleagues because they never leave their offices to venture out into the life of the school. The following are starter suggestions to help you increase your visibility. While some may not be universally applicable, you can use this list as a point of departure to create personal invitations and become visible in your school program. Use the ideas that work for you, discard those that do not, and develop your own style of relating personally to students, parents, teachers, and administrators.

Offer a Morning Welcome

In most schools, teachers have responsibility for meeting the buses in the morning and escorting children onto departing buses in the afternoon. Unfortunately, these personal opportunities are often perceived as demeaning and arduous obligations. As a result, these functions are called "duties" and viewed in a negative light, making it impossible for anyone to appreciate their positive benefits.

Help your school take a positive posture by changing the language associated with these events. Chapter One stresses the importance of language in identifying and defining who you are as a counselor. The same is true for other aspects of your school. If we refer to functions as "obligations" and "duties," we will perceive them in negative ways. By finding a language that accentuates the positive, we encourage helpful personal interactions.

You can begin by visibly helping with "morning welcomes," "meet and greet," "daily farewells," "hall safety," "lunchtime relief," and other aspects of student supervision in the school. For example, bus duty can be viewed as an opportunity to "meet and greet" children as they arrive at school each day. Some counselors are reluctant to assist with these responsibilities because they place them in roles of monitoring student behaviors and correcting misbehaviors. Who better to help teachers learn positive ways of relating with students than someone skilled in human relations, student development, and facilitative behaviors? By visibly relating to students in personal ways, you demonstrate positive postures for other professionals to emulate.

A beneficial by-product of visibility is the incidental data that you observe and record when out in the school. When students arrive in the morning, enjoy recess on the playground, eat lunch in the cafeteria, and leave for home at the end of the day, you can gather valuable information to assist children and teachers. An observant counselor uses these occasions to watch for signals from students who are experiencing difficulties at school or home. In this way, you can use ordinary, unobtrusive functions and activities to assess students and help parents and teachers focus on the personal, social, and educational needs of children.

Exchange Greetings

Take time each day to see as many of your teaching colleagues as possible. Early in the morning visit their classrooms and stick your head in the door to say, "Hello. How are you today?" When you pass teachers and students in the hallway, make an effort to recognize them in some way. A smile, nod, pat on the shoulder, and similar gestures, when personally and culturally appropriate, tell people that you are aware of their presence and value their company. These apparently simple behaviors are sometimes the most powerful invitations we send. Counselors who fail to attend to the presence of others become phantoms in their schools. People do not know who they are or what they do. It is hard to imagine that such personally invisible professionals would be effective helpers. In contrast, when you openly display acceptance and acknowledgment of others, people seek you out for your company and assistance.

One caution about personal greetings is appropriate here. Always be intentional and aware of your behaviors to avoid discriminating against selected students and teachers. Because we are human and face all the challenges and conditions that other people confront, we sometimes are handicapped by biases, prejudices, and negative behaviors that inhibit our personal relationships. It is essential to offer yourself personally in an equitable manner to everyone in the school. To do otherwise paints a fraudulent picture of yourself as a helping professional and alienates people who feel shunned by your discriminating behaviors.

Celebrate Events

Encourage your school and students to celebrate life. Send birthday cards to colleagues, announce student achievements over the intercom, and post announcements of upcoming events on the bulletin board. A visible counselor is one who actively promotes the celebrations and accomplishments of others. When students achieve their goals and improve their school performance, send a note home letting parents know about their children's progress. Show parents that you appreciate their support for the school. By choosing this type of visibility, you take a positive stance as a counselor, rather than that of constantly being a purveyor of bad news. All parents appreciate hearing about positive events in their children's lives.

Hold a Happy Hour

Schedule a party in your counseling center for the staff after school. Offer beverages and snacks, and plan relaxing, fun activities for teachers and support staff. To ensure a pleasant, positive atmosphere, enforce one simple rule: no shop talk. Encourage teachers to relax, laugh, and enjoy each other's company.

If the week has been particularly harried and stressful for your colleagues, walk the teachers through a few relaxation exercises and take them on a fantasy trip to Tahiti! Find a soothing tape of music and ocean sounds as background for your fantasy trip. This is a time for you and your teachers to socialize without discussing or dealing with school issues. It is also an excellent time for teachers who do not know each other to meet and greet informally. These personal interactions help establish professional relationships that will benefit students and the school in the future.

Invite a Colleague to Lunch

Take a teacher or your principal to lunch. This simple gesture may be the beginning of a long-term and valuable friendship. Breaking bread together is a traditional way of establishing beneficial alliances. Similar invitations might be bringing a box of candy for the faculty lounge, giving a living plant to the secretary for the school office, and visiting a colleague who is in the hospital.

The preceding suggestions are a few of the countless ways that counselors relate visibly to teachers and students in personal ways. The main idea in all these suggestions is to allow people to *see* you and *know* you personally. This is the first step toward professional helping relationships. People can relate more comfortably with you professionally if they have come to know you on a personal level.

Nevertheless, whereas visibility is important for people to know who you are, there are times when it may be more appropriate for your identity to remain unknown. Effective elementary and middle school counselors know when to promote themselves and when to remain silently, invisibly in the background.

Being Invisible

A visible image helps people know who you are and what you do. However, when your visibility becomes so pronounced and overwhelming, some people may withdraw from relationships with you. Sometimes, it is best to do your work, reach out to others, and seek assistance for students without fanfare and recognition. Artful counselors know the difference between being visibly inappropriate and invisibly appropriate in their personal and professional relationships. The following examples illustrate how invisible behaviors can accomplish intended goals.

In one elementary school, the teachers and staff were struggling to establish a warm working relationship. Teachers communicated very little except for the usual "student degrading" and "administrator bashing" that they exchanged in the faculty lounge. The principal and counselor had attempted to use warm-up activities and other strategies at meetings with the teachers, but these attempts failed to bear fruitful results. One day the counselor decided to put random gifts in teachers' mailboxes. The counselor did this secretly without anyone's knowledge. The gifts were small, unpretentious presents. A typical gift was a card saying, "It is nice working with you!" or a candy bar with a note that read, "Enjoy! Share with a friend!"

Naturally, when the first few gifts appeared, the recipients wondered who sent them. When asked, the counselor pleaded ignorance (some fibs are justified!). Occasionally the gift-giver put a surprise in the counselor's mailbox to throw off suspicion. As the weeks went by and more gifts were distributed, teachers became more deliberate in their efforts to discover the "phantom of the mailroom," but the identity went undetected. After a while, a strange and marvelous thing began to happen. Teachers started receiving cards and gifts that were not sent by the phantom! As the vaudeville comedian, Jimmy Durante, often said, "Everybody wants to get into the act!" What had begun as an invisible strategy to say and do simple, nice things for people had become a full-scale invitation to outsmart and outdo personal messages sent to each other. The result was that the staff had a common ground to talk, laugh, and enjoy each other's company, and school morale improved.

A middle school counselor demonstrated another example of invisible behaviors. The counselor learned that a particular student wanted to be a

Student Council representative. Unfortunately, the student believed that no one would nominate her. The counselor quietly began asking students about the Student Council nominations and whom they were planning to select. During these informal conversations, the counselor would inquire about this particular student and ask, "What do you think about her as a Student Council representative?" By simply asking the question, the counselor placed the student's name before her peers for consideration. Eventually the student was nominated and elected to the Student Council.

In every personal relationship, you determine the extent of your visibility. To make the most appropriate decisions, assess the value of your visibility regarding your identity in the school, and weigh that assessment against the value of your invisibility to the recognition and development of others. The accuracy with which you make these decisions about your personal relationships strengthens your posture and enables you to establish effective professional relationships.

RELATING PROFESSIONALLY

Successful elementary and middle school counselors capitalize on their ability to relate personally and use this ability to help them function at a high professional level. When perceived by their colleagues, parents, and students in more than personable and friendly ways, these counselors are viewed as competent professionals who know how to help people and facilitate beneficial relationships.

Not all counselors who function satisfactorily at personal levels are able to make the transition to the professional level. During my years as a counseling supervisor and counselor educator, I have consulted with school administrators who expressed concern about particular counselors and their lack of effective helping skills. Invariably, these consultations began with the administrator emphasizing that the counselor was well liked by the faculty and staff; often the administrator described the counselor as a "good person." The problem was that these counselors struggled to establish effective working relationships because they had difficulty communicating with staff about the counseling program, relating with parents, or following through on student progress.

As emphasized in the first few chapters of this resource, these areas of professional practice are all relevant to an effective comprehensive program of services. To establish strong professional relationships in your school, you want to seek input from others, share appropriate information, facilitate professional interactions, provide staff development, follow up on referrals, and assist the school in developing an orderly, healthy environment for learning. Let us examine each of these processes.

Seeking Input

Chapter One emphasizes the importance of winning the support of your administration and faculty and sharing ownership of the school counseling program. In addition to the formal interviews and questionnaires recommended in that chapter, you will also want to adopt informal systems of asking teachers, administrators, parents, and students for their opinions. This type of professional involvement can take many forms:

Individual Contacts

Visit teachers in their classrooms before and after school, and ask their opinions about ideas you have for the counseling program, students you have observed, or concerns you have heard them express at faculty meetings or on other occasions. Ask whether you can help them with anything. These interactions are excellent opportunities to inquire about guidance activities and topics that the teachers would like to integrate with their classroom instruction. The image to convey during these brief contacts is that you value teachers' opinions and want their suggestions for improving the school counseling program.

Group Discussions

There are many opportunities for you to receive input from teachers. For example, in elementary and middle schools where team-teaching is used, teachers meet regularly to plan and coordinate their instruction. If this is true in your school, find out the schedule for these meetings and ask teams whether you could sit in on these planning sessions. When the time is appropriate, ask them for input to help you plan services for the counseling program.

Faculty meetings are another way to seek group input. Ask your principal for a few minutes on the agenda of each faculty meeting. Use this time to listen to teachers' concerns, receive feedback about counseling activities, and generate ideas for improving the program. Accepting group input is risky at times, because teachers may tell you things you would rather not hear. Consider their ideas carefully, and if you can implement some, do so. Your acceptance and implementation of teachers' suggestions strengthen your credibility and status with the faculty. When you give clear programmatic reasons for not accepting some suggestions, teachers will respect your decisions.

Committee Input

The advisory committee advocated throughout this guide is another vehicle for receiving input. The more your advisory committee reflects the cultural and ethnic makeup of the school, includes parents and students, enjoys administrative support, and is viewed by the staff as having an essential role in program development, the more valuable its input will be to the counseling program. Your committee should help you articulate the range of services included in the school counseling program. With accurate input from the committee, you can define more clearly your role in the school, form working alliances with teachers, and enhance your professional relationships.

An advisory committee can also facilitate cooperation between the business community and the school. Many counselors establish strong relationships with local businesses that contribute products for the school to use in rewarding students and faculty for their efforts. Although the initial ideas for these types of relationships may come from you, their development and realization is the result of input and work by many teachers, students, parents, and community leaders.

Written Communications

At times, it is inconvenient to meet face to face with people, individually or in groups. Sending written notes is one method of letting teachers know you appreciate their support and want their input. Because counselor time is so valuable, it is tempting to design and print a standard form to use for these contacts, but this is probably not the most effective method. Instead, try a personal touch to achieve a professional result by sending a handwritten note. Form letters rarely receive the attention and regard that a brief handwritten message elicits.

Sharing Information

Similar to seeking input is the importance of sharing appropriate information with students, parents, teachers, and administrators. When you know when and what to share, you win the respect of people you serve. Chapter Eleven considers the legal and ethical issues involved; here I present practical methods and guidelines about sharing information.

Select Carefully

Whether you are counseling an individual, leading a group meeting, or sending a written communication, it is imperative to know what information to share. In making this decision, you determine whether the information in question is essential for the other person to have and how this person will use the information. Sometimes counselors share information freely because it is not confidential. Although some people might view this openness as cooperation, others might become concerned about our inclination to share so much. A more conservative posture would be to share information only when it is imperative to do so for the welfare of the individual and group. There is a delicate balance between collegiality and professional integrity, which you have to judge on a case-by-case basis.

Know Your Audience

When you share information carefully, you take time to get to know the professionals, volunteers, and others in your school and community. With this knowledge, you are better able to share different types and levels of information without fear that people will misconstrue or misinterpret messages.

Demonstrate Respect

When you are approached by teachers and others seeking information, always convey respect for their professional role and their interest in student welfare. If you are unable to share details with them at a particular time, let them know that you appreciate their interest and willingness to be involved and that, as time progresses, the situation may change. Promise to keep them as informed as possible and certainly to provide the information necessary to perform their functions effectively.

Following Up

Chapter Three discusses the importance of follow-up in coordinating school counseling services. The degree to which you successfully follow up on the cases referred to you by teachers, parents, and students measures to a large extent the success of your professional relationships. Counselors, on the one hand, who demonstrate results, ask about the progress observed by others, and share their observations appropriately are likely to win respect for their professionalism. On the other hand, when you accept referrals but fail to respond with information about services provided or progress observed, teachers, parents, and students eventually will cease seeking your assistance. Keep your professional relationships at a high level of functioning by staying in touch with your referral sources. The methods and guidelines suggested in earlier sections of this chapter can apply to your follow-up strategies.

Facilitating Support Groups

Another avenue for developing strong professional relationships is to facilitate support groups among teachers and parents. These groups are excellent vehicles for teachers and parents to help each other deal with the challenges of teaching and guiding children and adolescents. Your role is to advertise the groups, schedule a time and place for the meeting, and facilitate the discussions. This latter responsibility relies on your knowledge and use of communication skills rather than on any expertise you might have about teaching or parenting. Let us consider two types of support groups for teachers and parents.

Teacher Support Groups

The best experts to help teachers are other teachers. Even school counselors who have been teachers themselves do not have the level of credibility that a seasoned, effective teacher has. Support groups are one way of inviting teachers to share common concerns and give suggestions to each other of ways to resolve these concerns. Your role as group leader is to help members share ideas about a particular concern or issue, focus on the member who has raised the concern, and facilitate a decision about what suggestions will be implemented to see whether the problem can be alleviated. All the skills you apply in group guidance and group counseling are useful in leading these types of teacher groups. To help make the groups more receptive to teachers, consider asking a teaching colleague who is highly respected by the faculty to co-lead the group with you.

Parent Support Groups

These groups are similar to teacher groups except that they focus on child development and relationships in the home. As with teachers, parents helping parents is a much more effective strategy than one-on-one consultation with a counselor. Depending on the parents served by your program, you can hold groups in the daytime for parents who do not work or work an evening shift, or schedule groups in the evening for other parents. These support groups often produce beneficial by-products beyond the support for parents and the establishment of professional relationships. They also can serve as a mechanism to identify parents who could benefit from referrals to other community agencies, such as social services, the local Health Department, or a family counseling agency.

Leading In-service

Another way elementary and middle school counselors relate professionally with their teaching colleagues is through staff development and in-service plans and presentations. Earlier I stressed the importance of seeking input from teachers about in-service they would like to have during the school year. In many cases, you are the best person to present these workshops. Other times, you will want to locate a suitable presenter. Either way, the workshops you present or coordinate will display your skills in a visible way to your faculty and administration. In planning and leading workshops for your teachers, establish a few guidelines to structure and organize successful presentations. Here are some helpful hints:

1. *Be prepared.* Know your subject well and have all the necessary materials ready. If you use handouts, overhead transparencies, or PowerPoint presentations, make them clear, professional, and accurate. Have a colleague or friend proofread your materials because errors are distracting to participants and detract from the message of your presentation.
2. *Start and end on time.* Begin the workshop on schedule. Usually a warm-up or icebreaking activity sets a positive, comfortable tone for in-service

activities. Also, end the workshop at the designated time. By beginning and ending on time you demonstrate respect for people's schedules and recognize that they have obligations and responsibilities to meet. Teachers will appreciate your punctuality and respect.

3. *Avoid mandatory workshops.* Because you seek input from all teachers about their topics of interest, you know that they are not all equally interested in every topic. Make attendance voluntary unless school policy requires everyone's participation. We treat people professionally when we defer to their judgment about whether a particular activity will be beneficial for them.

4. *Arrange the meeting room to facilitate discussion and participation.* In schools where faculties are small, chairs can be arranged in a circle for workshops. For larger groups, an auditorium or theater setup is best. Use tables only when essential. They tend to be barriers to communication and may inhibit interaction among group members.

5. *Have refreshments and snacks ready for a break.* If you plan the workshop for more than an hour, plan a break about midway through. Offer soft drinks, coffee, tea, and snacks so teachers can enjoy refreshments and conversation.

6. *Try a little humor.* Show your personal side by telling a humorous story or two that relate to the workshop topic. Usually the most successful stories are ones about you. Avoid telling jokes merely for a laugh, and never use humor that belittles, degrades, or offends other people. Profanity, even to emphasize a point, is off-limits in workshop presentations. Ask other group members as well to share humorous experiences. These opportunities for self-disclosure can broaden perspectives and at the same time offer a "lighter side" view of what normally might be serious topics.

7. *Allow opportunities for discussion.* Teachers have much to offer each other. Your workshops will be more successful if you avoid a total lecture format. Use sharing activities and intersperse them with your presentation to alternate the flow and style of the in-service. You demonstrate professionalism when you accept the views and contributions of others.

8. *Call on the expertise of others.* When you plan the workshop, see whether any other faculty member is interested in the topic and willing to be a co-presenter with you. With some topics, such as using guidance in the classroom, the credibility of the presentation is enhanced if a teacher leads the discussion.

9. *Evaluate the workshop.* Design a brief evaluation form for participants to complete before they leave the session. Checklists are the easiest to use. Worksheet 9-1 is one example.

WORKSHEET 9-1

Workshop Evaluation Form

Please complete this evaluation of our workshop. Circle your responses and place the form on the table by the door. Thank you for your input!

1. This workshop was informative.	Yes	No	Unsure
2. The presenter(s) stayed on task.	Yes	No	Unsure
3. This is an important topic for me.	Yes	No	Unsure
4. The presenter(s) answered my questions.	Yes	No	Unsure
5. The setting was appropriate for this workshop.	Yes	No	Unsure
6. I will be able to use this information to improve my teaching or my relationships with students.	Yes	No	Unsure
7. The presenter(s) was (were) knowledgeable about the topic.	Yes	No	Unsure
8. The presenter(s) listened to other views.	Yes	No	Unsure
9. The presenter(s) was (were) well prepared.	Yes	No	Unsure
10. I would like more in-service such as this.	Yes	No	Unsure

Additional comments: _____

_____

_____

_____

Promoting Positive Discipline

Student discipline continues to be a major issue in our schools today. Teachers want to be able to instruct their students and devote time to individual learning. Disruptive behaviors take time away from teaching and learning processes.

Counselors who view themselves as essential professionals in the school community understand the importance of discipline and accept a role in helping teachers, students, parents, and administrators face this issue. As an elementary or middle school counselor, you can take an active role by promoting positive approaches to school discipline.

To this end, there are countless models available to help teachers and schools focus on student development, cooperation, and reinforcement rather than on punitive consequences of misbehavior. Programs and strategies such as *Assertive Discipline* (Canter & Canter, 1992), *Logical Consequences* (Dreikurs & Grey, 1993), and Invitational Learning (Purkey & Strahan, 2002) are a few of the resources you will find in the bibliography at the end of this book. The first step is to involve your administrators, the advisory committee, and faculty in choosing an approach that is compatible with school philosophy and community values. The next step is to plan and deliver in-service to educate the staff about the approach selected. In this staff development, teachers should also learn about a schoolwide behavior management plan. Exhibit 9-1 offers a few steps to serve as a sample framework for your school plan.

School discipline is a group concern. As such, everyone who works in the school—teachers, counselors, teaching assistants, custodians, cafeteria staff, bus drivers, volunteers, students, and administrators—need to cooperate in ensuring that the school is a safe and orderly place to work and learn. As the counselor, you can take a leadership role in this process. The only area

---

EXHIBIT 9-1

Behavior Management Plan

1. Guidelines for student behavior will be printed, distributed, and discussed with students at the beginning of the school year. Focus will be on the positive points of school discipline rather than on the penalties of misbehavior.
2. Each teacher will present and clarify guidelines for behavior in the classroom.
3. Initial instances of student misbehavior will be resolved between the teacher and student in accordance with school and classroom guidelines.
4. Continued instances of student misbehavior will result in one or more of the following actions:
   a. The teacher informs parents (guardians) of behavior and requests a conference.
   b. The teacher develops reinforcement procedures to recognize appropriate student behaviors.
   c. The teacher informs the principal of the behavior and steps taken thus far to resolve problem.
   d. The teacher refers the student to the school counselor.
   e. The counselor assesses and determines what services, if any, are appropriate.
   f. The counselor provides follow-up with the teacher or administrator or both.
   g. The teacher, parents, student, or principal reach agreement on corrective measures.
   h. A referral to the Exceptional Children's Program may be considered.

of discipline that is unsuitable for a school counselor is the administration of punishment. Such a role is contrary to the ethical and professional beliefs upon which school counseling is founded. In elementary and middle schools, where a positive approach to student behavior is emphasized and applied, punishment is rarely seen as a solution. For this reason, you will be of great service to your teaching colleagues and students if you assume a leadership role in designing procedures and strategies that promote positive discipline.

In addition to the behavior management plan, you can assist your school with positive discipline by

- Creating healthy, respectful environments in and around the school
- Developing procedures to improve student supervision during the school day
- Advocating for alternative programs in your school and school system
- Examining policies and programs that discriminate against individuals or groups in the school
- Designing group activities for teachers to use in classes to focus on positive student behaviors
- Developing and coordinating bus safety instruction
- Implementing parent education programs

BEING WITH VERSUS *DOING TO*

Counselors who foster positive, respectful personal and professional relationships with the people they serve establish a cooperative posture within their schools. All the activities and functions suggested in this chapter aim at helping you become an integral part of the school community and educational program. In this sense, a major goal is to form personal and professional relationships demonstrating that you and the school counseling program are essential to student development, effective teaching, and a healthy school environment. Simply put, you *belong* in the school.

To achieve a sense of belonging in your school, become actively involved in programs and services that go beyond basic counseling relationships with students. Become a leader of program development, an initiator of policy changes, a facilitator of support groups, and a presenter of in-service training to benefit the school and community. Most important, if you wish to *belong* to your school, nurture a spirit of togetherness and mutual benefit in all your relationships. This attitude is referred to as a spirit of *being with* and is contrasted to the more clinical, separate, and expert posture of *doing to* others (see Schmidt, 2002).

Counselors who encourage a *being with* stance in their schools are aware that the most beneficial helping relationships are the ones in which respect and trust are central characteristics, manifested by carefully chosen and appropriately applied approaches and strategies. In these *being with* relationships, we value mutually beneficial outcomes. When you help students, the result is that the school, the family, and you all move to higher levels of functioning.

The notion of *being with* expresses a positive attitude toward egalitarian relationships, respectful of the expertise of all participants. In contrast, *doing to* relationships place us above others as we "diagnose problems," "modify behaviors," "adjust contingencies," and perform other similarly detached functions. Elementary and middle school counselors who exhibit mutually beneficial *being with* attitudes are confident of their professional abilities and they accept the knowledge and expertise that teachers, parents, students, and others bring to a wide range of personal and professional relationships.

Throughout this chapter, you have read about ways to establish yourself as a vital, contributing member of an elementary or middle school program. In conclusion, the following list provides suggestions to create ideas for *belonging to* and *being with* your school and community. These starter ideas are dedicated to all the elementary and middle school counselors who have asked themselves, "What can I do to become a visibly vital professional in the school program?"

- *Give an apple.* On the opening day of school (or any other day), carry a basket of apples around as you greet teachers and staff members, and give everyone you meet a shiny red apple. After all, apples are the traditional fruit of education!
- *Dial-a-home.* Every day call one parent or guardian of a child in your school. Introduce yourself, let parents know who you are, and invite them to visit you at school.
- *Send birthday greetings.* Design and print birthday cards for faculty and staff and send cards during the year. Ask the principal about broadcasting student birthdays each day during announcements on the intercom or the school's homepage on the Internet.
- *Guard against insensitivity.* Help teachers avoid activities that discriminate against certain groups of students. For example, when you plan programs to honor parents or invite parents to school, help teachers prepare alternatives for students who are without parents.
- *Take a workshop on the road.* Plan a professional outing to a museum, university, laboratory, or other point of interest for teachers.
- *Give advice reluctantly.* Because counselors are professional helpers, people sometimes want easy answers to tough questions. Use your skills to help people explore and decide their own solutions to difficult situations.
- *Be available.* Post your schedule in visible places around the school and, barring emergencies, stick to it. Avoid using a "Do not disturb" sign on the counseling office door when you are in conference. If you do,

someone will be disturbed. Try alternative messages such as, "Sorry, counselor is in conference. Please come back at. . . ."

- *Confer regularly with your principal.* Let the administration know about the counseling program and observations you have made about students' and teachers' needs. Your principal is a key person to help you belong to the school.

- *Hold luncheon parties.* As your schedule permits, have lunch with groups of students. Listen to their observations about the school, their peers, teachers, the town, and other aspects of their lives. Through simple invitations, you will keep your "ear to the ground" and become more informed and aware of student concerns.

- *Offer refreshments.* Have a fruit bowl or a treat dish to offer a bit of refreshment to visitors in the counseling center when appropriate.

- *Send get-well wishes.* When students and teachers are ill for a period of time, send a note wishing them well, and ask whether you can do anything while they recuperate.

- *Show appreciation.* When a teacher or other staff member has assisted you in some way, let them know you appreciate it. Send a note or a simple gift saying "Thank you!"

- *Accentuate the positive.* When meeting with teachers or having casual conversations, always focus on what "can be done" rather than what is "impossible." Teachers are challenged by diverse student needs and sometimes their job is difficult and frustrating. Hear their frustration, but do not feed the fires of discontent. Instead, support their efforts to find reasonable, workable solutions.

- *Listen completely.* Sometimes we have a tendency to say "no" to a response before hearing it fully. Practice saying "no" slowly by listening to the entire request and considering it carefully before giving your response.

- *Advertise the program.* Use available media to promote yourself and the school counseling program. Write a column for the school newsletter, commandeer a bulletin board in the school hallway, send press releases to your local newspaper, set up a counselor's Web site, and let people know who you are and what you do.

- *Dismantle the bureaucracy.* Help teachers and students find solutions by cutting through the red tape whenever possible. Facilitate processes with local officials and agencies. A counselor who gets things done is a prized possession in any school.

- *Be inclusive.* Include all teachers in the school counseling program. In every school, a few disgruntled teachers and staff can make life unbearable for everyone else. Our tendency is to exclude these negative types. Take the high road instead, and invite their participation. You may find, despite all their difficult behaviors, they have many legitimate ideas and suggestions.

- *Brighten up the center.* Your counseling center is a reflection of your professional posture and attitude. Hang some pictures and living plants, rearrange the furniture, add fresh paint, and think of other ways to have your space emit a positive, optimistic, professional image.
- *Establish a resource library.* When you come upon beneficial materials and information, make copies available to the teachers. Start a resource library in the school. Give teachers handouts of useful information you have discovered in your readings or at workshops. Encourage teachers to share in similar ways with each other.
- *Kill paper monsters.* Schools are notorious for creating "paper trails" the length of forever. Sometimes counselors contribute to this unfortunate process. Use your advisory committee to examine ways of cutting down paperwork that teachers, administrators, and you have created. Streamline processes for reporting information, requesting permissions, and performing other functions.

These twenty ideas add to the guidelines and suggestions found throughout this book. Use them as they fit your situation, and develop new ones for your school counseling program. As you create new ideas, you will begin to identify countless ways that you can belong to the school and *be with* others in the process of helping. The next chapter explores ways that you can reach out to significant others—parents, grandparents, and guardians—and involve them in their children's development.

chapter 10

INVOLVING SIGNIFICANT OTHERS

This guide encourages you to include many other people in developing and implementing a comprehensive school counseling program. Your willingness to invite participation, share information, and include students, parents, and teachers relates to your ability to survive and thrive as an elementary or middle school counselor. This chapter places particular attention on the role of the home in supporting and participating in the helping relationships established in the counseling program.

A chapter title of "Parent Support" would have been too restrictive because you want to include all persons in the home who have an impact on the child's development. Parents, grandparents, guardians, and other adults who have an important role in the family should be included and informed about the child's concerns, needs, and progress in school. With the wide range of cultural differences found in our communities, significant family members often include participants beyond the mother and father. Latino families, for example, place substantial importance on the role of the father and other male figures in making family decisions. Indeed an uncle may take more of a leadership role in some matters than the mother does. Without knowledge and understanding of these and other cultural differences, you are at a disadvantage in using family support wisely and effectively to benefit the child.

This chapter focuses on a few ways to include parents and other significant adults in the educational and developmental process of their children. To do so effectively, you will want to achieve a high level of knowledge and understanding about the families and communities served by the school in which you work.

FAMILY AND COMMUNITY KNOWLEDGE

Effective counselors learn about the families and communities of children in their schools. This is a gradual process of learning about people's customs and values that interact with the mission of the school. We achieve this knowledge by meeting people, joining civic groups, interviewing children, reading cumulative records, and observing events in the surrounding community. Without this knowledge, you and the teachers establish your helping and teaching relationships in a vacuum, unrelated to the reality influencing the child's development. When this happens, schools (and counseling programs) become separate and isolated from the community. They become detached, suspicious institutions, failing to win cooperation and support from families.

In many cases, the families that make up today's communities seem to be a potpourri of relationships, unions, and groups that make it difficult to define exactly what we mean by home and family. Your knowledge and understanding about these different patterns help you appreciate children's views of their world and their position in it. Effective schools and counselors know the value of this knowledge and understanding.

When you embrace your school's communities, you learn about the varying cultures within, and invite families—parents and guardians—to become an integral part of their children's education. As such, you are in a stronger position to make a significant difference in the lives of these students. When you reach out to parents and significant adults in positive ways, you create a respectful stance toward the family and community. To move toward this position, you will want to take proactive steps to learn about your students' families and plan ongoing activities within your school to invite their participation. Strategies that enable you and your colleagues to learn about families and the community include interviewing students, using cumulative records, orienting parents, touring the community, visiting homes of students, and assessing the needs of parents. Each of these activities also contributes to your development of a comprehensive school counseling program.

Interview Students

One way to learn about families is through their children. If you are new to your school, plan a brief classroom guidance activity called "Me and My

Family" for each class you visit during the early part of the school year or in small groups in the counseling center. Talk about how families are different across the country, in the state, and in the town where students live. Show pictures to illustrate some of these differences. As part of the presentation, ask students to share information about their families or have them draw a picture of the people in their families.

Variations of the preceding activities are limitless. As you learn about the many different types of family structures from children, you might discover some of the cultural differences existing in your school. In some instances, you might identify children to meet with individually and learn about their home and culture. Some sample questions to use in this type of activity are in Exhibit 10-1.

Review Cumulative Records

Sometimes counselors are hesitant to review student records because they do not want to bias their opinions about children. Although this may be an appropriate practice, there is information in student records that can help you learn about family backgrounds and conditions that influence student achievement and development. To attempt helping relationships without this information may be an ineffective and inefficient use of your time.

EXHIBIT 10-1

Me and My Family

1. How many people live in your home? Who are the people that live with you?
2. Do any animals live at your home? What kinds of animals? What are the animals' names? Who takes care of these animals?
3. What does your home look like? How many doors, windows are on the outside of your home? What color is your home on the outside?
4. Where do you sleep in your home? Do you sleep alone?
5. Where do you go after school?
6. If you go home after school, who is at home when you get there?
7. What is the first thing you do when you get home from school?
8. Do you have jobs to do at home? How do you help the family by doing these jobs?
9. What do you do for fun and play at home? Tell me about the people you play with.
10. Have you lived in other homes? What other homes have you lived in?

To use student records appropriately and efficiently you must focus on the facts. Ignore opinions, anecdotes, and other superfluous material that is unsubstantiated by your observations and documentation from other sources. Until you have assessed the situation completely, delay making judgments or forming opinions about information. You might design a simple summary sheet to use when reviewing student records. Keep these summaries in your counselor's file to refer to as you establish counseling relationships with students. This may be particularly helpful if you serve a large student population. Worksheet 10-1 shows a sample summary sheet you could use.

Orient Parents

Plan times and activities for parents and guardians to visit the school and learn about programs and events coming up during the year. Schedule these orientations at different times during the day and evening, and repeat them for parents who are unable to attend when originally scheduled. There are parameters and policies within which your school must operate regarding these types of program and meeting times, but do what you can to determine whether the school can be flexible in its planning.

When sharing information at orientation meetings, consider having parents who have been involved with the school assist you with the presentation. Parents who are new to schools and anxious for their children will be more at ease listening to other parents who are pleased with the school program. If your school has a culturally diverse population, choose discussion in small groups led by volunteer parents who understand the language and cultural differences of the new parents. Plan strategies and organize your meetings to accommodate the needs and interests of those attending. Keep in mind that although these orientations are to help parents become familiar and comfortable with the school, they also increase faculty awareness about parents and neighborhoods.

Take a Bus Tour

Another way to educate yourself and colleagues about the communities served by your school is to organize a bus tour around the city or town. Learn what neighborhoods are served by your elementary or middle school, and ask the principal to plan a "field trip" for the staff during an in-service day, some late afternoon, or a Saturday. Ride through residential areas to view the streets, houses, and apartments where children and their families live.

Make it a pleasant experience by planning a luncheon at a favorite restaurant that features cuisine and customs of the neighborhood. Plan stops at points of interests, such as churches, athletic clubs, museums, libraries, and parks, so the staff can appreciate the facilities and amenities available to the students of your school. If a teacher lives in the neighborhood, let that person be the tour guide.

WORKSHEET 10-1

Cumulative Record Survey

Student: _____ Home phone: _____

Address: _____

Family members: _____

_____

_____

_____

Physical or medical notes: _____

_____

_____

_____

Education notes: _____

_____

_____

_____

Previous schools: _____

_____

_____

_____

Other information: _____

_____

_____

_____

When budget constraints prevent you from organizing a neighborhood tour, try soliciting sponsors from the business community. Check with your chamber of commerce and local merchants' association and tell them about your plans. Promise them coverage in the local newspaper or other media for their support of this program. You may find that local businesses are supportive of such school efforts.

In large school districts, one bus tour may permit you to visit only a small portion of the neighborhoods served by the school. If so, plan a different tour every year and make it an annual cultural event. Learning about students' homes sensitizes us and brings us closer to them. In this way, we improve our chances of establishing beneficial relationships in the classroom and in other service areas.

Visit Homes

In some cases, the best way to learn about a student's situation is to visit the family at home. At one time, this practice was a common tradition for teachers and principals. Today's challenges and the move away from neighborhood schools in many communities make these face-to-face meetings more difficult and less frequent. Still, on rare occasion, a home visit might be the only way to truly understand the family's perspective.

Survey the teachers in your school to see whether they are receptive to home visits. Start with your principal to ascertain whether the administration supports this idea and if local regulations and contracts allow it. Informally canvass your faculty to get initial reactions. If a social worker and nurse serve your school, recruit their assistance. Let teachers know that you are available to make home visits with them if they would feel more comfortable having someone accompany them.

Encourage your teachers to make home visits for positive reasons as well as for concerns about student behavior and progress. Part of teachers' resistance to making home visits may be that they usually bring bad news to the home. The school can lessen this resistance if the purpose of these is balanced between positive and negative reports.

Assess Parent Needs

Chapter Three discusses ways of surveying the needs of students, parents, and teachers as a means of determining program goals and objectives, planning a program of services, and coordinating your counseling activities. Similarly, a parent needs assessment helps you acquire knowledge about the home situation, which is beneficial when the school asks for assistance in handling student problems.

If teachers suspect that a family is hurting, you may need to assess the situation directly by calling or visiting the home. Stressful situations and tragedies in the family have a debilitating effect on student development and learning if they go unheeded. Contact the family and offer to locate necessary assistance. To do this effectively, you must establish a working knowledge of the community and its available resources.

The preceding suggestions provide a few ways through which you can learn about families and communities served by your school. This learning process places you in a position to solicit parent support for the school and the counseling program. By learning about families and communities, you can communicate effectively with parents and guardians, informing them of their children's progress and the programs available at school.

COMMUNICATION AND INFORMATION

In some elementary and middle schools, good ideas and excellent programs go unnoticed and unsupported by parents because of lack of information and communication. You can help your school by coordinating efforts to communicate clearly and accurately with parents by planning schoolwide functions, organizing group conferences, and sending written communication home with students.

Special Events

Elementary and middle school parents and guardians care about their children's performance in school and enjoy seeing them show off their talents. You and the teachers can display student talent by planning special events and inviting parents to attend. These events can be schoolwide, such as a school bazaar to earn money for materials and equipment, or they can be limited to a single class, such as a kindergarten display of "new art forms."

When you arrange special events, use these opportunities to inform parents about other happenings and programs taking place in the school. For example, if your school holds a raffle to earn money, you could set up tables, staffed by students, parents, and teachers to distribute information and answer questions about the counseling program. In the same way, if you want to attract parents to the school for an open house to visit with teachers and learn about the instructional program, you could advertise door prizes for those who attend. Identify the main purpose of the event, plan ways to invite parents, make the invitation attractive by including incentives, and use every occasion to promote your school and the school counseling program.

Worksite Visits

Some parents work long hours and have so many obligations that getting to school to hear about their child's progress is unlikely if not impossible. One avenue that your school can follow to help these parents and guardians is to arrange with local factories and industries for you to meet with parents during work hours. One school system in North Carolina arranged with an area textile mill to have parents released for conferences in the mill with counselors once a semester during the school year for an update on their children's progress. Most businesses and industries will view a half-hour release time for this type of consultation as time well-spent and invested. If there are companies who employ parents from your community, this type of program may be worth considering. Talk with your principal and advisory committee to see whether this idea is worth pursuing.

Test Reports

Most elementary and middle schools across the country participate in achievement and aptitude testing. Test companies usually include home reports that explain results to parents. Sometimes schools do not send these test results home, or if they do, there is little explanation or discussion to help parents and guardians understand them. As counselor, you have a responsibility to see that the instructional staff uses test results wisely and appropriately and parents receive and understand their home reports.

One way of disseminating test results is to send them home with children's report cards. If this approach is used, an explanation should be included. This explanation needs to be clear and accurate, written in a layperson's language so parents are able to interpret the results. At the same time, you might extend an open invitation for parents who want an individual conference to receive further explanation and additional information about their child. You may need to call some parents directly to tell them the report is coming home and to invite them to meet with you at their convenience.

Group sessions are another method of sharing test results with parents. They are helpful because you can inform several parents at one time about the test results and how to interpret the information on their child's home report. In these sessions, the information you share about test results is general; ask parents to see you individually if they have specific questions about their child's scores.

Parent Conferences

Another vehicle for communicating with parents and guardians is through face-to-face conferences. In elementary and middle schools, you can schedule these sharing sessions routinely throughout the year. You can assist your school in the development of productive parent conferences in two important ways:

- Encourage the administration to schedule regular opportunities for teachers and parents to meet.

- Provide teachers with appropriate in-service training to acquire the necessary communication and leadership skills.

Regular conferences during the year enable teachers to establish working relationships with parents and guardians rather than calling on them only when problems surface. In addition, teachers can be encouraged to communicate with the home throughout the year by calling when students have been absent with a long illness, sending congratulatory notes when family members are recognized for their achievements, inviting parents, grandparents, and guardians to have lunch with children at school, and planning other ways of promoting goodwill between home and school.

By providing in-service to teachers, you help them strengthen communication and problem-solving skills with parents. Focus these sessions on active listening skills, facilitative behaviors, and decision-making strategies. In addition, help teachers learn about the importance of clarifying their roles, agreeing on a plan of action, and assigning responsibilities. One suggestion for a workshop outline is to outline specific stages of a parent-teacher conference:

1. Establish rapport by helping parents feel welcomed, comfortable, and valuable as equal partners in this helping relationship.
2. State the purpose of the conference. Be clear and precise in stating the reason for the meeting. In most instances, a conference occurs for one of three purposes:
   Planning—to design a plan to handle an upcoming event, such as a student's transfer to a new school.
   Sharing information—to report on data or other information about the student, such as testing results.
   Problem solving—to address some issue of concern to the parent or teacher, such as the student's classroom behavior.
3. Explore, discuss, and explain information and observations relative to the topic of the conference. Give parents specific, observed, and factual information. Avoid generalizations that you cannot substantiate.
4. Listen to parent observations and opinions about the child and the school. This information can help you understand the child's perceptions better.
5. Generate ideas and recommendations from the parents and teacher(s) to address issues raised in the meeting. These ideas can strengthen the plan of action you choose.
6. Narrow down alternatives and select ones that are agreeable to all concerned. Assign responsibilities to the teacher(s), parents or guardians, student, yourself, and other persons involved in the agreement and plan.
7. Close the conference with a summary of the agreement, a plan for follow-up, and a time for a second conference if needed. Ask all participants whether they have other items to discuss before adjourning.

8. Adjourn the meeting by thanking everyone for his or her participation and genuine concern for the child's welfare.

In addition to the stages detailed above, use in-service opportunities to offer helpful hints and enhance teachers' leadership skills for working with parents and guardians of students. Your suggestions can be presented in a handout during the workshop or posted around the room to use as catalysts for group discussion. Here are a few ideas:

- *Invite parents to become equal partners.* Use the pronoun *we* as you discuss the issues and solutions explored. In this way, parents will feel that they have an important role and valuable information to contribute.
- *Remember that parents are the experts on their children.* Listen carefully to their observations and respect their knowledge of the home situation.
- *Choose a comfortable setting for the meeting.* Sometimes parents are uncomfortable in schools. Do whatever possible to ease tensions and relax the atmosphere.
- *Avoid placing barriers, such as tables and desks, between you and parents.* If you need a table for writing, sit at the corners, or as close to the parents as possible.
- *Be prepared.* If records, test data, and other information are needed for the conference, have all materials ready and at hand. Getting up to search for information in the middle of the meeting breaks the flow and continuity of the relationship.
- *Be truthful with parents.* Exaggerations and untruths destroy confidence and credibility. Parents will appreciate your openness and honesty. Avoid being brutally frank or telling parents what you think they want to hear, so you "gain an upper hand" or "weaken their resistance." We build healthy working relationships on trust and respect, neither of which is compatible with uncaring, thoughtless behaviors.
- *In some conferences, particularly with middle school students, you may want to have the child sit in on part or all of the meeting.* Decisions about this should be made before the conference. Discuss it with the parent or guardian when you schedule the meeting.
- *When the conference is adjourned and parents leave, write a brief summary of what was decided and who was assigned responsibilities.* Keep a separate file of this information for all your conferences with parents and guardians.

Letters and Communiqués

Written messages provide another method of communicating information to the home. These might be letters that you mail to parents, notes that students bring home, articles you write in school newsletters, announcements on the school's home page, and reports that individual students receive from you and their teachers. All of these forms of communication can help to let parents know about happenings at school, student progress, and other important information. Your goal of being a visible counselor should include these types of communications.

In designing and implementing various strategies, remember that the messages and articles you write and distribute are a reflection both of you as a professional and of your school counseling program. Here are some guidelines for achieving effective communication with the home:

1. *Proofread carefully.* Sometimes readers miss an entire message because they focus on one misspelled word or grammatical error. Be accurate and ask a colleague to read your work before sending it out.
2. *Look professional.* Give your correspondence the best possible image. Ask the school secretary and media coordinator for assistance in designing and producing a polished product. Use colorful paper for brochures, add graphics, put appropriate links on your Web site, and try other ways of making your messages visually attractive.
3. *Check your vocabulary.* Write for your audience, not for yourself. Choose a language that is understood by all parents and avoid educational jargon at all times.
4. *Use positive phrases.* Keep your letters and announcements upbeat. Even when letters must convey difficult news for parents to hear, choose optimistic words and phrases to put forth the school's posture of hope and promise. By gaining parent support, barriers and obstacles are more easily overcome.

Beyond formatting and designing and writing your letters and other correspondence to the home, plan how you will distribute this information. Decisions about how to send notices home to parents are practical considerations influenced by the nature of your correspondence, the cost of mailing, the appropriateness of the Internet, and the dependability of students to deliver school notices home. These considerations will certainly have an impact on the success of your communication. For example, you might write an excellent announcement inviting parents for conferences with teachers, only to have a handful of parents show up because the word never reached home.

When a letter is critically important, it is best to mail it—perhaps registered mail if you want to be sure parents receive it—or deliver it in person. If you think students will deliver the message, give it a try. Students may want to know what the letter is about, particularly middle graders. If so, tell them. If you cannot tell students what they are delivering, it is best to mail the information.

When you use students as delivery agents and want to be sure the information reaches its destination, offer incentives to students—a treat, decal, or other reward. In the message to parents, ask them to tear off the bottom receipt, sign it, and give it to the child, who will return it to school.

Another way to communicate your role to parents, while informing them of guidance and counseling activities with their children, is to send home student worksheets completed during a classroom guidance activity. Attach the worksheet to a memo explaining the nature of the activity and ask parents and guardians to talk with their child about the lesson. At the end of your memo, place a form for the parents to sign and have their child return it to you at school to receive an award, such as a sticker, a special treat, or a free pass to the counseling center. Exhibit 10-2 gives an example of a memo to parents.

EXHIBIT 10-2

Memo to Parents

Dear *(Ask students to write the names of their parents/guardians)*:
Today in school we learned about friendships and the ways that we can make friends. In our discussion, students were asked to talk about some of the friends they have and what they do to make and keep friends.

Please ask your child about this activity and about what he or she learned. After you talk about this activity, sign the form below and your child will return it to me at school for a reward.

If you have any questions about this activity or other services of the school counseling program, please call me. Thank you for your support!

_____

The School Counselor

- -

I have talked about the friendship lesson with my child and have learned about the activity that was presented at school.

_____

(Parent/Guardian)

_____

(Date)

PTA and PTO Presentations

Ask your principal about presenting at PTA or PTO meetings during the school year. These presentations can be short announcements about school counseling services and upcoming programs, they can spotlight a student project, or they can focus on information and skills for parenting.

A question and answer panel with the principal, counselor, and teachers is another way of sharing information with parents while soliciting their input into the school program. These exchanges illustrate a school's openness and willingness to share ideas and discuss concerns in a public forum. If your school plans this type of presentation, be sure to set the parameters and areas for questions. This structure will give the presentation a specific focus so that you can cover a few topics adequately rather than trying to address too many topics insufficiently. The success of one of these sessions will encourage your school to plan future panels and include additional topics for discussion.

When making presentations to PTA or community groups, use the guidelines suggested earlier for school-home communications. The programs you present and speeches you make, as you have seen throughout this guide, advertise who you are and what you do. For this reason, you will want to put your best foot forward. Here are some additional tips for planning and presenting successful programs to parents:

1. *Arrive early.* Always give yourself time to survey the meeting place, set up your materials, check out the microphone, and take care of other structural matters, such as the arrangement of chairs for the audience. Presentations sometimes fall short of success because of environmental factors, which could have been adjusted if discovered early enough. If you finish setting up and have time while the audience is arriving, shake hands, introduce yourself, and greet people as they come into the meeting place. This simple gesture places you at an equal, receptive level with your audience.

2. *Dress professionally.* Always look your best and choose outfits that are attractive, yet not flashy or overpowering. Your appearance should not overshadow what you have to say. The message is more important than the package it comes in.

3. *Be prepared.* Have all materials and equipment for the presentation ready on time. Check the equipment. It is discomforting to a presenter and an audience to be set for the "show" and have the projector or computer malfunction.

4. *Keep a brisk pace.* Plan presentations that move smoothly and highlight the most important points as you speak. In most presentations of twenty to thirty minutes, you will have a couple of key points that you want the audience to hear. If most people leave remembering these main ideas, your presentations will be successful.

5. *Move around.* Avoid standing in one spot or behind a podium unless it is necessary. By walking around you alter your proximity to members of the audience and allow yourself the opportunity to make eye contact with different people. This subtle change in distance and eye contact enables you to include people in your talk and illustrates the "being with" posture described earlier in this book. Moving around also encourages the audience to follow you with their eyes and invites them to participate in your presentation.

6. *Summarize.* At the end of your talk, highlight once more the main points and key ideas you have presented. You have something important to say; be sure to present it more than once.

7. *End on time.* It is a cardinal sin to keep an audience longer than they expected. When you are introduced, glance at the time and remember to stay within the schedule. If you go too long, no matter how good you are, some people will tune you out and miss the point of your message. Sometimes, when other items are on the meeting agenda, the time allotted for your presentation will have to be cut. Be ready to adjust your program to meet the needs of the situation. In short, be flexible.

8. *Practice.* Finally, before you present and as you are preparing your talk, try it out on yourself and others. Check the timeframe and make adjustments as needed. If you are new at giving presentations, ask people close to you, a spouse or colleague, to listen to the talk and give you helpful reactions and comments.

The previous paragraphs present a few suggestions to facilitate and enhance school-home communication. These suggestions invite parent and guardian participation and involvement in the school and give ownership of the school to the community. Through this kind of cooperative spirit, your school can benefit from another avenue of parent support, that of volunteer programs.

Volunteers

As mentioned briefly in Chapter Three, parents, grandparents, guardians, and other people can provide valuable time and support to school programs, including school counseling services. Administrators, teachers, and counselors who truly believe in the notion of a school community recognize the wealth of resources and assistance lying beyond the schoolhouse doors. Encourage your school to open its doors and invite these groups to contribute to the quality of the educational program. The possibilities are countless, limited only by the imagination and willingness of the school to tap these resources. Here are some ways that volunteers can serve.

Tutors

Because of the diverse needs of students in schools and the challenge faced by teachers to meet all these demands, there will never be enough support services for all children. Volunteer tutors help individual students and relieve some of this demand on teachers' time. In schools that recruit many tutors, a volunteer coordinator may be necessary to keep track of schedules, notify tutors of changes at school, plan training sessions, and communicate between the school and volunteers as appropriate.

Media Assistants

Keeping up with all the materials in a comprehensive media program is a major challenge. Volunteers in elementary and middle schools can help media coordinators catalog materials and service equipment, as well as assist students in the center.

Guidance Assistants and Presenters

Parents and others can help teachers and counselors in guidance activities with small groups and in classes. Sometimes volunteers might share personal or professional expertise that relates to a guidance lesson. For example, a visiting grandparent could tell stories to primary children about friendships formed over a lifetime, or a mother who is a police officer could talk about her career in law enforcement.

Supervisors

As noted earlier, student safety and supervision is a major concern in all schools regardless of their size. Having volunteers in the school increases the number of eyes and ears available to assure a safe environment for children. The school administration should participate in the orientation of volunteers to discuss school policies and procedures and the role of paraprofessionals in the school. Be sure to invite the administration to plan all orientation functions.

Parents and others can also assist teachers with supervision during peak times when student traffic is high and monitoring is essential. These times include bus arrival and dismissal, lunchtime, and recess.

Clerical Assistants

You can use volunteers for clerical functions such as typing, copying, making bulletin boards, creating instructional materials, and other activities. The school secretary is an excellent person to coordinate these services and train volunteers.

There are many other ways that volunteers can help teachers meet the needs of students. Use your advisory committee as a resource to plan volunteer programs in the school, remembering always to involve your principal in all decisions about volunteer participation. Worksheet 10-2 presents a volunteer application form, which can be handed out at the first PTA or PTO meeting or sent home with students at the beginning of the year.

WORKSHEET 10-2

Volunteer Application Form

Check the appropriate responses and fill in the requested information. And thank you for volunteering in our school!

_____ Yes, I would like to help in school as a volunteer.

Name:_____

Home Phone: _____

Work Phone: _____

_____ I am available to volunteer during school hours.
_____ I am available to volunteer in the evening or on weekends.

My volunteer interests are:

_____ Tutoring students	_____ Doing clerical tasks
_____ Assisting in Media Center	_____ Driving on field trips
_____ Presenting career information	_____ Helping teachers with classroom
_____ Reading to students	guidance
_____ Repairing the building	_____ Organizing fund raisers
_____ Supervising students	_____ Sprucing up the school yard
(buses, cafeteria, etc.)	_____ Contacting businesses for
_____ Technology skills	donations (prizes, rewards, etc.)

PARENT EDUCATION PROGRAMS

Elementary and middle schools effectively help children through developmental stages and learning processes when they win support from and seek active involvement by parents and guardians. School programs intended to assist parents facilitate parental support and involvement. Because children today face increasingly difficult challenges and pressures, parenting, and all of its roles and responsibilities, has become a complex adventure. Programs to assist and support parents in this process are an essential part of school counseling services. In addition to presenting at PTA or PTO meetings and sending communications home, schools can take an active role in assisting parents by offering parent education opportunities.

Parent education programs use different formats and structures depending on the nature of the group, the training and expertise of the group leader, and the leader's style and preference for particular types of groups. When you organize and present parent education programs, there are typically two approaches from which to choose: discussion groups or instructional programs.

Discussion Groups

Usually, counselors trained in group procedures are comfortable leading parent groups in discussions about topics of mutual interest and concern. Group members can suggest topics or the counselor can preselect them. For elementary school parents a sample list of topics might be

- Mealtimes
- Sibling rivalry
- Family chores
- Allowances
- Bedtime
- Television
- Computer games and Internet surfing
- Parent-teacher communication
- Ready for the school bus
- School anxieties

You could add the following topics, which may be of interest to middle school parents as well:

- Friendships
- Homework
- Physical changes
- A new school
- Extracurricular activities
- Parent-child communication
- Adolescence and independence

Discussion groups are successful when group members feel comfortable with each other and the leader's skills are adequate to the task. When parents do not know other group members, or a range of diverse topics is not an appropriate format to use, you might consider instructional approaches for your parent education programs.

Instructional Programs

Many parent education programs are marketed commercially for you to purchase for your counseling program or you can design your own. A few popular programs are

- *Systematic Training for Effective Parenting,* by Don Dinkmeyer, Jr., and Gary McKay, American Guidance Services

- *Assertive Discipline for Parents,* by Lee Canter, Canter and Associates
- *Active Parenting,* by Michael Popkin, Active Parenting Publishers
- *Parent Effectiveness Training,* by Thomas Gordon

In addition to these programs, books and materials on Transactional Analysis, logical consequences, and behavioral approaches are available for teaching parenting skills. Many of these are listed in the Bibliography at the end of this book.

You should choose an instructional program according to the structured format of the group, the learning goals and objectives, and specific activities incorporated into the learning process. If you are not familiar with a specific approach to parent education, investigate what approaches other counselors in your school system have used successfully. Locate a training program to attend or join a group currently being held in your school system or community. After you have reviewed different programs, received appropriate training, and determined which is best for you and your school, you will be in a better position to plan and implement successful parent education sessions.

Program Planning

When you have researched and determined which of the various approaches to parent education are best suited for your school counseling program, plan a strategy for introducing the program, recruiting participants, and evaluating your success. Consider the following procedures:

1. Win commitment from the principal and teachers. The time you allot to run these groups has to come from somewhere in your busy schedule. Talk about the program with your advisory committee and ask assistance to guide you toward a schedule that is acceptable to your administration and faculty. In some schools, counselors run daytime and evening groups to accommodate the work schedules of parents. Sometimes counselors arrange evening groups at parents' homes and rotate the meeting place for each session.

   In some communities, parents may have difficulty arranging transportation to a school or other location to attend sessions. If possible, you can bring the program to a convenient meeting place. One elementary counselor ran parent groups in the recreation room of a housing project for parents who lived in that community. Whatever arrangements you make for your program, clear them through your supervisor and the school principal.

2. Through surveys and informal contacts, ask parents about the types of programs and groups they are interested in attending. There is little point

in taking the time and effort to design and implement a program to which few people respond. Do your homework and estimate your audience.

3. Advertise the program through school newsletters, local radio shows, PTA or PTO meetings, and other avenues to make sure word gets out. Sometimes the first couple of groups you run will be sparsely attended. However, when you are successful, the word will spread and future programs will become better attended.

4. Use the same leadership skills you apply in group counseling and guidance to your parent group. Facilitate discussion and place every parent in the role of an expert. De-emphasize your own expertise and rely on the suggestions and collective wisdom of the group.

5. Limit the number of participants for each group to maximize discussion. You can give presentations at PTA or PTO meetings on specific parenting topics to large audiences, but ongoing parent discussion groups should be limited to fifteen to twenty members.

6. Set a schedule for every meeting date and time at the beginning of the program. Having a schedule in advance helps parents plan their calendar and assures good attendance at the sessions. Start each session promptly and end on time.

7. Let everyone participate. Use your group skills to keep discussions going and prevent individuals from dominating the meeting. Create a spirit of belonging by giving everyone an opportunity to contribute.

8. Summarize each session and ask parents for feedback before ending the meeting. Begin each new session with a brief review of the previous meeting.

9. Ask parents to complete an evaluation of the program during the last session. Worksheet 10-3 is a sample evaluation of a parent education program. Summarize these evaluations and present a report to the principal and faculty. Sharing results of these evaluations with your colleagues will win their support for future programs.

This chapter considers a variety of ways that you can develop healthy working relationships with parents and guardians. Sometimes, because of the confidential nature of helping relationships formed by counselors with elementary and middle school children, communication with parents becomes delicate. Developing positive communications throughout the school year with your parents will assist you during these sensitive, difficult times. In these instances, your knowledge of legal and ethical guidelines is of paramount importance. Chapter Eleven reviews legal and ethical issues related to counseling in schools.

WORKSHEET 10-3

Parent Education Evaluation

Please complete this questionnaire to help me evaluate the parenting group and plan future programs. Thank you!

1. Did you enjoy participating in this program?	Yes	No	Sometimes
2. Were you comfortable in this group?	Yes	No	Sometimes
3. Was the information helpful to you?	Yes	No	Sometimes
4. Was enough time allotted for discussions?	Yes	No	Sometimes
5. Did the counselor respect your views?	Yes	No	Sometimes
6. Were you encouraged to help other participants?	Yes	No	Sometimes
7. Were your questions answered?	Yes	No	Sometimes
8. Have you successfully used any information learned in this group?	Yes	No	Sometimes
9. Would you join another group in the future?	Yes	No	Sometimes
10. Would you recommend this program to other parents?	Yes	No	Sometimes

Additional comments: _____

_____

_____

_____

chapter 11

PLAYING FAIR
and ACCORDING
to the RULES

As services expand and student populations become more diverse, school counselors face increasingly difficult and complex legal and ethical issues. Understandably, these situations relate to the role of schools in today's society and challenges faced by students, parents, and teachers. For you as a practicing school counselor, the responsibility of making the most appropriate, correct decisions is dependent on a clear knowledge and understanding of legal and ethical guidelines. Such understanding begins with knowing the difference between ethical and legal issues.

School counselors establish their working relationships with students and other clients in accordance with legal parameters and ethical standards. Although these two sets of guidelines are frequently in agreement, there are times when they appear to be in conflict with each other. At these times, your own professional knowledge and judgment will be the most important guide.

You interpret each legal and ethical situation within the context of school policies and your responsibilities for serving students, parents, and the local administrative unit. To place yourself in a knowledgeable position and make appropriate decisions about legal and ethical issues, learn about state and national laws as well as local policies that relate to the practice of counseling in your school setting. At the same time, you will want a clear understanding and working knowledge of professional ethics for school counselors. The ethical guidelines commonly followed by school counselors are the Ethical Standards of the American Counseling Association and the American School Counselor Association.

This chapter examines legal and ethical considerations you might encounter as an elementary or middle school counselor. If you are not already knowledgeable and versed in these issues, you may want to obtain current readings, attend conferences, and participate in pertinent workshops. Strengthening your knowledge base protects you, your clients, and the school and is a responsible position to take. Books and other readings are available to help you attain this knowledge. In addition, the professional journals frequently focus on such topics of interest to counselors.

A first step in becoming informed is to learn about local, state, and national laws and policies that govern schools. As a professional counselor who practices in a school setting, you provide services according to regulations set by your school administration, policies enacted by the local school board, state laws and procedures, and federal laws. All these come under the heading of legal considerations when you face decisions involving a law, policy, or other regulation. To be informed in this area, you will want to know about legal parameters and have access to resources that will guide you in making decisions on a case-by-case basis.

LEGAL CONSIDERATIONS AND RESOURCES

Many resources are available to help you explore the breadth and complexity of legal issues faced by today's counselors. This chapter focuses on specific resources to help you gain knowledge about local, state, and federal laws and policies. The first resource person to contact is your school principal.

The School Principal

Ask your principal to locate manuals and guides for you to learn school regulations and local policies. These materials include a copy of the student handbook, a faculty manual, school board policies, a school principal's guide to state law, and other resources the principal will share. Documents such as these present the policies and regulations by which your administration manages the school. As a professional hired by the school system, you want to adhere to these policies and regulations; in particular, you want to be aware of potential conflict between these regulations and your ethical standards. If you have questions in this regard, ask your principal to discuss these issues with you. In these discussions, listen carefully to the principal's point of view. You may not always agree with his or her viewpoint, but knowing it will be helpful when legal and ethical guidelines are unclear or in conflict. In practice, you balance your adherence to school policies with your concern for student welfare and development. Sometimes it may be appropriate to illustrate for the principal how local regulations are inhibiting rather than facilitating student well-being and educational progress. This is an appropriate role for you to take.

Overcoming differences of opinion about how regulations affect student development will be less difficult and stressful if you and your principal begin with a good working relationship. For this reason, it benefits you and the students to communicate consistently with your administrator about the school counseling program, the issues addressed, and services provided. By maintaining open communications with your principal, you improve the likelihood of negotiating changes in school procedures and policies when they are detrimental to student welfare. Open communication also places you in a stronger position to win the support of your principal when local policies raise ethical dilemmas regarding counseling services for elementary and middle school students. The responsibilities you have to students, parents, and the school may not always be in harmony with one another. Therefore, having the support of your principal to help you satisfy each of these responsibilities is essential.

Your Counseling Supervisor

If your school system has a supervisor or director of school counseling services, ask this person for published state manuals related to the practice of school counseling. Determine which regulations of your local school board and policies of the state are followed for the school counseling program.

Your supervisor should be able to obtain information about actions related to school counseling handed down by state and federal courts. Because of the different levels and jurisdictions of courts, it is important to know which rulings apply to what situations. One avenue in which to present this information is through a workshop on current legal rulings that pertain to school counseling. Your local school board attorney, a judge, or a district attorney can be an excellent resource to help plan and deliver this in-service. You also might ask the counseling supervisor to plan in-service that would help you and other counselors learn about your role and responsibilities when being subpoenaed to court. As counselors become more involved in counseling children about family separations, abusive situations, sexual development, and other sensitive issues, they might be subpoenaed to testify in legal hearings and procedures. Workshops and seminars presented by expert counsel can help you learn about your rights, legal proceedings, and appropriate ways of responding as a court witness.

In some states, privileged communication statutes protect student-counselor relationships. Find out whether such protection exists in your school system and what exceptions or conditions, if any, there are in your state. Privileged communication relates to the ethical practice of confidentiality, but sometimes counselors misunderstand it. When a law grants privileged communication, the client is protected, not the counselor. Students protected by privileged communication in their relationships with school counselors can waive this privilege if they so desire, and in some states parents are involved in this process for minor children. Be sure to learn all you can about privileged communication, the pertinent statutes in your state, and how they affect the practice of counseling in your school.

The School Board

In school systems governed by local boards of education, regular meetings of the board review and act on policies to govern and regulate school practices. Attend your local board meetings if permissible. Check the agenda when released and see whether any items pertaining to the school counseling program are on it. Sometimes school systems post the agendas in the central office before meetings or announce them in the local newspaper.

By staying informed, you are able to design and implement counseling services that conform to local policies and procedures. At the same time, you learn about local regulations under consideration, which may hinder or help the delivery of comprehensive guidance and counseling services. By keeping in touch with local regulatory issues, you take a strong position to advise decision makers, such as board members, about school counseling services and the legal and ethical responsibilities of counselors.

In addition to attending school board meetings, you may find that the board attorney is a vital support person when legal matters interact with your helping relationships. As mentioned above, the board attorney is an excellent resource to inform you about your role and responsibilities when testifying in court as a witness. Attorneys also can provide information about an array of subjects that influence or interfere with counseling services in schools. Matters related to exceptional children's rights, parent custody and access to children at school, privileged communications between students and counselors, due process, counselor malpractice, and limitless other topics can be addressed by competent attorneys.

Situations faced by counselors are not always simple to answer in legal or practical terms. Sometimes conflicts occur, for example between a principal and a counselor, because of how each person perceives his or her role, authority, and responsibilities. Imagine that a teacher suspects physical child abuse with one of the students. This teacher has brought the evidence to you, the school counselor. In your system, it is proper procedure to bring such cases to the school principal immediately, and you do so. The principal listens and says, "I know this family. This is not abuse; it is simply firm discipline." The principal makes it clear: "This will not be reported to the child protective services agency." Both you and the teacher feel otherwise. What should you do?

According to the law, you are required to report any situation when you have sufficient reason to believe a parent or caretaker has abused a child. All states have laws that require school officials to report suspected child abuse. Knowing this, however, may not be sufficient in helping you and the teacher make a decision to act against your principal's orders. What you need is guidance from a local policy that clearly shows the legal responsibilities of all school personnel to follow state and federal laws regarding child abuse. You may also need to consult your supervisor or the personnel director in the school system. In cases of suspected child abuse, the report is usually required within a specific time frame. Therefore, you may not have time to research the legal position of the school system on this matter. For this reason, it is all the more important that you have a working knowledge of local school regulations and the authority of the school principal, other administrators, and yourself. As noted in Chapter Eight, suspicion of child abuse requires a report to an investigation agency.

Most school officials—administrators and board members—want school counselors to provide comprehensive services to students, parents, and teachers, and they want those services to meet the expectations of local policy, state mandate, and federal law. Hence, school systems generally are willing to provide in-service training and make available legal experts who can educate counselors, teachers, and other professionals about appropriate regulations and their responsibilities. In addition to the training that the school system provides, you should seek further information from the professional counseling associations.

Professional Associations

State and national counseling and educational organizations offer an excellent avenue for acquiring resources about legal issues and professional responsibilities. As mentioned earlier, the American Counseling Association, the American School Counselor Association, and their state divisions provide opportunities for counselors to learn about the legal and ethical views of our professional organizations. This information will help you compare local school policies with the positions of various counseling associations. In some ways, this comparison will help you prepare a case to convince your principal and school system of adjustments needed in policies that are seemingly in conflict with the legal views or ethical standards of the counseling profession.

The exchange of information during workshops and in conference sessions on legal and ethical issues is invaluable because you can learn a great deal from colleagues about how to handle local situations that create dilemmas. By attending state conferences, national conventions, and local workshops, you can learn from colleagues who are counseling in other elementary and middle schools and facing issues similar to those you are confronting in your school. Take advantage of these opportunities to increase your knowledge, and place yourself in a position of being able to prevent legal and ethical entanglements.

As noted earlier, experts who are trained and knowledgeable in matters of law can best address legal issues. Although you may want to attain a working knowledge of the law and how it relates to the practice of school counseling, your best resource in times of conflict will be the specific law or policy in question and an expert in the practice of law. Ethical considerations, however, are less precise than legal mandates (many of which are also imprecise) and are guided by our knowledge, understanding, and acceptance of professional codes and standards.

ETHICAL CONSIDERATIONS

The American School Counselor Association, a division of the American Counseling Association, has presented a code of conduct to maintain and regulate standards of practice for school counselors. In its ethical standards, ASCA defines six areas of counselor responsibility: responsibilities to students, parents, colleagues and professional associates, the school and community, and one's self. To be fully informed, you want to obtain and review a complete copy of this ethical code, which you can download from the ASCA Web site. The following sections offer a brief summary of counselor responsibilities as outlined in the ASCA ethical standards.

Responsibilities to Students

School counselors are primarily concerned with the total development of students, including their educational, vocational, personal, and social growth. You accept responsibility for informing students about procedures and techniques used in counseling relationships and encourage students to explore their own values and beliefs in making decisions and plans about life goals.

School counselors are responsible for knowing about the laws and regulations regarding student welfare as they seek to protect the rights of all children. To protect the confidentiality of information received in your helping relationships, release information according to existing laws and policies and always use student records and data in an accurate and appropriate manner. At all times, you should select and use tests and other assessment procedures according to published practices.

Counselors inform appropriate authorities when a student's behavior indicates a clear and imminent danger to his or herself or others. Necessary referrals must be made when your assistance is no longer showing adequate progress with students receiving counseling. Such referrals, of course, are contingent upon your knowledge of existing resources in the school system and community.

Responsibilities to Parents

Although counselors in elementary and middle schools have the ethical obligation to protect the rights of children and confidential relationships established with students, they also have a responsibility to involve parents and keep them informed of services that are available to their children. According to the ASCA code, counselors recognize the rights and responsibilities of parents, and they establish cooperative relationships with parents to ensure the progress and development of students. However, these rights and responsibilities are not always clearly defined, and today's challenging social issues, such as child neglect and abuse, coupled with continuously changing family structures place you and your school in precarious ethical and legal positions. For this reason, be knowledgeable about your school's views on parental involvement in all services for children and about your role as the counselor. In general, your role should include the following:

1. Know local policies and state laws that pertain to counseling with minors and to guidance and counseling services in schools.
2. Communicate frequently with your principal about your program of services and about the nature of concerns that children bring to you. Although information about particular children is confidential, you generally inform principals of the types of concerns that students are having in school.
3. Inform parents about the school counseling program by making presentations at PTA or PTO meetings, making brochures available, writing a column for the school newspaper, and inviting local media to cover special events in the school during the year. When parents know you and are aware of their child's progress in school, they are more likely to accept confidential relationships between you and their child to some degree.
4. Seek permission from children to involve their parents in the helping process. With young children in elementary and middle schools, the support and involvement of parents is critical in determining the success of a counseling relationship. Young people do not have sufficient control of their lives to make all the decisions necessary for moving the helping process forward. Parent input is essential in most cases. When appropriate, you should encourage children to inform their parents about their concerns and permit you to communicate and involve their parents in the helping relationship. *When a child is in danger, you should inform and involve parents and guardians.* An exception is when the parents or guardians themselves are responsible for the imminent danger, such as child abuse. At these times, you follow local and state regulations for reporting to the proper authorities.
5. Another responsibility you have toward parents is to provide accurate and objective information. When it is appropriate to share information

with parents, you should give an accurate, complete, and unbiased accounting of the situation. Interpreting test data, discussing school policies, and sharing other information reliably and accurately builds parent confidence in you and the school. One cardinal rule is that when you are unsure of the accuracy of data or other sources, say so, and assume responsibility for following up and obtaining the most current and correct information.

Responsibilities to Colleagues and Professional Associates

To provide comprehensive services for students, you work with an array of professionals in the school and community. The degree to which you form successful partnerships with these professionals is a measure of the regard and respect you earn as a counselor. Your relationship with other professionals, beginning with your teaching colleagues, must be beyond reproach, because an effective counseling program cannot exist without sufficient collaboration among all professionals in the school.

Be respectful toward teachers and administrators in your school. Let them know that you hold their profession in high regard and admire them for accepting the challenge of educating all children. Inform teachers and administrators about your role in the school and the ethical guidelines by which you practice. Be open, trustful, accurate, and objective when communicating and consulting with school staff members.

Use the knowledge and expertise of teachers and other professionals to make appropriate decisions in your role as counselor. Teachers, media coordinators, psychologists, social workers, and nurses offer a wide range of expertise and knowledge. By seeking assistance from these professionals, you avoid overextending yourself and the risk of providing services and information beyond your level of competency.

One responsibility inherent in cooperating with others is to be informed about the roles and capabilities of professionals with whom you work. Learn about the other specialists who serve your school and find out about their training and professional skills. Acquire this knowledge as well for professionals outside the school to whom you refer children and families. You have an ethical responsibility to know your referral sources and to seek professionals and agencies that are highly competent, appropriate, and effective with their respective client populations.

Gathering this type of information takes time. One way to begin is to follow up regularly with the referrals you make. Ask children and parents you have referred to other professionals and agencies about the services they have received. Call the referral agency and, if appropriate, ask for a progress report. Base future decisions of whether to continue using various community resources on the follow-up you receive about past referrals.

At all times, your relationship with community agencies and professionals should consider the welfare of the students, parents, and teachers with whom you work in the school. It is improper to place your own personal and professional interests before those of the counselees you serve, particularly when working with referral agencies and professionals in the school and community. The paramount consideration should be: what is best for the client?

Responsibilities to the School and Community

As an employee of the school system, you have certain legal and ethical responsibilities regarding your role as an elementary or middle school counselor. As noted earlier, a working knowledge of the rules and policies governing the school and the counseling program is essential to function appropriately. At the same time, it is imperative to follow these regulations in your practice as a school counselor. You are a representative of the school system and must abide by the rules of the institution.

Ethically, counselors have a responsibility to students first and the school second. At times, you may have conflict between your ethical responsibilities and the regulations mandated by the school. When this happens, point this out to the school administration. By showing your principal, for example, how a school policy is limiting or jeopardizing your effectiveness and ability to function, you may be able to get a regulation changed and have a positive effect on many students. The potential for this type of conflict is another reason to have an open, cooperative relationship with your school administration.

On rare occasion, a school policy that contradicts your ethical standards cannot or will not change, and you will face a difficult professional and career decision. It comes down to two basic questions: Should I continue in this counseling position or resign? If I remain in this position, do I behave against policy to do what I believe to be best for students?

Ethical codes and legal regulations do not always provide us with clear answers. Each case we handle is unique, and policies and laws are always subject to interpretation. Sometimes you might decide that the best and most appropriate action to take is to behave against policy. If so, you risk losing your job. Only you can decide whether this risk is worth taking. As counselors, we encourage our counselees to take risks in their lives and develop their fullest potential. Sometimes we must take risks, too, and heed our own advice.

Responsibilities to the Profession

As a member of the counseling profession, you join thousands of counselors who serve in a variety of settings and institutions. Although these may differ in the populations they serve, their primary mission and the nature of services offered enable their clientele to reach common goals for human development and learning. For this reason, counselors from every area of practice—schools, universities, mental health centers, prisons, hospitals, and other settings—collectively establish a stance and posture by which the general public views the entire counseling profession. All practicing counselors, regardless of the institutions in which they function, have an obligation to behave in the most responsible and ethical manner. At the same time, each counselor also reflects his or her particular counseling area.

The behaviors you choose and the manner in which you function in an elementary or middle school will add to or detract from the credibility and worth of the school counseling profession. This is a notable challenge because everything you do and say will make a positive or negative difference in the way that people view you as a counselor and in their perceptions of your profession. In past works, I have described this challenge as the belief that *everything counts* (Purkey & Schmidt, 1996; Schmidt, 2002). Each personal and professional action, interaction, and decision you make has the potential for either a negative or positive impact on some person or group. Realizing this responsibility and accepting the challenge of behaving in a dependably ethical and knowledgeable manner are the hallmarks of professionalism.

Another avenue for demonstrating your professional responsibility is through the accountability processes you use when assessing your school counseling program. In this book, you have been encouraged to measure what you do and how well you do it in your role as an elementary or middle school counselor. When doing program evaluation, conduct yourself in an ethical manner by collecting data in appropriate ways and reporting results accurately, completely, objectively, and according to acceptable research practices. Counselors who exaggerate outcomes or omit data in an attempt to paint an untrue picture of their program or themselves behave in an irresponsible and unethical manner.

A starting point to plan your professional and program evaluation is by doing a self-examination. An honest self-examination summarizes your strengths and weaknesses in areas of professional knowledge and practice and presents a profile of you as a professional counselor.

Related to an accurate reporting of program evaluation results is the practice of presenting yourself to your clientele and the public in a clear, truthful manner. This means giving accurate information about your training and credentials as well as understanding your level of competence and skills in delivering appropriate services. Misrepresentations about your background and training are improper, and you should immediately correct such information when mistakenly conveyed by yourself or others. For example, if you are introduced to the parent-teachers association as a "certified family counselor" when you hold no such credential, it is your responsibility to correct this information for the audience before beginning your presentation.

Identifying your level of skill and practicing within the boundaries of your competencies are not always as simple as correcting misinformation about your background. For example, in a critical situation you might be the only professional available to help. Due to the immediate circumstance, you must take action quickly. In such cases, you intervene to the best of your ability and seek assistance from more qualified professionals as soon as possible. Behaving in accordance with your level of training and making appropriate referrals are ways of demonstrating responsibility to yourself as a professional.

Responsibilities to Yourself

The ASCA ethical code states that school counselors should function within the boundaries of their professional competence and accept responsibility for the consequences and outcomes of their decisions and actions. Behaving in any other way places you, your counselees, and the institution in physical, emotional, and legal jeopardy. In addition to practicing within your professional limitations, you also want to choose approaches and techniques that have the probability of generating positive outcomes with minimal risk to clients and yourself. You are committed to choose the most beneficial services that will enhance rather than hinder the development of others.

Your behavior in a competent manner demonstrates a high level of self-responsibility and is evident by your commitment to professional development. Keeping abreast of issues in school counseling, attending conferences and workshops, returning to school, and reading professional literature are a few ways to remain current and improve your skills. Chapter Twelve explores in detail some additional approaches to caring for yourself in personal and professional ways.

Thus far, this chapter has reviewed legal and ethical issues to consider when establishing your school counseling services. These considerations are important in establishing a framework for professional practice, but they will not provide clear, precise answers for every situation. Although ethical standards do not supersede the law, legal knowledge is not always sufficient to guide your decisions about the most appropriate course of action to take. Because each case is different and the welfare of the student or other client is paramount, your judgment always plays a pivotal role in legal and ethical issues. The concluding section offers general guidelines to establish your own professional framework for making appropriate decisions and demonstrating sound judgment. Use these suggestions as a guide to develop your own list of ethical standards.

GENERAL GUIDELINES OF ETHICAL PRACTICE

Counselors and other school professionals face ethical and legal decisions daily. As society becomes more complex and challenges facing the school become more pressing, these decisions become more compelling. By establishing your own professional guidelines, you increase your consistency and dependability in the decisions you make and the actions you choose. These qualities lend credibility to your performance as a professional school counselor because students, parents, and teachers come to rely on you and trust your judgment.

Over the years, businesses and industries have searched for appropriate and pragmatic ethical standards. Many businesses have adopted the Four Way Test of the International Rotarian Society for establishing ethical relationships. The four key questions of this test can be adapted to provide a framework for ethical practice in professional counseling as well. Ask yourself the following questions in all your helping relationships:

1. *Am I being truthful?* We have seen that providing accurate information is essential to ethical practice. Counselors who function at the highest level behave genuinely and honestly at all times. They handle information appropriately and respect confidentiality in accordance with ethical guidelines. At times, you may need to withhold information for the protection and welfare of a counselee, but you choose to omit or withhold information only with utmost care and respect for the individual.

2. *Am I being fair to everyone involved?* Fairness is frequently a matter of perception. It is also a condition to assess in examining your own behavior. One way to assure a high degree of fairness is to seek input from everyone involved. By including all parties, you increase the likelihood that people will agree with the decisions made.

3. *Will my actions result in cooperative relationships?* The goal of every helping relationship is to enable people to work jointly toward a common, beneficial goal. In counseling, you have an obligation to establish cooperative relationships with all who are involved in the education process. When you avoid seeking input from others or diminish their contribution to the helping process, you threaten the success of your relationships and damage your credibility.

4. *Are my actions beneficial to all parties?* Every action you take should produce results that enhance human development. Behaviors that demean, degrade, and dehumanize in any way, shape, or form cannot be ethical, responsible actions. In contrast, when you function at the highest level of ethical practice you take every precaution to assure that your behaviors lead to beneficial outcomes for everyone involved, including the school.

In addition to the four key questions of the Rotarian Four Way Test of ethical behavior, there are other considerations to include in your guidelines for professional functioning. These include making your services clearly known, knowing when to refer, understanding the voluntary nature of counseling, following through on cases, understanding your own values, informing parents, seeking appropriate assistance, and caring for yourself personally and professionally. Consider each of these areas of ethical behavior as you develop your program.

Advertising Your Services

In this guide, you are encouraged to be visible as a counselor in your elementary or middle school and advertise who you are and what you do. As you prepare materials for distribution to students, parents, teachers, and other groups, check the accuracy of this information. Counselors who announce their functions and services through appropriate channels and according to ethical standards are careful to describe their role and function clearly and correctly. The brochures you create, the news releases you send out, Web sites you develop, and interviews you give should be carefully prepared and presented so there is little doubt about the services of the school counseling program and your role as the school counselor.

Moreover, you want to present yourself as a professional counselor by accurately describing your level and area of training when requested to give this information. School counselors who are properly trained in their graduate studies have studied a range of human development theories, numerous helping skills and processes, measurement and evaluation theories and techniques, and a variety of other knowledge bases. As a practitioner, you borrow methods and strategies from several disciplines, including human development and learning, sociology, psychology, group dynamics, and educational research. With this broad background of study, you are able to provide many beneficial services in your schools. Yet your expertise and level of competency have limitations, and you should practice within these boundaries. In sum, you know when you have gone far enough.

Knowing When You've Gone Far Enough

How long should you continue seeing a student for individual counseling? I once heard a consultant respond to this question by commenting that a counselor should refer the student if the counseling relationship lasts more than five or six sessions. It is important to set parameters on the duration of your counseling relationships, but I am troubled by simple quantitative responses such as this one. There are many factors to consider in making a decision about how long a counseling relationship should continue and when it is appropriate to refer. In your practice as an elementary or middle school counselor, you want to develop guidelines for making these important and sometimes difficult decisions. Here are a few questions to ask:

1. Do I have the knowledge and skills to help this person explore the problem, examine alternatives, make decisions, and act accordingly?

2. Is there another professional who is better able to help than I am and who is available and accessible to the person needing services?
3. Do I need to involve parents (guardians) in this helping relationship?
4. By seeing this person on a regular basis, am I denying other people services or neglecting other vital functions in my role as a school counselor?
5. Am I making progress with this person and can I show evidence of this progress?

Children in elementary and middle schools often need someone on a regular basis to listen to them and guide them toward appropriate decisions. Not all these children require intensive therapy; they simply need a caring person to be their confidant, ally, and friend. How much time you are able to give to these regular clients is a question only you can answer. The essential factor should be whether the services you provide make a positive difference in the life of a student, in classroom relationships, in educational development, and in the overall function of the school.

Developing guidelines for addressing these questions will help you be consistent in the services you provide. Ask members of your advisory committee for their opinions and suggestions about how to determine the length and duration of your counseling relationships with students. Of course, students also have something to say about this issue based on their level of commitment and voluntary participation in the helping process.

Understanding Volunteerism in Counseling

The notion of "voluntary" counseling has been discussed and examined at length among counselors in all professional settings. The issue is of particular importance in institutions where counselees are a captive audience. Schools are among these institutions because students are required to attend and, in some cases, they are required to receive services. Classroom guidance, orientation services, and annual registration are a few activities that include all students. Individual and group counseling relationships, however, also may be expected for some students who have behavior problems, learning difficulties, or other concerns that inhibit their progress. How you handle these expectations and at the same time respect the rights of students is a measure of your ethical and professional practice.

When students are referred involuntarily for services, the initial steps you take in developing a relationship are critical. It is essential that all students view your assistance as genuine and potentially beneficial for them. In this regard, you should find out what the student would like to see changed in his or her life or in school. As you and the student explore these wishes, you will be able to determine what goals are possible within the scope of the helping relationship. In some cases where students are particularly resistant to your help, it may be necessary to establish a personal relationship before expecting them to accept your professional assistance. If after a reasonable time you are unsuccessful in winning their acceptance, it is appropriate to seek assistance from other professionals.

On rare occasion, students will refuse help, even from the most competent and caring of counselors. A student who does not want to be involved in a helping relationship, who absolutely refuses to participate in any form of a relationship, should not be coerced or pressured to continue. Referral to another professional is an option to consider, but elementary or middle school children may not respond any better to other professionals than they do to you. A second option is to provide indirect services by assisting the parents, teachers, and students in the class. Services such as parent education programs, teacher consultation, and classroom guidance may help others discover new, appropriate behaviors to choose in relating to the child in question. Because of changes on the part of others, the child may begin to make adjustments in his or her views and behaviors. Whatever route you choose, it is important to follow through on all referrals even when the student resists or rejects your assistance.

Following Through

You probably receive many referrals from students, teachers, and parents. By following through on all these referrals, you behave in an ethical manner and you function at an effective level of professional practice. To do so, you must have a good referral system and a process for following up on the cases you receive.

Often the referrals you receive as a counselor are spontaneously made by teachers. You may be walking down the hall, having lunch, or getting your mail in the front office when a teacher says, "I have a student that needs counseling." Because you have many responsibilities and provide services throughout the school, these spontaneous referrals are sometimes difficult to remember. Help yourself and your teachers by keeping a small notebook, "Things to Do," handy during the day. By writing these messages down, you accept responsibility for receiving the referral, which is more efficient than handing teachers a referral form and saying, "I would love to help. Please fill this out." It is also a better way of facilitating professional relationships. Although referral forms have their place, they are not always practical; a notepad will demonstrate to teachers that what they have shared with you is important and that you value their input and time.

Understanding Your Values

Another aspect of helping that relates to ethical practice is a clear understanding and appreciation of your values and their effects on counseling relationships. The ethical code says that counselors should refrain from forcing opinions and values on students and others whom they counsel. Yet it is impossible not to have one's values color and influence personal and professional relationships. At the same time, you also must follow the policies and guidelines established by your school, which has its own set of values.

A few suggestions may help you in handling this value-laden issue. First, know where you stand. A clear understanding of your values helps you assess how others view you and how they perceive the assistance that you offer them. Second, withhold your values and beliefs unless sharing them facilitates the counselee's progress toward a beneficial goal. When you share your beliefs, do so openly and honestly and allow others to disagree. Third, provide several options for the counselee to choose. Encourage students to list as many alternatives as possible, and refrain from judging these options solely on what *you* believe.

When working with students, some values that enter the relationship invariably will be those of their parents. With young children, these family values raise another issue related to ethical practice—the involvement of parents.

Informing Parents

Legal precedent may preclude ethical standards when considering the involvement of parents in counseling relationships with children. As we noted earlier in this chapter, you have an obligation to know your state laws and local policies regarding parent permission. Sometimes there is a delicate balance between your duty to protect the rights of the child and the ethical and legal obligations to honor the rights and responsibilities of parents. In counseling elementary and middle school children, it is good practice to involve the parents or guardians as soon as possible in the helping relationship.

With the exception of instances where imminent danger is apparent and *immediate* notification of authorities and parents is the rule, counseling relationships with school children should eventually include parent (guardian) participation at some level. Children in elementary and middle schools do not control their lives to the extent that adolescents and adults do. For this reason, progress in a helping relationship with young children can be greatly enhanced by the involvement and support of parents. In most cases, children will give you permission to include their parents in the helping process. If possible, children should be involved in planning how to inform their parents and what to tell their parents. By combining forces, counselors and parents can offer children stronger and more consistent support in resolving conflicts and addressing concerns. Parent input is also essential when a decision is needed to refer a child to other services.

Seeking Assistance from Others

Earlier, this book presented those occasions when you will not be able to provide optimal services and must refer students for additional services within or outside the school. To offer these referrals ethically and professionally, you need to know about the agencies and practitioners you are recommending. You also want to give parents the opportunity to select a referral resource if possible.

Avoid giving only one option simply because you think it is the "best" alternative. Keep a file of agencies and professionals in the surrounding community and note which ones provide services to families and children. Follow up with those to whom you refer cases and evaluate the effectiveness of their services. When offering suggestions to parents, give as many options as possible, be open about your impressions of these agencies and professionals, and share results that other families have reported. Then ask parents to choose one they think will meet their needs. At this point, you might ask parents whether they would like assistance in setting up the initial appointment, arranging transportation, or seeking financial aid.

All of the issues and processes presented here will help you make appropriate and ethical decisions as an elementary or middle school counselor. Worksheet 11-1 provides a checklist to follow when you face the most challenging situations and decisions.

WORKSHEET 11-1

Ethical Decision-Making Checklist

____ Identify the issue or problem.
____ Gather essential information.
____ Consider your value system. What do you believe?
____ Understand your responsibilities and obligations.
____ Inform the appropriate people (for example, administrators, teachers, parents).
____ Review ethical guideline(s).
____ Seek consultation.
____ Consider the options and corresponding consequences.
____ Determine best course of action.
____ Take action.
____ Evaluate the outcome.

Caring for Yourself

A final thought on ethical and professional practice relates to your own health and well-being. Counselors who practice at the highest level of professional functioning do so because they take care of themselves. They maintain their physical, mental, and emotional health, which allows them to behave at a highly skilled level. This is extremely important in the counseling profession: take care of oneself so that you can offer appropriate care to others. The final chapter of this survival guide explores this notion of self-care more fully.

chapter 12

HELPING YOURSELF *to* HELP OTHERS

A variety of services and activities constitute a comprehensive school program, and most require a high level of training and skill. Equally important, these functions require counselors to be fit physically, mentally, emotionally, and socially. When you are in top physical form, think highly of yourself and others, behave in a rational manner, and welcome interactions with people, you are in condition to meet the challenges of your profession. You are most able to help students, parents, and teachers effectively when you enhance your own personal well-being and professional development.

Throughout this *Survival Guide,* we have explored together countless ways to organize, plan, and deliver counseling services in schools. These ideas and suggestions have the potential to help you design appropriate services and establish effective helping relationships. This potential is optimally realized when you, as a person and professional, function at the most hopeful, beneficial, and productive level in your own life. To achieve this level of functioning, you begin by helping yourself. Caring for others begins by demonstrating genuine care for oneself.

This final chapter explores the art of caring for oneself. Perhaps it is the most important chapter of this book because to survive as an elementary or middle school counselor you first must endure the challenges of your own life and succeed in your own personal and professional development.

We win the confidence of those we seek to help when they perceive us as capable of helping ourselves. By caring for ourselves, we become capable of extending ourselves and caring for others in authentic ways. This ability to relate with others in thoughtful, understanding, and considerate ways is a hallmark of effective counselors and is more important than any single skill or area of knowledge we possess. Noted author and pioneer in the counseling profession, Gilbert Wrenn (1973) summarized the value of this ability when he wrote, "To me the most striking personal discovery of the past decade has been that people respond to my degree of caring more than to my degree of knowing" (p. 249).

A first step in developing your personal and professional self is to assess where you are at present. As emphasized throughout this guide, effective counseling requires an accurate assessment of people and situations. Similarly, the ability to care for yourself correlates with your knowledge of where you are and where you want to go in life. To assist students, parents, and teachers with the challenges of education and career development, you must have an accurate accounting of your own purpose and direction in life, including your personal relationships and professional goals.

SELF-ASSESSMENT

Successful counselors recognize that they have similar needs and face the same challenges as the students, parents, and teachers who seek their services. When counselors fail to see these similarities, they are unable to assess their personal and professional levels of functioning because they do not know where to begin. They view other people as needing counseling and are blind to their own developmental needs because they are unwilling or unable to assess where they are in their own life.

Numerous formal and informal methods for evaluating and assessing where you are in your own personal and professional development exist. No single method is any better than another. For this reason, a key to accurate self-assessment is to establish guidelines with which to evaluate continually where you are and where you are going in life. Here are a few ideas to get started:

1. *Design self-questionnaires to focus on particular aspects of your development.* Use self-help checklists from magazines and newspapers and adapt them to develop your own assessment sheets. One caveat to note is that most questionnaires and self-assessments found in popular magazines are unscientific instruments. Their validity and reliability as assessment tools are, at best, questionable. For this reason, you should not rely on their scoring procedures. The scores are unimportant. Rather, it is the individual questions on these surveys that are helpful in developing an individual assessment

process. Scoring these questionnaires is not as important as your overall reactions and responses to specific questions. For example, an item that asks, "Do you smoke?" may be assigned a maximum score for poor health, but the score has little meaning if you do not recognize smoking as a personally destructive and inappropriate habit.

2. *Set goals and choose behaviors to improve in areas that will benefit you personally and professionally.* As you set personal and professional goals and continually assess these aims, you are in a stronger position to assist other people in reaching their objectives. But if you are misdirected and disorganized in your life, you are unlikely to achieve credibility and instill confidence in students and others who seek your assistance. Counselors who set and assess their life goals are more inclined to be goal-directed in their professional helping relationships. In addition, they act at a greater level of intentionality, choosing from several alternative behaviors, approaching situations from different points of view, and selecting their helping skills to suit the individual needs of counselees (Schmidt, 2002). Set goals for yourself in both personal and professional arenas.

3. *Monitor the ingredients you put into your plans for success.* Setting goals and making plans are essential steps to achieving personal and professional objectives, but these steps are incomplete unless complemented by beneficial ingredients. You illustrate these ingredients when you express genuine concern for the welfare of others, accept responsibility for your actions, respect individuals, groups, and institutions, and extend your faith and trust toward others. Simply having a plan for action is not enough. Without these beneficial ingredients, plans have the potential to become paths of destruction rather than the helping relationships intended. When you function without high regard for the welfare and well-being of others, you choose behaviors that degrade, demean, and defraud your counselees, yourself, and the counseling profession. To guard against this, always practice in the most ethical manner and consistently monitor the purpose and direction in all your relationships.

4. *Seek input from people whom you trust.* You enhance the accuracy of self-assessment when you include the perceptions of those who know you best. As you evaluate behaviors and goals, ask colleagues and friends to offer their impressions of your performance and the characteristics that help or hinder your relationships. Naturally, a single response from one friend or colleague may not tell much, but if several people offer similar observations, their views are worth considering. Accept these observations, compare them with your perceptions, and make decisions and changes you believe will be worthwhile in your personal and professional development.

From your study of human perception and development, you understand that the human eye is often narrow in scope and distorted in focus. Counselors and other professional helpers know this better than most people. For this reason, you should seek out the perceptions of others, compare these views with your own, and make decisions based on sufficient sources and observations. This process of seeking and accepting input from friends and colleagues contains an element of risk because we do not always like what we hear. In most cases, however, the collective observations you compile from others will validate your beliefs about yourself and enable you to select characteristics and traits you want to change.

5. *Start small and update your plan for personal and professional development on a regular basis.* Choose a few behaviors or traits to target in your plan of action. In addition, select objectives that you can accomplish in a reasonable time. For example, if you want to learn a new skill, set a goal of reading a few articles or books about the technique before you invest time and money to enroll in school or attend a national seminar. Take preliminary steps toward reaching your grandest goals. By doing so, you set up a gradual process of working toward incremental goals and increase the likelihood that you will succeed.

Write your plan down and review it regularly. By writing your goals, you make a personal commitment to yourself. It is much like having a contract, an agreement, with yourself. Goals that are unwritten are easily forgotten and cannot be reviewed with consistency. In contrast, you can erase and alter written plans as needed, but they exist as reminders of the purpose and direction you have chosen in your personal and professional lives. Worksheet 12-1 suggests a contract for your personal and professional goals.

These few starter steps are intended to help you establish a routine for assessing your self-development and taking charge of caring for yourself. Each of these guidelines presents decisions about personal and professional development. Both areas of your development are important. When you take care of your personal development and focus on your professional needs, you are in a better position to reach out and help others.

Sometimes counselors spend so much energy focusing on their professional responsibilities that they neglect their personal welfare. They forget that equal attention to both areas of development is essential. When we neglect our personal well-being, in spite of our attention to professional development, we do not have the physical, emotional, and mental stamina to keep up with the rigorous pace of our helping relationships. Similarly, when we look after our own personal welfare but neglect our professional knowledge and skills, we cannot expect to function at an effective level of counseling practice.

The next two sections focus on the responsibility you have to care for your personal self and assure optimal professional development as an elementary or middle school counselor. Not all the ideas presented in these sections will fit your individual needs and job situation. Choose those that do and discard the others, or save them for a later time. A key to helping yourself develop to optimal personal and professional levels is the belief that you can encourage others to do only what you are willing and able to do

WORKSHEET 12-1

Personal and Professional Goals

During the next _____ days/months, I will accomplish the following goals:

Personal Goals
1. Physical well-being _____
2. Social well-being _____
3. Emotional well-being _____
4. Other goals _____

Professional Goals
1. Intellectual growth _____
2. Skill development _____
3. Collaboration with others _____
4. Other goals _____

yourself. Helping students, parents, and teachers accept change and confront challenges means that you and I, as professional helpers, are willing and able to do likewise. If not, we may need to let others provide the help instead, and spend our energy on our own well-being.

Although personal and professional caring go hand in hand, our own personal development should be considered first. It is through our personal success that we accept professional goals with the confidence that we can accomplish them. Let us now examine more closely this area of personal caring.

PERSONAL CARING

To a large degree, effective helping relationships are dependent on personal interactions between counselors and their clients. For this reason, your own personal strength and success are essential contributors to the outcome of your helping relationships. If you are healthy, physically capable, emotionally stable, and responsible in your social interactions, you are more able to establish and follow through with services than counselors who are frequently in ill health, socially uncomfortable, and emotionally strung out. To maintain a high level of performance in all these areas, take the time and pay attention to your own well-being. Caring for your physical self is an appropriate place to start because bodily health affects emotional and social well-being.

Physical Well-being

How healthy are you? If you have health problems, can you do anything about them? If so, *are* you doing anything about them? As noted earlier in this chapter, an effective counselor is one who takes care of the physical self and establishes a plan and routine to live a healthy life. Counselors who take control of their physical condition and assume responsibility for their health are more likely to be respected and trusted for the professional guidance they offer others. In contrast, counselors who do not take charge of their physical well-being are in a less favorable position to win the trust and confidence of the students, parents, and teachers they aim to help.

There are numerous reports informing us how to live in healthier ways. We read them in newspapers, hear them on radio, see them on television, and learn about them from the Internet. In spite of the abundance of information, many people continue to follow paths of self-destruction with the foods they eat, the beverages they drink, and the drugs and other substances they allow into their bodies. If we eat poorly, drink too much, smoke cigarettes, and take unnecessary medications, we join the legions of people who diminish the value and importance of maintaining a high level of physical health. As a result, we are less likely to reach optimal levels of professional functioning.

To take charge of your physical health, start by doing a quick self-assessment and evaluate your attitudes and behaviors about your physical well-being. Assess where you are and where you are going, and determine whether there are ways to improve your direction and goals in this area of your personal life. Make a checklist to assess your current state of physical health:

1. *Do you take time for exercise or recreation?* Most of what we read today indicates that modest, moderate exercise is beneficial to our physical well-being. Walking a few times a week or exercising a few minutes a day helps us stay in shape. In addition, physical activities such as dancing, playing tennis, riding bicycles, and other programs enhance our stamina and tone our muscles.

Counseling is a demanding profession that often stretches one's patience and endurance to ultimate limits. By being in top physical condition, you are likely to maintain optimal levels of functioning on the job. In elementary and middle schools, this is very important because young children and pre-adolescents have high energy levels, which require durability on the part of teachers, counselors, and administrators.

2. *Do you eat well?* Most Americans love food, and usually the food we adore most is high in fat, sugar, salt, and other deadly ingredients. Counselors who are overweight, underweight, or undernourished usually consume foods that are fatty, high in sugar and salt, and void of any nutritional value.

This type of behavior cannot continue if they expect to be effective helpers, encouraging students and others to take charge of their lives by behaving in responsible and healthy ways.

Balance and moderation are the keys to eating well and enjoying what we eat. By planning and eating nutritiously balanced meals, you allow yourself occasional opportunities to deviate and enjoy snacks or desserts in moderation. If you have purpose and direction in your life, you are able to take command of your eating habits with the same intentionality that you take charge of your counseling program and services.

3. *Do you use unnecessary or illegal drugs?* Do you smoke or drink alcohol excessively? Habitual, self-destructive behaviors contradict the beneficial posture needed to maintain one's physical health. Counselors who take drugs, smoke, and drink to excess choose irresponsible behaviors, both personally and professionally. These destructive behaviors, while taking a physical toll on the body, show little regard for socially acceptable and responsible actions. When counselors and other helpers hold these attitudes, they jeopardize their standing in the community and reflect poorly on the counseling profession.

4. *Do you follow your physician's instructions?* Most people need medical assistance sometimes to care for their physical well-being. When you are under a physician's care, do you follow instructions accordingly? By taking the appropriate medication, watching your diet, getting sufficient rest, and behaving in other responsible ways, you demonstrate commitment to good health and a willingness to take charge of your life.

Visiting dentists, physicians, and other health care providers to assess one's physical development and well-being are part of an overall plan for healthful living. These visits do not take the place of your own responsibility to have an appropriate plan of self-care. For example, making regular appointments at a health clinic does not relieve you of the responsibility to eat well, exercise, stay active, and treat your physical self with utmost care and respect.

Caring for your physical self in responsible ways enables you to elevate your emotional self to an optimal level of functioning. In many ways, our emotional selves are related so closely to our physical well-being that it is impossible to determine whether either is more important, or which one should receive our attention first. Sometimes people ignore their physical health because emotionally they are so distraught or incapacitated that they have little regard for their own welfare. In contrast, we sometimes ignore our physical well-being because we are so emotionally committed to enabling others to reach their optimal potential. For this reason, emotional well-being is another area to consider as we assess our degree of personal caring and development.

Emotional Well-being

Being emotionally and psychologically healthy means thinking about yourself and relating with others in beneficial and constructive ways. By maintaining your emotional health, you demonstrate a high regard for yourself and others, respect for your capabilities and limitations, and responsibility for your own behavior.

Self-responsibility is critical to your emotional health, especially in your role as a professional counselor. In school, where there are many demands on you to perform and resolve problems, daily pressures can be tremendous. Understanding your role, knowing your strengths, and accepting your limitations enable you to handle these job pressures. In addition to achieving this level of self-knowledge and maintaining your physical health as emphasized earlier, you are able to focus on a few key behaviors for developing and caring for your emotional well-being. The first of these behaviors is to avoid blame.

Avoiding Blame

With so much going on in elementary and middle schools and so many people concerned about the welfare of children, mistakes will happen on occasion. At these times, when feelings run high and situations are critical, some people will try to place blame elsewhere. Counselors who are emotionally healthy avoid the issue of blame and instead seek to find alternative solutions and new directions that enable people and programs to move forward. In this way, we are more concerned about correcting a situation than punishing those who are to blame.

At the same time, emotionally healthy counselors accept responsibility for their own actions and encourage others to do likewise. We do not accept blame or responsibility for actions over which we have no control. When we do assume responsibility, we monitor our own physical and emotional stress to make appropriate decisions.

Handling Stress

Sometimes life is hectic and stressful, but we can plan measures and take action to handle it in appropriate ways. Identifying stressful factors, learning relaxation techniques and other stress-reducing approaches, and seeking assistance from others are a few ways that you can take responsibility for your emotional well-being in stress-related situations. A first step is to identify negative factors in your life and measure how they are contributing to your level of stress. Many questionnaires and checklists are available to help you with this assessment. Generally, there are broad areas of health and behaviors to examine. As mentioned before, any single checklist or indicator produces only one factor to consider. In evaluating stress factors in your life and on the job, the following indicators and questions may help you:

1. *Physical.* Have you have been experiencing unusual and disturbing symptoms lately? These might include muscle tension and pain, dizziness, nervousness, skin rashes, headaches, stomach problems, fatigue, excessive sweating, chest pains, loss of appetite or excessive eating, high blood pressure, back pain, frequent illnesses, general sick feeling, or sexual problems.
2. *Behavioral.* Have some of your behaviors changed recently? Do you have difficulty falling asleep at night, get confused easily, lack concentration at work, delay making decisions, forget things frequently, get angry over minor inconveniences, become impatient with yourself or others, find yourself preoccupied, have frequent accidents, smoke or drink heavily, experience frequent nightmares, or have regular arguments at work or home?
3. *Emotional.* Have you wondered about your state of mind lately? Are you overly concerned with what people think about you or your performance as a counselor? Do you feel "hyper" much of the time, show your frustration easily, become depressed frequently, act impulsively without much thought, avoid being with other people, feel overwhelmed with responsibility, cry for no apparent reason, get irritated often, worry about things, or have wide mood swings?

Each of us experiences these behaviors and feelings on occasion. When they become a major force in our lives, however, they inhibit us from developing in healthy ways and performing our duties in an effective manner. Occasionally, situations become so intense that we may not understand the stress we are experiencing. When this happens and we feel we are losing control, it is time to seek assistance from others.

Seeking Support

You have learned in this guide that competent counselors have a clear understanding of their knowledge and skills and at the same time recognize their limitations. You demonstrate your own competency by achieving this level of self-knowledge and understanding, and knowing when to seek assistance for yourself. Because we are highly trained in human development and helping processes, we sometimes forget that counselors might also need assistance on occasion. We are not immune to the tragedies and traumas of life. Understanding this and willingly asking for help when we are suffering, experiencing a crisis, or simply standing still in our personal or professional development is a hallmark of survival.

It is helpful to identify trustworthy colleagues in whom you can confide when you need support. Teachers, administrators, and others whose judgment you respect are excellent sources of comfort and guidance. These people might not be professionally trained counselors, but they are a valuable resource when you need assistance. They also may be the first step in your search for professional counseling when you face critical concerns in your life.

Taking Time Alone

It helps to spend time alone occasionally in moments of self-reflection, meditation, and rest. Being an active counselor, reaching out to others on a continuous basis, and implementing a rigorous schedule of program activities can be exhaustive. Planning time to be alone in quiet activity allows you to recharge your batteries, examine personal and professional goals, make decisions about new directions, and adjust your plans accordingly.

By taking time and doing things for our own benefit, we demonstrate value for our personal well-being. A solitary walk, a good book, peaceful music, and countless other opportunities exist for us to take stock of our lives, get in touch with ourselves, and evaluate who we are and where we are going.

During the school day, which is often filled with scheduled services and critical situations, set aside a few brief moments to be alone and gather your thoughts. Assess the day's progress thus far and prepare for the remaining events. These times of reflection enable you to check your perceptions and make adjustments to meet the professional challenges that lie ahead. In this way, you strengthen your commitment to interact in beneficial ways with others and are prepared to enter worthwhile social relationships. This brings us to a third area of healthful living—your social well-being.

Social Well-being

People are not meant to be alone. We need the company of others. Sharing experiences and celebrating life are vital elements in the process of caring for one's personal self. Counselors and other helping professionals have a particular obligation to nurture and care for their social well-being because through this process of social acceptance they develop trusting relationships. When we are aloof and distant, we discourage people from approaching us openly and honestly. At the same time, we thwart our own development by limiting social interactions and thereby narrowing the scope of our perceptions. Such a narrow field of vision reduces the alternatives available for us to take positive action as helping persons. As noted earlier, you should not restrict yourself to one approach or style of helping others. Rather, it is better to broaden your options in providing appropriate care.

Another danger that exists when we limit social interactions is the possibility of our tolerance of human difference and uniqueness becoming restrained. It is difficult to accept people who are culturally different, physically challenged, or behaviorally eccentric when we have had little exposure or contact with the variance of human existence in the world today. Elementary and middle school counselors who care for their social well-being willingly join others in the celebration of life and form beneficial relationships with a wide audience of students, parents, and teachers. In this way, by focusing on your social well-being you raise the level of your professional functioning.

Chapter Nine explores ways to build social and professional relationships with teachers and others in the school. A review and expansion of these ideas will help you focus on your social well-being:

- Volunteer in the community. Civic organizations provide valuable assistance to children, families, and schools. By joining these groups, you increase your visibility as a school counselor and enhance opportunities for social interaction.
- Identify social groups that pursue hobbies and activities of interest to you. If you enjoy playing bridge, making crafts, boating, or other activity, locate a group in the community that shares your interest. If no group exists, start one and invite other people to join with you!
- Initiate contacts with students and teachers who are new to your school. Learn about their backgrounds. Invite them to lunch and socialize with them in other ways to demonstrate your availability.
- Plan special events. Ask a group of students, parents, and teachers to organize special celebrations during the year. These can coincide with national celebrations, such as Thanksgiving, or can be unique to your school, such as an annual talent show or a "Founder's Day" to remember the historical beginnings of the school.
- Search and deliver. In every school, there are people, students and teachers, who are alone and lonely. See what you can do to identify people who would benefit from a kind invitation, and deliver one to them! Purkey and Novak (1996) presented a variety of ideas for sending positive messages in their book *Inviting School Success,* and Purkey and Stanley (1997) presented a treasury of inviting ideas to use in schools. Use these and similar resources to learn about sending beneficial messages and invitations to persons in your school.

Caring for one's personal self is the first step toward professional development. By focusing on your physical, emotional, and social well-being, you place yourself in a strong position to elevate your professional functioning, the ultimate goal of all counselors. To achieve this ultimate goal you also must care for yourself in professional ways.

PROFESSIONAL CARING

At the beginning of this *Survival Guide,* you read that its purpose was to offer practical ideas and strategies to assist you in becoming an effective elementary or middle school counselor. The introduction optimistically offered the contents as an opportunity for you to move beyond survival and toward a higher level of functioning as a professional. Throughout the chapters of this book, many ideas and suggestions have encouraged you to choose approaches that fit your personal style and professional setting. These ideas and the encouragement offered are contingent on your willingness and ability to plan programs and deliver appropriate services. To do so, you must establish a functional level of professional knowledge and competence. In sum, you must care for your professional development with the same intent and commitment that you care for your personal well-being. This level of caring begins with your knowledge of counseling and related areas of human development.

Intellectual Development

Counseling in schools presents a continuing challenge influenced by changing educational, social, and cultural factors. To meet these challenges requires a high level of training and a commitment to continue your education throughout your career. The training you received in your graduate studies laid a foundation upon which to build an expanding knowledge for future practice.

School counselors who believe that their formal graduate studies, at the master's, advanced, and doctoral levels, are sufficient to meet the ever-present concerns and issues of students and schools today are mistaken. Changing family structures, evolving sexual attitudes, debilitating substance and alcohol abuse, and advancing technologies and scientific discoveries, among other changes, require up-to-date knowledge and information on the part of all of us. An expanding knowledge base allows you to make intelligent choices about appropriate approaches, techniques, and strategies to support student development, encourage parent involvement, and enhance teacher performance in your school.

As noted in Chapter Eleven, a first step is to assess what you know and how well prepared you are. By assessing your knowledge and skills, you are committed to pursue learning and enrich your professional development. Some activities to include in your continuing quest for intellectual and professional development are returning to school, attending workshops, and reading.

Returning to School

Contact universities and colleges in your locale and see whether they have counselor education programs or other areas of study to continue your education. Courses in psychology, family relations, child development, counseling, and a host of other disciplines will keep you informed about the latest research and developments in your profession.

Attending Workshops

Look for announcements about upcoming workshops and seminars that present information for your school counseling program. Sometimes community workshops sponsored by health agencies, churches, and other groups offer valuable information for counselors and teachers. Professional organizations, such as your state school counselor association, are excellent resources for these types of experiences. By joining state and local organizations, you place your name on mailing lists to receive current announcements about educational opportunities.

Reading

Counseling is a young and emerging profession. It is also a profession that, as noted earlier, embraces a number of disciplines and knowledge bases. Hence, the literature for school counseling is expansive. To stay current, you will want to read from a wide range of sources, including the counseling journals, books on professional helping and self-development, and scientific resources on discoveries about human development and learning. As a counselor who practices in a school setting, you may want to subscribe to educational journals and magazines to keep up with trends in the teaching profession.

In addition to these professional readings, you also will benefit from learning about trends in child behavior, cultural changes in society, and scientific advancement through magazines, newspapers, recordings, and other media. You might want to subscribe to one or more of the popular magazines read by children and preteens. By reading their literature, you stay in tune with fashion, music, television, and other trends that influence juvenile behavior. In this way, you enhance your ability to communicate with these students.

Returning to school, enrolling in online or distance education courses, attending workshops, and reading a wide range of information are a few ways to care for your professional self. By keeping abreast of professional, social, and cultural trends, you strengthen relationships with students, parents, and teachers and raise your level of professional competency.

Counselor Competence

Because counseling is an emerging profession and its primary focus is to assist people in their development, the necessary and essential competencies inherent to the profession are continuously under examination. This evaluation process occurs across the profession and with individual counselors as well. The suggestions offered in this chapter about returning to school, attending workshops, and reading a wide range of information can help you monitor your level of professional competence and expand your knowledge base. In addition, two areas of functioning, echoed throughout this guide, will enable you to care for yourself professionally. These two areas are scheduling time and being accountable.

Scheduling Time

Throughout this chapter you have been encouraged to take time to enhance and enrich your personal and professional development. In reading many of the suggestions offered, you may have wondered, *Where do I get all this extra time?* If so, you have probably realized that there is no "extra time" because each of us has the same amount. We all would like to have more time but, truthfully, we are not going to get any more than the twenty-four hours a day allotted to each of us. Successful counselors understand this reality, yet they are able to balance their personal and professional lives by using their allotted time efficiently.

As noted earlier in this guide, no single element is more important to a successful counseling program than the appropriate use of time. This is particularly true when you serve large student populations, more than one school, or communities hindered by low economic development, crime, drug use, and other debilitating social factors. In addition to the suggestions given in Chapter Two for balancing your school counseling program, here are ten "time-controllers" to increase your efficiency:

1. *Make the call.* Counselors, like umpires and referees, frequently face tough decisions. Time is critical. When confronting timely decisions, list the most viable options and the pros and cons of each choice. Examine your list, focus on major points, and choose one of the alternatives. Do not put off your decision.
2. *Strive for imperfection.* A common stumbling block for many of us is the desire to excel. We sometimes think that if we cannot do it perfectly, it would be best not to do it at all. Avoid this pitfall by planning your tasks in phases. Set short-term goals and time limits to accomplish major projects. Aim for completion rather than perfection. On the one hand, a perfect project, never started, can never be completed. On the other hand, an imperfect, completed project can always be improved.
3. *Remain underwhelmed.* Because we serve so many audiences and have such broad responsibilities in schools, it is easy to become saviors to everyone and for everything. Keep control of your time; use resourceful faculty, students, and parent volunteers to assist with services. Practice saying "No, thank you." When your plate is full, let people know you can take no more until you have finished what you have started.
4. *Reinforce yourself.* Attack the task you like the least and stay with it for a predetermined amount of time. You may surprise yourself in completing it before the time is up. Give yourself a reward when you finish these and other tasks. A two-minute walk around the school grounds, a brief encounter with a jump rope on the playground, a cup of tea with

teachers in the lounge, and other rewards are simple ways of congratulating yourself on a job well done.

5. *Arrange your space.* Neatness may count, but it is not as important as organization. Keep materials you use most often in an accessible location so you do not waste time searching for these essential, frequently used items.

6. *Pad your memory.* Keep a small notepad on your desk or in your pocket and write down tasks that you think of during the day. By having this list, you avoid spending time trying to remember, *What was that important thing I was going to do today?*

7. *Cluster your tasks.* Group your tasks during the day so similar and related ones can happen at the same time. For example, if you need to do follow-up phone calls to parents and agencies, make all your calls in one block of time. Set aside ten minutes, a half-hour, or whatever you need, and make the calls during that time at one sitting.

8. *Write down your goals.* Planning is a well-intended process, but unless you write down your major goals, you are less likely to accomplish them. Spend a few minutes at the end of each day writing down your major tasks for tomorrow. Rank these tasks in order of importance and schedule time to accomplish each one. When you run out of time and tasks remain, carry them over to the next day.

9. *Access technology.* Use computers and other technology to assist in delivering services efficiently. Word processing, computer-assisted learning, the Internet, video-taped instruction, and other programs can be used to broaden services in the school.

10. *Keep an accurate accounting.* Maintain a calendar of your appointments and your daily plans. A good calendar not only helps you use time efficiently but also is an excellent resource for being accountable.

Being Accountable

Chapter Three discusses the importance of evaluating your program of services and how accountability is essential to future program development and your credibility with the school staff. You exemplify professional accountability by the consistency and dependability with which you behave in a responsible way. How you spend your time, the effectiveness of your services, the attitudes and behaviors you exhibit in the school and community, and the regard you demonstrate for yourself and others are a few of the countless ways accountability is measured. Here are some ideas for strengthening your professional accountability:

1. *Watch your image.* Your reputation precedes you. All that you do on behalf of others in the school and community creates the image that people have of you as a professional and of school counseling in general.

2. *Be accurate.* Always give accurate information. When in doubt, say so, and research the question thoroughly before responding. People will respect your honesty and admire your conscientious effort.

3. *Keep your promises.* Follow through on commitments made to students, parents, and teachers. If you know there will be a problem in keeping a commitment, let people know immediately. Excuses may help you save face, but when relied on too frequently they paint a picture of undependability.

4. *Follow up.* Keep in touch with people who seek your assistance. Stop by and check on students who have seen you in the beginning of the year, send notes to teachers and ask them about concerns shared with you earlier, call parents and look in on the home front. In addition, make occasional contact with professionals in the community who have provided effective services to your students and families. They will appreciate hearing from you.

5. *Take the high road.* Courtesy and civility are two essential hallmarks of professional counselors. Treat everyone with high regard and respect, regardless of their status or their attitude toward you. A true professional never stoops to the ranks of the malcontent. Counselors who reach the peak of professional performance and accountability always maintain a posture of optimism, trust, respect, and intentionality (Schmidt, 2002).

CONCLUSION

School counselors offer a variety of skills and a broad area of knowledge with which to help students, parents, and teachers establish beneficial relationships. Elementary and middle school counselors are in an ideal situation to enable students to achieve a solid beginning in their educational, personal, and social development. As a member of this profession, you have accepted this challenge.

This resource is a guide to help you survive as well as flourish in the exciting profession of school counseling. It offers ideas for establishing comprehensive school counseling programs, organizing efficient services, reaching out to special populations, handling crisis situations, relating to students, parents, and teachers, and caring for yourself as a person and counselor. Although all the ideas in this book may not suit your needs or fit your setting, they might help you discover or create more appropriate and practical ideas for yourself and your program. If so, the purpose of this *Survival Guide* has been served.

You have chosen a most rewarding profession as an elementary or middle school counselor. The success you experience and the rewards you receive will be largely dependent on your ability to help yourself help others. Those of us who are able and willing to help ourselves are most likely to be able and willing to help others. By taking time to read and use this book as well as other resources to give strength and direction to your professional development, you have demonstrated a willingness to help yourself. I commend you for this effort and for your positive regard for the counseling profession.

Thank you for accepting my invitation to explore "survival" as an elementary or middle school counselor. I wish you all the best as you move toward becoming a flourishing school counselor. May you have continued success in your personal and professional development throughout life.

Resources

BIBLIOGRAPHY

Allan, J., & Anderson, E. (1986). Children and crises: A classroom guidance approach. *Elementary School Guidance and Counseling, 21,* 143–149.

American School Counselor Association (1998). *Ethical standards.* Alexandria, VA: Author.

Association for Supervision and Curriculum Development (1955). *Guidance in the curriculum.* Washington, D.C.: Author.

Bello, G. (1989). Counseling handicapped students: A cognitive approach. *The School Counselor, 36,* 298–304.

Bloom, J. W., & Walz, G. R. (Eds.). (2000). *Cybercounseling and cyberlearning: Strategies and resources for the millennium.* Alexandria, VA: American Counseling Association.

Bonnington, S. B. (1993). Solution-focused brief therapy: Helpful interventions for school counselors. *The School Counselor, 41,* 126–128.

Bowman, R. (1987). *Test buster pep rally.* Minneapolis, MN: Educational Media Corporation.

Bowman, R. P. (1986). The magic counselor: Using magic tricks as tools to teach children guidance lessons. *Elementary School Guidance and Counseling, 21,* 128–138.

Bruce, M. A. (1995). Brief counseling: An effective model for change. *The School Counselor, 42,* 353–363.

Bruce, M. A., & Hooper, G. C. (1997). Brief counseling versus traditional counseling: A comparison of effectiveness. *The School Counselor, 44,* 171–184.

Campbell, D. (1990). *If you don't know where you're going, you'll probably end up someplace else* (Rev. ed.). Allen, TX: Thomas More.

Canter, L., & Canter, M. (1992). *Assertive discipline: Positive behavior management for today's classroom.* Santa Monica, CA: Canter and Associates.

Clemente, R., & Collison, B. B. (2000). The relationships among counselors, ESL teachers, and students. *Professional School Counseling, 3,* 339–348.

Coy, D. R. (2001). *Bullying.* ERIC/CASS Digest. Greensboro, NC. ERIC/CASS Clearinghouse. (ED459405)

Davis, T. E., & Osborn, C. J. (2000). *The solution-focused school counselor: Shaping professional practice.* Philadelphia, PA: Accelerated Development.

de Shazer, S. (1991). *Putting difference to work.* New York: Norton.

Dreikurs, R., & Grey, L. (1993). *New approach to discipline: Logical consequences.* East Rutherford, NJ: Plume.

Glasser, W. (1992). *The quality school: Managing students without coercion.* (2nd ed.) New York: HarperCollins.

Good, T. L., & Brophy, J. E. (1994). *Looking in classrooms* (6th ed.). New York: Harper Collins.

Gordon, T. (2000). *Parent effectiveness training.* New York: Three Rivers Press.

Lumsden, L. (2002). *Preventing bullying.* ERIC Digest. Eugene, OR: ERIC Clearinghouse. (ED463563)

Maultsby, M. C. (1986). Teaching rational self-counseling to middle grades. *The School Counselor, 33,* 207–219.

Morrow, G., (1987). *The compassionate school: A practical guide to educating abused and traumatized children.* Englewood Cliffs, NJ: Prentice Hall.

Myrick, R. (1997). *Developmental guidance and counseling: A practical approach* (3rd ed.). Minneapolis, MN: Educational Media Corporation.

Myrick, R. P., & Bowman, R. (1991). *Children helping children: Teaching students to become friendly helpers* (Revised ed.). Minneapolis, MN: Educational Media Corporation.

Pedersen, P. (2000). *A handbook for developing multicultural awareness* (3rd ed.). Alexandria, VA: American Counseling Association.

Pedersen, P. (2002). Ethics, competence, and other professional issues in culture-centered counseling. In P. Pedersen et al., *Counseling across cultures* (5th ed.). Thousand Oaks, CA: Sage Publications.

Purkey, W. W. (1970). *Self-concept and school achievement.* Englewood Cliffs, NJ: Prentice Hall.

Purkey, W. W., & Novak, J. M. (1996). *Inviting school success* (3rd. ed.). Belmont, CA: Wadsworth.

Purkey, W. W., & Schmidt, J. J. (1996). *Invitational counseling: A self-concept approach to professional helping.* Pacific Grove, CA: Brooks/Cole.

Purkey, W. W., & Stanley, P. H. (1997). *The inviting school treasury: 1001 ways to invite student success.* Greenville, NC: Brookcliff.

Purkey, W. W., & Strahan, D. B. (2002). *Inviting positive classroom discipline.* Westerville, OH: National Middle School Association.

Range, L. M., Campbell, C., Kovac, S. H., Marion-Jones, M., Aldridge, H., Kogos, S., & Crump, Y. (2002). No-suicide contracts: An overview and recommendations. *Death Studies, 26,* 51–74.

Range, L. M., & Knott, E. C. (1977). Twenty suicide assessment instruments: Evaluation and recommendations. *Death Studies, 21,* 25–58.

Roberts, W. B., & Morotti, A. A. (2000). The bully as victim: Understanding bully behaviors to increase the effectiveness of interventions in the bully-victim dyad. *Professional School Counseling, 4,* 148–155.

Rogers, J. R., Lewis, M. M., Subich, L. M. (2002). Validity of the Suicide Assessment Checklist in an emergency crisis center. *Journal of Counseling & Development, 80,* 493–502.

Satz, M. (1989). Balancing a middle school counseling program: A potpourri of ideas. *American Middle School Education, 12*(3), 59–65.

Schmidt, J. J. (1997). *Making and keeping friends: Ready-to-use lessons, stories, and activities for building relationships.* San Francisco, CA: Jossey-Bass.

Schmidt, J. J. (2002). *Intentional helping: A philosophy for proficient caring relationships.* Columbus, OH: Merrill/Prentice Hall.

Schmidt, J. J. (2003). *Counseling in schools: Essential services and comprehensive programs* (4th ed.). Boston, MA: Allyn and Bacon.

Schmidt, J. J., & Medl, W. A. (1983). Six magic steps of consulting. *The School Counselor, 30,* 212–215.

Shore, K. (1999). Success for ESL students. *Instructor, 110*(6), 30–33.

Stanard, R. P. (2000). Assessment and treatment of adolescent depression and suicidality. *Journal of Mental Health Counseling, 22,* 204–217.

Sue, D. (1978). Counseling across cultures. *Personnel and Guidance Journal, 56,* 451.

Thompson, C., & Rudolph, L. (2003). *Counseling children* (6th ed.). Belmont, CA: Wadsworth.

Wallerstein, J. (1983). Children of divorce: The psychological tasks of the child. *American Journal of Orthopsychiatry, 53,* 230–243.

Winston, S. (1991). *Getting organized: The easy way to put your life in order* (Rev. ed.). New York: Warner Books.

Wittmer, J. (Ed.) (2000). *Managing your school counseling program: K-12 developmental strategies* (2nd ed.). Minneapolis, MN: Educational Media Corporation.

Wrenn, C. G. (1973). *The world of the contemporary counselor.* Boston: Houghton Mifflin.

WEB SITES

This resource list includes many Web sites that may be helpful to elementary and middle school counselors. Care has been taken to list only sites that have been reviewed, but you must use appropriate caution when ordering and purchasing materials from any Internet site. Neither the author nor publisher endorses any product or information presented on the sites listed here. This resource list presents examples of how counselors can access information over the Internet. There are seemingly limitless Web sites with helpful information, yet caution is necessary. Every school counselor who uses the Internet has professional and ethical responsibility to ensure the accuracy and appropriateness of information obtained when offering it as a resource to students, parents, and teachers.

The Web sites are organized by chapters, but several sites may have information that pertains to more than one chapter.

Chapters 1 and 2

http://www.schoolcounselor.org

The American School Counselor Association is the primary professional organization for school counselors. This site includes the National Model for School Counseling, legislative links, publications, and ASCA's definition of comprehensive counseling programs.

http://www.counseling.org

The American Counseling Association is the parent organization for all professional counselors. This site offers valuable information about research, ethics, certification, and counselor roles and responsibilities.

http://www.sagecraft.com/puppetry/

The Puppetry Home Page is a free resource for information about the world of puppetry.

http://www.puppeteers.org/index.html

Puppeteers of America, Inc., is a nonprofit organization founded in 1937.

Ericcass.uncg.edu/digest/2001–07.html

A research site to find articles about leading and managing comprehensive school counseling programs.

Chapter 3

http://www.cnw.com/~deets/guidance.htm

This site offers information about educational, personal, social, and career development, and includes counselor planning, curriculum, community, and services related to school counseling.

http://www.invitationaleducation.net/

The International Alliance for Invitational Education is a not-for-profit organization. Members are an international network of professional helpers who seek to apply the concepts of invitational education to their personal and professional lives.

http://aac.ncat.edu/documents/atsc-cmptncy.htm

This site offers resources and information on competencies in assessment and evaluation for school counselors.

http://middleweb.com

This site presents models and articles related to middle school issues, including transitions, time management, advising, social support, character education, discipline, leadership, and student mentoring.

http://www.peerhelping.org/

This is the National Peer Helper Association Web site.

http://www.peer.ca/peerprograms.html

Mentors Peer Resources is a source for examples of effective peer programs designed for grades K–12.

http://nbcc.org

This is the site for the National Board for Certified Counselors.

http://guidancechannel.com

The Guidance Channel is a very broad site addressing issues and providing information related to school counseling.

Chapter 4

http://www.nasbe.org

National Association of State Boards of Education presents research and articles surrounding educational issues, assessment, and lifelong learning.

http://www.clcrc.com

The Cooperative Learning Center offers information about cooperative learning theory, procedures, implementation, and research. This site includes a question and answer board for issues related to cooperative learning.

http://www.asgw.educ

The site of the Association for Specialists in Group Work focuses on group counseling issues of training, diversity, best practices, professional development, counseling environments, special populations, and research.

http://www.racc-research.org

The Research and Assessment Corporation for Counseling, Inc., addresses current research, global issues, future trends in counseling, promotion of research, research guidelines, and grants in counseling.

Chapter 5

http://aac.ncat.edu

The Association for Assessment in Counseling's site offers information on counseling developments, general testing information, tester responsibilities, multicultural assessments, and testing ethics. This site also provides a test locator, test reviews, testing articles, and links to other testing databases.

http://www.qualityschools.com/

The Quality Schools Web site presents the principles of Dr. William Glasser's Choice Theory and suggests practical applications for schools.

http://www.nasdse.org

The National Association of State Directors of Special Education provides information on testing, laws, reporting, and interpreting tests related to special education students. This site also offers a discussion board.

http://www.unl.edu/buros/

The Oscar and Luella Buros Center for Testing site offers test reviews, test finders, and sales, in addition to providing information on development and evaluation, recognition and accreditation, history, and research studies.

Chapters 6 and 7

http://www.schoolpsychology.net

School Psychology Resources Online offers resources related to disabilities, special education laws, parenting of children with disabilities, assessment, evaluation, teaching ideas for the disabled, and behavior intervention strategies. This site also has information about suicide.

http://wwwamcd-aca.org

> Site for the Association for Multicultural Counseling and Development.

http://www.counseling.org/consumers

> This ACA site focuses on crises in school with facts and ways to cope with trauma. The site provides a national 800 number crisis help line to access local resource guides for information and services to help manage crises.

Chapter 8

http://time2act.org

> Time 2 Act is a site that focuses on a variety of concerns that commonly arise in middle school. Some of the key topics are eating disorders, illnesses, abuse, violence, cliques, cults, gangs, health and nutrition, minority issues, parenting, and teen pregnancy. This site is a good resource for informational articles and additional links to related topics.

http://www.allkidsgrieve.org

> All Kids Grieve is a site addressing childhood grief through curriculum support and group counseling.

http://www.etr.org/recap

> The Resource Center for Adolescent Pregnancy Prevention presents "programs that work," which target male and female at-risk sexual behavior, sexually transmitted diseases (STDs), and pregnancy prevention. Service learning programs, peer education programs, research, and programs directed at making choices are also included.

http://www.health.org/kidsarea/

> U.S. Department of Health and Human Services and Samhsa's National Clearinghouse for Alcohol and Drug Information is a site directed at children in grades three to eight to learn about substance abuse and parents with alcoholism. The site contains games and activities. The site is also in Spanish.

http://www.ncsu.edu/cpsv

> The Center for the Prevention of School Violence in North Carolina provides useful articles, Internet links, counseling tools, parent resources, and alternative-learning information related to school violence.

http://www.unitedway.org

> The United Way publishes community resource guides for counties across the country. Once on this site, you can enter your county and access all available agencies, services, resources, and programs in the local area.

http://www.renew.net

The Renew Center for Personal Recovery focuses on issues dealing with crises, setting up crisis prevention plans, and response training. The site provides access to current programs.

Chapter 9

http://www.counseling.org/enews

The American Counseling Association's electronic journal can be used to locate articles related to working with teachers and administrators, enhancing counseling outcomes, and parenting. New articles regularly focus on issues central to school counseling.

Chapter 10

http://www.npin.org

The National Parents Information Network (NPIN) is an information site for parents on all education related topics. The site also has a question and answer board.

http://www.ncpie.org

The National Coalition for Parent Involvement in Education is focused on developing partnerships and resources for parents, families, school personnel, and the community to work with the disabled.

Chapter 11

http://www.counseling.org/resources/ethics.htm

The American Counseling Association site posts the complete ACA Code of Ethics, standards of practice, a guide to ethics, information regarding processing complaints, references, and answers to frequently asked questions.

http://www.schoolcounselor.org

The American School Counselor Association site posts information regarding ethical standards of school counselors, ethical roles and responsibilities of school counselors, and the roles of paraprofessionals in school counseling programs.

http://www.edlaw.net

Edlaw, LLC, and the Edlaw Center address developing legal issues in counseling, school records, special laws, and laws regarding students with disabilities. This site also includes an electronic library on related legal and ethical issues.

Chapter 12

http://www.guidancechannel.com

The Guidance Channel offers a general database with a wealth of information related to all aspects of counseling, including professional development and team building.

http://www.education-world.com

Education World provides access to seemingly endless information on counseling and related topics. There are links to many counseling databases to locate articles and information concerning all areas of counseling. Education World also offers a link to the U.S. State Department of Education to access information on all the schools and universities, government educational agencies, and educational organizations in the country. In addition, Education World provides a counseling-specific discussion board.

Index

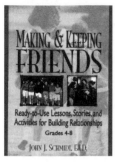

Making & Keeping Friends: Ready-to-Use Lessons, Stories, and Activities for Building Relationships, Grades 4–8

John J. Schmidt, Ed.D.

ISBN: 0-7879-6626-6

Paperback/ 265pages/ 1997

Making and Keeping Friends places in your hands a proven, ready-to-use curriculum for group discussion and guidance lessons dealing with friendship, conflict resolution, and self-development. This program gives your students a specific framework and language for examining their own behaviors and developing healthy relationships. Organized into nine sections, each focuses on important ideas about inviting friendships.

The book presents a specific process for creating and developing relationships, and places responsibility on the individual student to create "messages" that invite friendships. It shows students, step by step, how to form strong, lasting friendships by being more inviting toward themselves and toward others.

The material in the book is divided into nine sections, which include more than 70 activity sheets and role-play scripts to accompany each lesson. The sections are:

- Understanding Friendship

- Becoming Friends

- Learning About Invitations

- Four Levels of Encouraging or Discouraging Friendship

- Knowing Yourself

- Creating Invitations to Friendships

- Making Choices & Resolving Differences

- Choosing Positive Behaviors

- Sending Yourself Invitations

As a further help, each section begins with Group Leader Instructions, including an overview, objectives, and a description of the activities, role-plays, and special vocabulary used. "Gold Nugget" ideas throughout the program help stimulate student discussion about friendship, and simple cartoons bring life to ideas about inviting and disinviting behaviors.

Life Skills: 225 Ready-to-Use Health Activities for Success and Well-Being (Grades 6–12)

Sandra McTavish

ISBN: 0-7879-6959-1

Paperback/ 288 pages/ 2003

"Teachers of middle or high school health and physical education will find this book an excellent resource for developing classroom activities and generating class discussion."

— **Stephen C. Jefferies, publisher,** *Today's Physical Education Online*

"It is clear that McTavish understands the adolescent mind and the needs of this diverse group of learners. Her text will support educators who want to reach adolescent learners with curricular inventions that promote life knowledge and life skills, key requisites of success and well-being."

— **J.R. Bruce Cassie, head of the Northeastern Ontario Field Centre and associate professor, University of Toronto**

This practical and easy-to-use-book tackles the key issues that all health teachers must cover including drugs, alcohol, smoking, sex, love, relationships, marriage, stress, food-related issues, and much more. A comprehensive resource for classes (grades 6–12), this book provides ready-to-use exercises covering a wide variety of key life skills. Each section includes numerous one-page worksheets to help students learn about, understand, and assess their knowledge of a wide variety of life skill issues.

For quick access and easy use, the worksheets are organized into eight sections and are printed in large 8½" x 11" format that lays flat for photocopying. Here is a preview of some of the sections you'll find:

Drugs, Alcohol, and Smoking: Trends in smoking, second-hand smoke, reasons why people smoke and ways to help people quit, facts about drug use, the classification of different drugs, alcoholism, fetal alcohol syndrome, as well as drinking and driving.

Love, Relationships, Marriage, and Family: The role of friends in our lives, negative aspects of cliques, dating and love, love and infatuation, qualities in an ideal mate, problems in marriage, why marriages end, family life cycles, and nontraditional families.

Life Skills: High and low self-esteem, long- and short-range goals, learning assertive behavior, dealing with difficult people, conflict resolution, what makes a good leader, effective communication and time management skills, and problems with violence.

The School Administrator's Complete Letter Book with CD-ROM, 2nd Edition

Gerald Tomlinson

ISBN: 0-7879-6589-8

Cloth-CD/ 416 pages/ 2003

"School administrators at every level will benefit from *The School Administrator's Complete Letter Book with CD-ROM*. In the face of ever-increasing job complexity, the tools in this book provide school leaders with tools to better communicate with diverse constituencies."

— Dr. Gerald N. Tirozzi, executive director, National Association of Secondary School Principals

The School Administrator's Complete Letter Book with CD-ROM, Second Edition, offers a comprehensive selection of model letters and memos for a wide variety of educational purposes and situations. This book and its accompanying CD contain a gold mine of tested, usable letters and other communiqués, some of which can be used practically word-for-word from the book, while others can be adapted to your specific needs.

The book's letters and memos represent the contributions of more than 60 outstanding school administrators throughout the United States — including superintendents, principals, supervisors, guidance counselors, and others — all of them with well-earned reputations for solid, professional communication.

Many types of letters are included — letters for a variety of occasions, addressed to parents, teachers, students, other school administrators, teacher applicants, businesspeople, and the community at large. In addition, this handy resource is clearly organized, designed for easy use, and filled with the best letters of the best communicators in modern American education. The CD-ROM makes the letters easy to modify to fit your own situations.

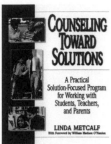

Counseling Toward Solutions: A Practical, Solution-Focused Program for Working with Students Teachers, and Parents

Linda Metcalf

ISBN: 0-7879-6629-0

Paperback/ 304 Pages/ 1994

For counselors and teachers at all levels, here is a new, positive program for changing individual behavior that helps empower students of all ages to deal with their own problems and gain self-esteem in the process. Step by step, *Counseling Toward Solutions* shows how to help individual students begin their own change process by noticing when a problem does *not* occur rather than focusing on the problem or what caused it. This approach — called Solution-Focused Brief Therapy — is often used by private counselors and therapists and is now being applied in the schools with great success.

You will find guidelines for dealing with specific problems ranging from incomplete homework to abuse and depression . . . techniques to develop small group dynamics . . . ways to help staff other than counselors use the approach . . . plus over 80 reproducible student handout pages and dozens of delightful illustrations throughout. Also included are directions for adapting solution-focused brief therapy to group settings and a handy appendix packed with additional cartoons, quotations and ideas suitable for classroom bulletin boards, certificates of success, and note-writing examples for teachers, students and parents.

Complete Group Counseling Program for Children of Divorce

Sylvia Margolin

ISBN: 0-7879-6631-2

Paperback/ 240 Pages/ 1996

Help children who are struggling to cope with and accept changes in their families. This unique resource gives you 12 ready-to-use, school-tested group sessions including guidelines for establishing divorce groups, ideas for beginning and ending each session, suggestions for responding to the confusion children may express, and case studies with actual examples of the children's questionnaires and artwork. You'll also find valuable time-savers, including reproducible notices, permissions, and other forms, letters to parents and teachers, and a questionnaire and information handout for parents — some offered in Spanish for communicating with Spanish-speaking parents.

Each of the 12 group sessions provides ready-to-use lesson plans and reproducible activity sheets that can be copied as many times as needed:

• General Background on Divorce

• Why Parents Marry and Divorce

• Changes

• Two Houses

• Feeling Angry

• Feeling Guilty

• The Grieving Process

• Legal Issues

• Stepparenting

• A Happy Marriage

• Review

• Achieving Closure

In short, you'll find this book will give you a proven, step-by-step plan for helping children better understand and cope with changes in their lives and develop the self-esteem and confidence they need to succeed in school and beyond!